Masterpieces of American Furniture
1620-1840

MASTERPIECES OF AMERICAN FURNITURE

1620-1840

A Compendium, with Photographs,
Measured Drawings
and Descriptive Commentary

BY LESTER MARGON, A.I.D.

ARCHITECTURAL BOOK PUBLISHING CO.

New York

Copyright © 1965 by Architectural Book Publishing Co., Inc.

All rights reserved. No part of
this book may be reproduced
without written permission
of the publisher.

Published simultaneously in Canada
by Saunders, of Toronto, Ltd.
Toronto 2B.

Library of Congress Catalog Card Number: 64-8125

Printed in the United States of America

CONTENTS

Foreword	7
Acknowledgments	10
Chapter 1	
ANTIQUES AND THE MUSEUM	11
Chapter 2	
ORIGINS OF THE COLONIAL	61
Chapter 3	
PRE-REVOLUTIONARY DAYS	95
Chapter 4	
RELIGION INFLUENCES DESIGN	141
Chapter 5	
STYLE AND THREE GREAT DESIGNERS	
Duncan Phyfe • John Goddard • Samuel McIntyre	177
Chapter 6	
AFTER THE REVOLUTION – VICTORIAN	203
Chapter 7	
FURNITURE DESIGN IN OUR TIME	245
Index	251

FOREWORD

This is a polemic consideration of the main events, principles and substance of American furniture from 1620 to 1840. It is not a history of furniture in pedagogic terms. The text consists of seven personal evaluations and deliberations by the author on the subject matter and the influence that Colonial furniture continues to exert on furniture today.

Lester Margon has spent a full lifetime in furniture. Working in commercial factories as an apprentice and advancing to superintendent, he has served on the staff of the foremost furniture organizations in Chicago, Sheboygan and Grand Rapids.

Graduating from Cooper Union, he became one of seventeen draftsmen and designers then in the employ of W. & J. Sloane in New York. He remained there for seven years. Following that he became associated with several of the most exclusive decorating firms as designer, delineator and interior decorator, including The Hampton Shops and Schmieg-Kotzian. For many years he was director of his own Interior Design Shop in New York, specializing in the furnishing of hotels and motels. Possibly his best known assignments were the Sky Top Motel on the heights of Newburgh, N.Y., and the Hamilton Hotel in Utica, N.Y. For many years he has been an Active Member of the American Institute of Interior Designers.

Lester Margon is an inveterate student, having studied at Cooper Union, New York University, Columbia College, the New School of Social Research, Mechanics' Institute, Stevens Institute in Hoboken and

Pratt Institute. He has received numerous awards, among which are a First and a Second Medal from the Beaux Arts in national competition representing New York University.

He has visited almost every museum and private collection of furniture in this country. Beginning in 1925 as representative of the furniture industry of Grand Rapids to the Exposition Les Arts Décoratifs in Paris, he has made seven subsequent tours throughout Europe, going from Naples in Italy to the northern points of Bergen and Trondjhem in Norway; visiting England, France, Belgium, Switzerland, Germany, Austria, Italy, Denmark, Norway, Sweden, Holland, Czecho-Slovakia and Roumania. On his travels he has made over 500 measured drawings of furniture masterpieces, possibly the largest collection of documentaries in existence. In Europe many of these pieces were bombed out and these drawings remain the only authentic records.

Lester Margon is the author of two furniture books, *Construction of American Furniture Treasures* and *World Furniture Treasures — Yesterday, Today and Tomorrow*. Both are out of print but still in demand. Critics have praised these books highly.

Professor Fiske Kimball, late Director of the Philadelphia Museum of Art said: "*Construction of American Furniture Treasures* is an unique book, full of Lester Margon's incredibly complete and inimitable drawings."

Mr. Edwin J. Hipkiss, former Curator of Furniture and Decorative Arts at the Museum of Fine Arts in Boston, wrote: "In my opinion the good selections and drawings exceed anything heretofore attempted in this country."

Mr. Richard F. Bach, for many years associated with the Metropolitan Museum of Art, added: "I shall refer people to your books as an excellent compendium of source material."

In this new book, he traces the story of Colonial Furniture from the Jamestown and Plymouth settlements and testifies to its continuous effect on furniture design to 1840, and in fact to the present time. The text is direct, deliberate, unequivocal, illuminating and controversial. The fifty measured drawings of the individual pieces of furniture are varied and accurate, of a high character and encompassing a wide scope. No attempt has been made to produce shop drawings showing every screw and joint and dictating the method of procedure for possible reproduction. That is certainly not the idea or purpose of this collection. Believing that measured drawings of furniture offer the most satisfactory method of showing the design, details and the "feel" of furniture was the reason for undertaking this task.

Foreword

Sizes are approximated, sections indicated where necessary and construction shown where deemed needful. In some cases enlarged details have been included and delineation of carvings and turnings illustrated. All this has been done so that a better understanding of this furniture may be ascertained for study, appreciation and inspiration. The 100 supplementary photographs have been included to enable comparison to similar pieces of the same or related epochs. Most of the furniture included has not been measured before and many of the pieces had to be specially photographed for reproduction here. Therefore we are of the belief that this volume contains new and fresh sources of material for your use and edification.

Having reached that enviable position where he is no longer commercially involved, Lester Margon can now sit back and regard the furniture situation in this country today, clearly and dispassionately. Having no ax to grind, he can express himself freely and without restraint. Many of his deductions and conclusions are definitely dialectic. That is healthy. In the last chapter he discusses the shortcomings of what has been called "Modern Furniture" and laments the grabbag tactics of many furniture manufacturers. He clearly defines what he considers the basis of good design in furniture and questions this artificial obsolescence. Joyously he heralds the promising signs of the return to Traditionalism. These are questions that are on the minds of everyone who is interested in furniture design — the student, the home craftsman, the collector, the architect, the interior designer, the decorator, the contract planner, the furniture manufacturer, the furniture salesman, the homemaker and the layman. In fact, furniture is such a universally used product that we cannot think of anyone who is not interested.

NOTE: In the 100 additional photographs which supplement the measured drawings, a few European photographs have been used so that comparisons may be made with the Colonial American Furniture.

ACKNOWLEDGMENTS

WE wish to express our sincere thanks and appreciation to the following museums throughout the country which have given their permission to reproduce the excellent photographs and make measured drawings of some of the treasures in their furniture collections. This hearty cooperation, on a courtesy basis, has made it possible for the publishers to bring forth this volume.

Lester Margon, A.I.D.

THE MUSEUMS INCLUDE

    The Metropolitan Museum of Art, New York, N.Y.
    The Art Institute of Chicago, Chicago, Ill.
    The Philadelphia Museum of Art, Philadelphia, Pa.
    The Detroit Institute of Arts, Detroit, Mich.
    The Brooklyn Museum, Brooklyn, N.Y.
    The Rhode Island School of Design, Providence, R.I.
    The Wadsworth Atheneum, Hartford, Conn.
    The Shaker Museum, Old Chatham, N.Y.
    The Museum of the City of New York
    The Los Angeles County Museum of Art
    Old Sturbridge Village, Sturbridge, Mass.
    The New York State Historical Association,
        Cooperstown, N.Y.
    and The Museum of Fine Arts, Boston, Mass.

Antiques and the Museum

LIST OF ILLUSTRATIONS

(Asterisks indicate photographs accompanied by measured drawings.)

CHIPPENDALE ARMCHAIR*
Metropolitan Museum of Art
CHIPPENDALE SIDE CHAIR
Los Angeles County Museum of Art
UPHOLSTERED SETTEE
Metropolitan Museum of Art
TAMBOUR DESK*
Wadsworth Atheneum
DESK, DROP-FRONT
Detroit Institute of Arts
TALL SECRETARY
Wadsworth Atheneum
MIRROR AND CHEST*
Art Institute of Chicago
PANEL MIRROR
Art Institute of Chicago
"CONSTITUTION" MIRROR
Metropolitan Museum of Art
POLE SCREEN*
Museum of Art, Rhode Island School of Design
POLE SCREEN AND CANDLE HOLDER
Detroit Institute of Arts
GEORGIAN SCREEN
Victoria and Albert Museum
PHILADELPHIA HIGHBOY*
Metropolitan Museum of Art
POWEL HOUSE DRAWING ROOM
Metropolitan Museum of Art

AMERICAN GALLERY
Museum of Fine Arts, Boston
CHEST ON CHEST
Philadelphia Museum of Art
TULIP CHEST*
Art Institute of Chicago
SUNFLOWER CHEST
Brooklyn Museum
MAPLE HIGHBOY*
Los Angeles County Museum of Art
WALNUT HIGHBOY
Metropolitan Museum of Art
HIGH CHEST
Brooklyn Museum
PINE KITCHEN DRESSER*
Philadelphia Museum of Art
KITCHEN CORNER
Philadelphia Museum of Art
PENNSYLVANIA GERMAN INTERIOR
Metropolitan Museum of Art
TRI-PART BOOKCASE*
Brooklyn Museum
SECRETARY BREAKFRONT
Philadelphia Museum of Art
SECRETARY AND BOOKCASE
Detroit Institute of Arts
FOUR-POSTER BED*
Detroit Institute of Arts

1

ANTIQUES AND THE MUSEUM

This preamble places emphasis on the importance of Colonial American furniture treasures from 1620 to 1840 in the museums throughout the country because they are the houses of good-keeping for these masterpieces. Not only have many great collections of antiques been entrusted to these institutions; the museums also are the logical receiving stations for the best examples of the works of these early designers and cabinetmakers. Here they are carefully preserved, painstakingly restored when necessary and presented in a fashion that is praiseworthy — often in rooms transported from old and historic houses or shown against befitting backgrounds. Here are recreated actual living quarters of yesteryears for present-day viewing and appreciation. Many of these facsimile settings are astonishing, done with sympathetic understanding and a flair for display.

Probably the first organized exhibition of American Colonial furniture was a feature of the Hudson Fulton Celebration in New York City in 1907. It was then that Mr. Bolles, one of the earliest collectors of Americana, exhibited his entire miscellanea at the Metropolitan Museum of Art. Some years later, Mrs. Russell Sage purchased this collection and presented it in its entirety to the museum. Besides the Bolles Collection, the Metropolitan Museum can boast of the excellent Blair Collection. At the Art Museum of the Rhode Island School of Design in Providence, the famous Pendleton Collection may be seen. It is exhibited in a house especially designed and built for Mr. Stephen O. Metcalf, who endeavored to combine the proportions and interior design of the best houses in

Rhode Island at the beginning of the eighteenth century. The collection is rich in American pieces as Mr. Pendleton, through the long years in which he engaged in collecting, had the primary object of obtaining the best American antiques extant, and it covers the period from 1690 to 1790.

Mr. J. Pierpont Morgan purchased the fabulous collection of good and bad antique furniture assembled by the minister and antiquarian Wallace Nutting and presented many of the better pieces to the Wadsworth Atheneum in Hartford, Connecticut. There this furniture has been placed in special settings with appropriate accessories. In the Boston Museum of Fine Arts may be seen the great M. & M. Karolik Collection, the fame of which has been broadcast. In the Philadelphia Museum of Art the Geesey Collection is featured; the Pennsylvania German furniture presented by Mr. & Mrs. Lamont Du Pont and Mrs. Pierre S. Du Pont may be seen in the rooms from the House of the Miller of Millbach, which indeed afford an excellent background.

The Francis du Pont Winterthur Museum near Wilmington, Delaware, contains certainly the largest and the finest assemblage of Colonial American furniture in existence. Here may be seen 150 rooms, alcoves and corridors, yet it retains its lived-in atmosphere, for there are no glass cases, forbidding velvet ropes or labels at Winterthur. The collection is rich and the quality of the pieces is transcendental. Reservations must be made well in advance, as only a limited number of guests can be admitted. Here you spend the day, have lunch and are graciously escorted through by hostesses who are trained guides. The effect is like walking through a house whose owners have just left, whether the year be 1640 or 1840, or whether the locale be Massachusetts or Virginia.

Unfortunately, many museums today have so much Colonial American furniture in their possession that, because of lack of gallery space, only a portion of their collections can be shown. This difficulty is being overcome by periodically changing the pieces on view, affording a greater variety in the displays and creating the maximum of public interest. When this procedure is made known, visitors can look forward to seeing something different on each succeeding visit. This rotation of pieces in the collections of Colonial American furniture is exemplary and should be widely encouraged.

In each of the foremost museums, where furniture and the decorative arts are featured, there are to be found curators, dedicated men and women, well trained and authoritative in knowledge and experience, who are making this their lifework. It will be sufficient to mention only a few,

Antiques and the Museum

past and present, who have served in this worthy capacity, including Professor Fiske Kimball, Mr. Vincent D. Andrus, Mr. Gregor Norman-Wilcox, Mr. Richard F. Bach and Mr. Edwin J. Hipkiss. There are many others; the list is too long to include them all.

Most important is the fact that this fine furniture is being exposed to the view of the public, is readily accessible and thereby affords the student — the interior decorator as well as the furniture manufacturer — the opportunity to study and appreciate the merits of Colonial antique furniture. Many institutions, like the Williamsburg Restoration, have given the rights for the reproduction of their furniture to reputable manufacturers who are doing a splendid job. Some museums permit reputable and competent delineators to make measured drawings on the premises with excellent staff cooperation. Splendid large photographs of individual pieces and room settings may be ordered and special photographs taken when required for book and magazine reproduction. Certainly full credit will be given in all cases. Special permission must be secured for any and all published reproduction of photographs of museum collections. There are some museums that prohibit any sketching or making of measured drawings of their furniture. Others permit drawings to be made for the exclusive use of home craftsmen, with the expressed understanding that there will be no commercial implications at any time.

Colonial American furniture is so highly prized because of its design, construction, workmanship, historical significance and association with our national development. For these reasons we believe that this furniture should rightfully become a part of the public domain. The owners of fine antiques have a pertinent duty to expose them for the study, education, appreciation and gratification of the public. What better way can this be accomplished than by presenting these treasured pieces of furniture to the museums for safekeeping and preservation? Whereas the great collections and large donations may get the most publicity, no less worthy are those individuals, known and unknown, who bequeath their treasures to the museums in memory of loved ones who have passed beyond the pale. However, we all know that a profusion of fine Colonial antiques is still playing truant in private homes, sheltered and secluded from public viewing. It is only reasonable to expect that with the rapid changing of times and conditions many of these antiques will eventually find solace in the protective custody of the museums by way of gifts, legacies, purchases and through funds set up for this purpose.

The manor house is fast becoming obsolete. The mansions are giving way to the erection of towering apartment buildings in the cities as well as in the suburbs. The one-family house is hearing its death knell. Due to the population explosion, property is becoming too costly for private occupancy. The necessity of driving an hour each day back and forth to work on freeways is too nerve-racking and hazardous. As the children go out of town to college and get married, the big house with the surrounding grounds loses its attraction. People are moving back to the city and taking smaller apartments. Say what you will, the chores of tending to a private house are manifold. People are becoming too busy these days with extracurricular activities to regulate large households. Servants are almost impossible to secure and most difficult to keep. The push-button age has taken possession of us and we look for the easiest way out. Housework has become almost an abhorrence to many women. Perhaps it is a reflection on this tremulous age that we find it so difficult to concentrate on anything. We are distracted on every side and try to avoid having to do anything save the absolute necessities. We are the victims of our own escapism with the result that many things remain undone. Sedatives cannot come to the rescue. They only tend to put off the day of reckoning. We must again learn to become masters of ourselves, to sit down, to relax, to concentrate and think — try to determine where these avalanches of credit cards are leading us.

In rare cases gracious living and entertaining still persist but they are gradually being relegated to that stratum of society where the lady has little else to do and has the facility and the means of attending to these social and household undertakings. Even under these favoring circumstances the tensions can become too great. In many homes, the placement of antiques becomes a problem. They appear incongruous in the modern setting, especially in apartments where every inch is at a premium. One might compare it to introducing an elderly person into the midst of a crowd of young people: they just do not belong together. While it is perfectly valid for some antiques to retain their usefulness and rigidity in everyday use, such may prove to be a rather precarious undertaking. Good reproductions are more practical and stand up better. The contention is that antiques from 100 to 200 years ago are too precious for everyday service. They should be relegated to the museums to be exhibited and preserved for posterity.

Before going any further, one question should be clarified. What is an Antique? The new *Webster's Collegiate Dictionary* defines it as "A piece of furniture made at a much earlier period than the present." This may be correct to a limited degree but its scope is too general, basing its worth solely on the proposition of age. A belated Act of Congress

Antiques and the Museum

admits foreign-made furniture into this country tax-free if it was made prior to 1830. Again we cannot accept this premise, as it is based specifically on the age of the furniture imported. It is our understanding that a piece of furniture can only have value as an antique if, besides age, it also has style, character, fine construction and is recognized by experts as a work of excellence that expresses the artistic development of the period.

The fact of the matter is that furniture periods do not begin or end according to definite dates. Authorities disagree as to the exact duration of some periods; it is well that dates should be considered approximate, as there is always an overlapping. Periods are gradual developments, duly influenced by preceding styles which tend to overlap into the succeeding epoch. They are brought into being by many exigencies such as fashion, historical events, governmental progress and new discoveries, and above all by the fresh and violent influx of new talents. The will and determination of leading architects, designers and cabinetmakers can bring about drastic innovations, especially if their prowess is substantiated by personages of wealth, influence and distinction. This is indeed a fascinating subject that should be investigated further, which could lead to conclusions of which we are not now entirely cognizant.

Often it is not possible to set an exact date on pieces of Colonial American furniture, due to the lack of documentary evidence or historical associations or inability to identify the place of manufacture. There are, however, other means of arriving at approximate dates, among which are determining the woods used, the particular type of construction as well as the general aspect of the design. Helpful information sometimes can be found in newspaper advertisements of the period, inventories, bills of sale, records of auctions, stipulations set forth in wills and even in descriptive passages found in novels of the time. Another source of information, but one that is often most unreliable, is the spoken evidence offered by descendants from family tradition. In this we are all inclined to lend a ready ear and to accept as gospel truths old wives' tales of how this or that bit of furniture, now resting peacefully in the attic, belonged to a dear departed grandfather's mother of some hundred and fifty years ago. They certainly would not part with it, no sir, not for anything in the world, except money. Old letters also can throw some light as to the genuineness of an antique and should receive considerate attention.

It is just as well to be prudent and accept the opinion of an expert, who by reason of study and experience, coupled with a thorough knowledge of antique furniture, can set the date fairly accurately and suggest its place of origin. He just knows. With him it may be a matter of having a predilection based on erudition. Unless a piece of furniture is actually signed or bears the identification marks of a particular cabinetmaker, it is customary to use the term "circa," meaning that the object was made about such and such a time, somewhat similar to wines of indeterminate vintage. All this fuss about dates is irrelevant. The important thing is to ascertain whether or not the particular antique in question embodies the salient characteristics for which the period has become identified. Has it the quality of design, the excellence of workmanship and the correct construction which we have come to recognize in these antiques?

After a certain piece of furniture has been tentatively ascertained as belonging to a definite period, it does not necessarily imply that it actually was made by the hands of its foremost cabinetmaker or that it may even be a product of his shop. Take for instance the case of Duncan Phyfe, who worked and prospered in New York from 1795 to 1847. So many varied articles of furniture have been attributed to him that it would have been humanly impossible for him even to have supervised the production of this tremendous output. Therefore, for the records it is sufficient to say that this furniture in this locality may be described as belonging to the "School of Duncan Phyfe." It seems to be so futile to haggle over such matters that really can never be resolved.

Unfortunately the supply of genuine Colonial American antiques in this country is fast dwindling to a minimum, due to the population explosion, territorial expansion, the inevitable ravages of time and the fact that more people are becoming interested in antiques than ever before. It is not only that many of the choicest pieces have been secured by the museums and there is no possible source of replacement. Even though auctions do advertise and offer for sale what they term genuine antiques, let the uninitiated be aware. There is really no conclusive way of knowing unless you are a connoisseur in this particular field. Otherwise, it is best to listen to the advice of an appraiser and even then think twice. Be skeptical! Always view the pieces before they are put up for sale and make inquiries of the gallery as to what positive proof they have as to the authenticity of the furniture offered. The sad fact is that many of these unheralded pieces are either reconstructions or even reproductions.

The thorough antiquarian knows the characteristics of fine furniture and can often tell at a glance whether or not a piece is an original. However, there is so much faking going on, such as imitating patina, bleaching of surfaces, denting and making false wormholes, all to fool the unknowing purchaser. Since it is a fact that the ravages of time do enhance the charm of antiques, the efforts to secure these effects can be overdone and thus help one to determine that the piece is a fake. Look underneath and see if there is any raw wood showing or if there are indications that a circular saw has been used. There are so many ways of detecting the counterfeits!

By reason of the incessant search for and the lure of the antique, the bottom of the barrel has been well scraped. If the pieces offered for sale are genuine antiques, they should bring a high price which only the wealthy collector can afford. The desire to purchase rare antiques for personal use or aggrandizement is in itself an affront to good taste and judgment. Of course it is the collector's privilege to purchase whatever he can afford but how much more altruistic it would be for him to purchase the antiques and then turn them over to a museum for safekeeping! The list of such donors is long but there is always room at the top. Then too, such gifts are tax-deductible.

Undoubtedly, much furniture believed to be genuine and treasured by people in their homes is spurious. They do not know because they took a dealer's word for it and never had the pieces investigated or appraised. Just as the making of Utrillo paintings is the sixth biggest industry in France, just so the manufacture of fake antiques in the United States is a very large part of the furniture industry. The sad fact is that many of the newly fabricated antiques are so cleverly made that these flagrant decoys often baffle even the initiated. So adroitly done are these facsimiles that one would be confounded to place the genuine beside the deceptive and decide which is which. Many dealers do not know themselves and unwittingly offer for sale pieces of furniture that are unwarranted. Then too there are dealers who know but deliberately take advantage of the client and secure high prices for items that are unworthy. Therefore it is well to deal only with firms whose reputation is paramount. In many cities there are Antique Dealers Associations whose membership is restricted and who guarantee the authenticity of all the antiques which their members offer for sale.

Museums generally have on their staff or in their workrooms persons who are experts and can recognize immediately the status of an antique. Their decision can be relied upon. No museum will ever put on exhibition any antique if there is the slightest question as to its credentials. Sometimes overzealous workmen will unknowingly remove that precious patina which time has endowed on a piece and destroy the evidence of age and usage. This is lamentable because it makes the antique appear to be a recently produced piece of furniture. Believe it or not, this original patina not only has artistic value but can increase to no small degree the selling price. In most cases the term "Museum Piece" denotes an antique of superlative quality, exceptional merit and unrivaled grandeur, making it worthy of being exhibited in a museum.

Another worthy service which some museums offer to the public is to set aside certain hours during the week when people may come by appointment and bring their personal treasures to get an opinion as to their artistic worth. No financial appraisal can be made but the merits of a piece can be substantiated. It will be a boon to the inexperienced young collector to be assured that his possessions do have merit, a matter he has long desired to have determined. Thus the museum offers another service to the community. In many museums there are special study rooms where students may come and view their favored antiques in privacy and at close range and work there. More and more the art museums are playing an important role in civic activities, giving lectures and promenades through the galleries under proficient staff leadership. Their auditoriums are being used for dance recitals, concerts and theatrical performances, all at a moderate admission fee. Therefore it behooves everyone who is interested in the cultural milieu of his community to become a member of the museum. The fee is generally about ten dollars a year. It must be noted that many museums conduct regular art schools with courses that are accredited. Other museums have courses for children and adults who are interested. The Rhode Island School of Design, the Brooklyn Museum School and the school at The Art Institute of Chicago are only a few that come to mind.

Antiques and the Museum

We have selected ten measured drawings of American Furniture Treasures along with supplementary photographs from Museum Collections throughout the country. They illustrate the exceptionally high quality of pieces that are valued for their design, construction, workmanship and artistry. Representing the finest in the realm of antiques, they are exemplary because of their exceptional grandeur and magnitude. As such, they are indeed worthy of museum sponsorship and exhibition.

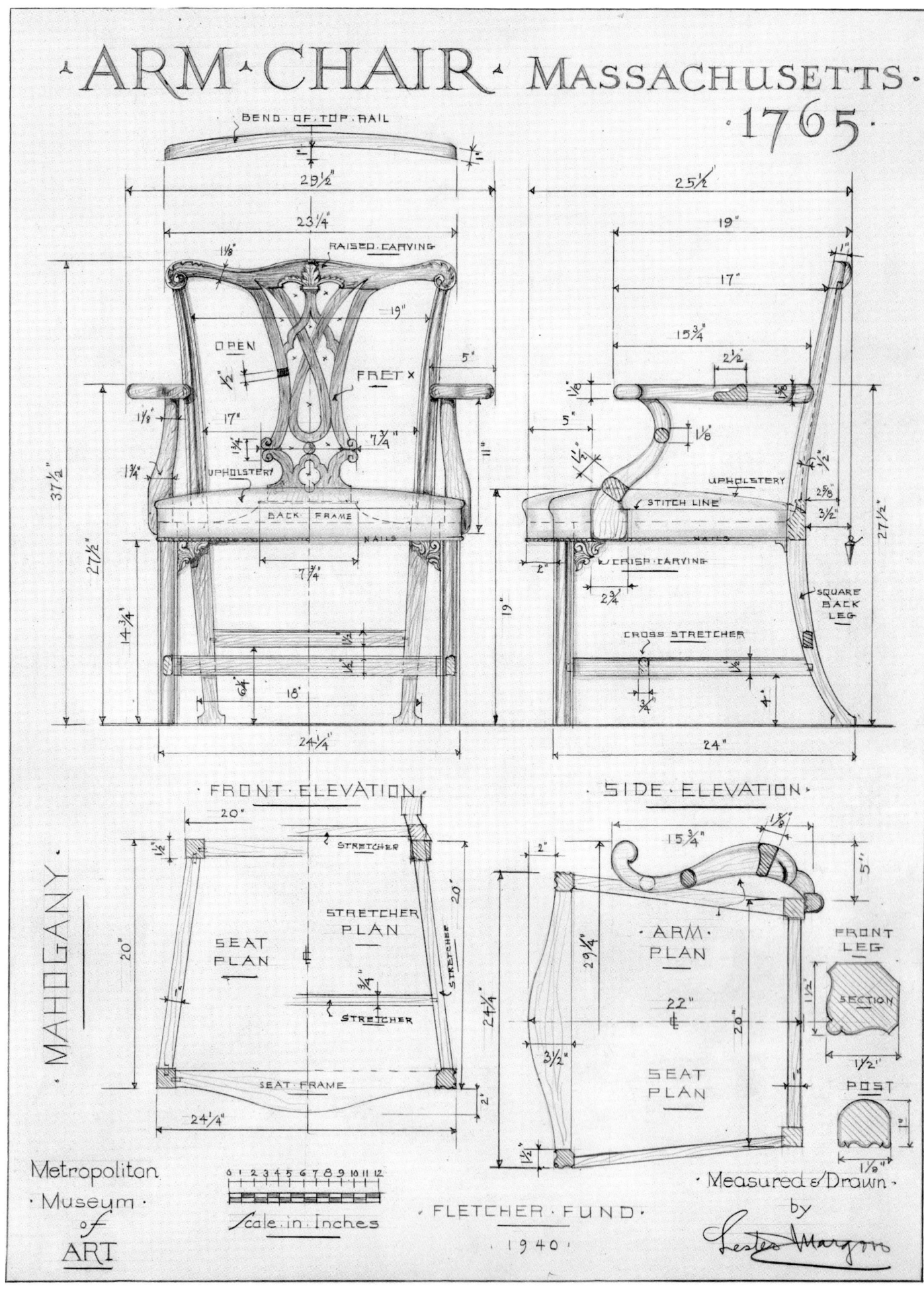

CHIPPENDALE ARMCHAIR
Metropolitan Museum of Art   Fletcher Fund 1944

This Chippendale-style armchair comes from Boston, Massachusetts, 1765-1770. It is a fine chair with an excellent perforated splat and a shaped crest. Note how the vertical members of the splat flow into the crest without a break, creating a perfect graceful entity. The straight legs and the plain stretchers are typical and the bits of acanthus leaf carving at the knee and on the crest are low and crisp. The curve and shape of the arm are particularly gratifying and add much to the chair's seating comfort. The English and the French designers were masters of this art but the Colonial American craftsmen vied with them in producing this excellent chair. It has often been said that a good chair is worth its weight in gold. If such be the case, this armchair would fit well into the category. The fact of the matter is that many of these American chairs excel the European prototypes by reason of their restraint and common sense. One of the greatest things in designing is to know when to stop.

CHIPPENDALE SIDE CHAIR
Los Angeles County Museum of Art

This Chippendale mahogany side chair with a pierced splat centering on a lozenge, fan carved cresting, has plain cabriole legs with ball-and-claw feet and "stump" back legs. The cresting ends in scroll "ears," turned backward. It was made by Eliphelet Chapin (1741-1807), of East Windsor, for Oliver Wolcott, signer of the Declaration of Independence and one-time governor of Connecticut. The date is *circa* 1780 and the place East Windsor, Connecticut. This is indeed a chair that has historical associations. It is a museum purchase of the Denis Bequest.

UPHOLSTERED SETTEE
Metropolitan Museum of Art

This elegantly fashioned settee is from the Sylmaris Collection. It is of the Chippendale School in mahogany. The outer and center cabriole legs are interesting and well fabricated. Probably made in New York about 1775, it is impressive in its curvatures and elegant in the upholstery. It is a piece that would fit graciously into the urban drawing rooms of the period. Its seating propensity is good and the brocade shown here is befittingly propitious.

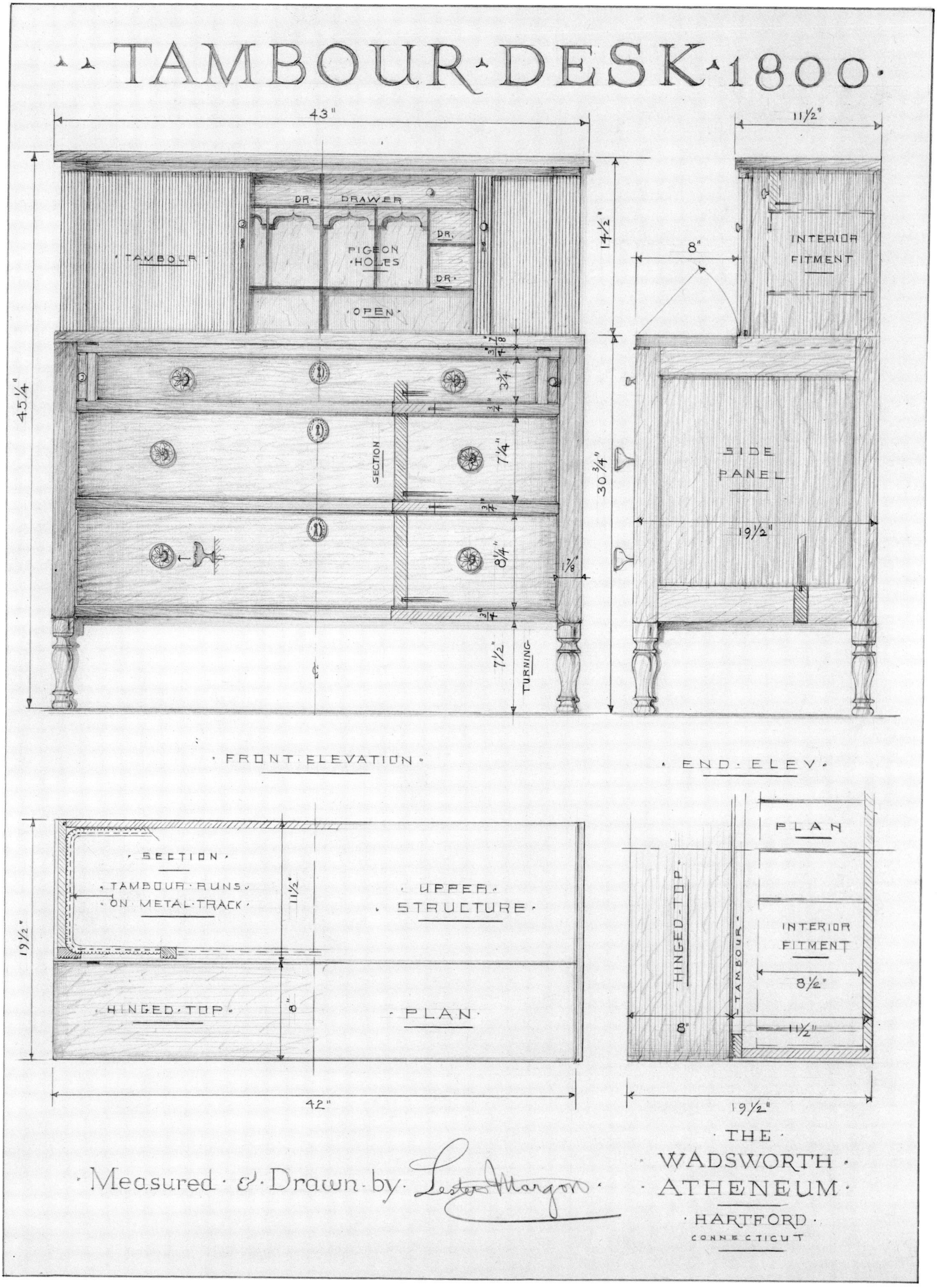

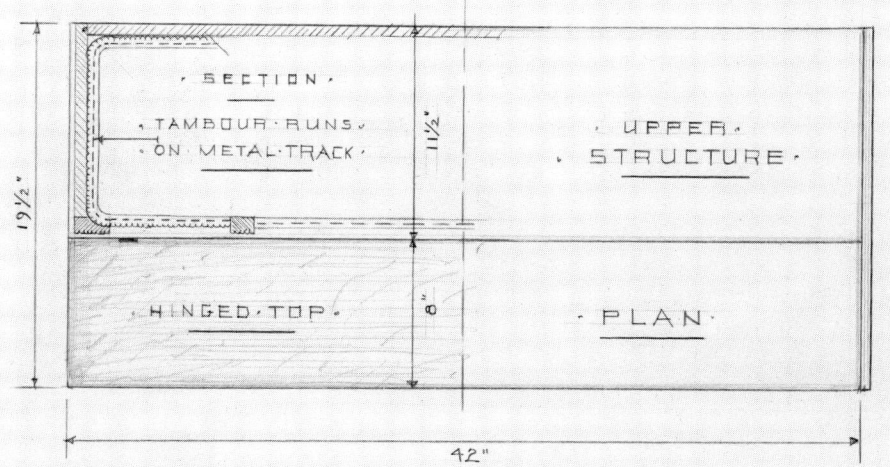
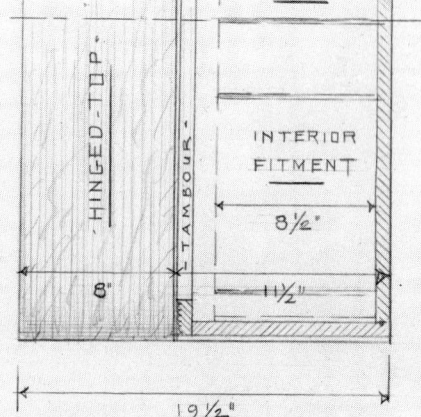

TAMBOUR DESK
Wadsworth Atheneum

This elegant desk of Hepplewhite design is of mahogany and dates from *circa* 1800. It may be considered a masterpiece of urban cabinetwork. Its simple dignity, with the moderate-grained mahogany and the imposing ormolu rosette pulls, is the acme of refinement. The term "tambour" refers to a series of small strips of wood that have been glued on a piece of canvas or strong cloth, in such a manner as to permit the doors to glide easily on a track so that it may open. In this particular case the tambour works horizontally, thereby bringing the small drawers and the pigeonholes inside of the desk into view. The hinged top, when opened, provides an adequate writing surface. Besides being a desk the piece is a good-size chest with three long drawers. The writing top when opened is supported by two pull-outs. Though rather sedate in appearance this tambour desk has great distinction by reason of its careful planning and fine proportions. A piece of furniture need not be presumptuous to be praiseworthy.

DESK
Detroit Institute of Arts

This auspicious drop-front desk of mahogany, *circa* 1775, has a commodious interior arrangement of drawers, cupboards and pigeonholes. The lower part is a shaped chest of drawers. The squatty cabriole legs with the ball-and-claw feet appear to be pressured by the weight. This type of desk has been generally identified by the name "General Winthrop." A very similar model in the collection of the New York Historical Society is said to be the one on which General Washington signed Major André's death warrant.

TALL SECRETARY
Wadsworth Atheneum

Mr. J. Pierpont Morgan used great taste and discretion when he selected a group of pieces from the huge assemblage of Colonial American furniture which Wallace Nutting had collected. He presented this furniture to the Wadsworth Atheneum, where it is so well shown. This tall secretary is from Pennsylvania and shows these craftsmen in a more advanced and sober mood, *circa* 1750. This is indeed one of the best examples of what has been called "This Pennsylvania Dutch Stuff." The interior is complete with small drawers and pigeonholes. This is in effect a three-piece structure, consisting of a chest of drawers, a slope-top desk and a cupboard above.

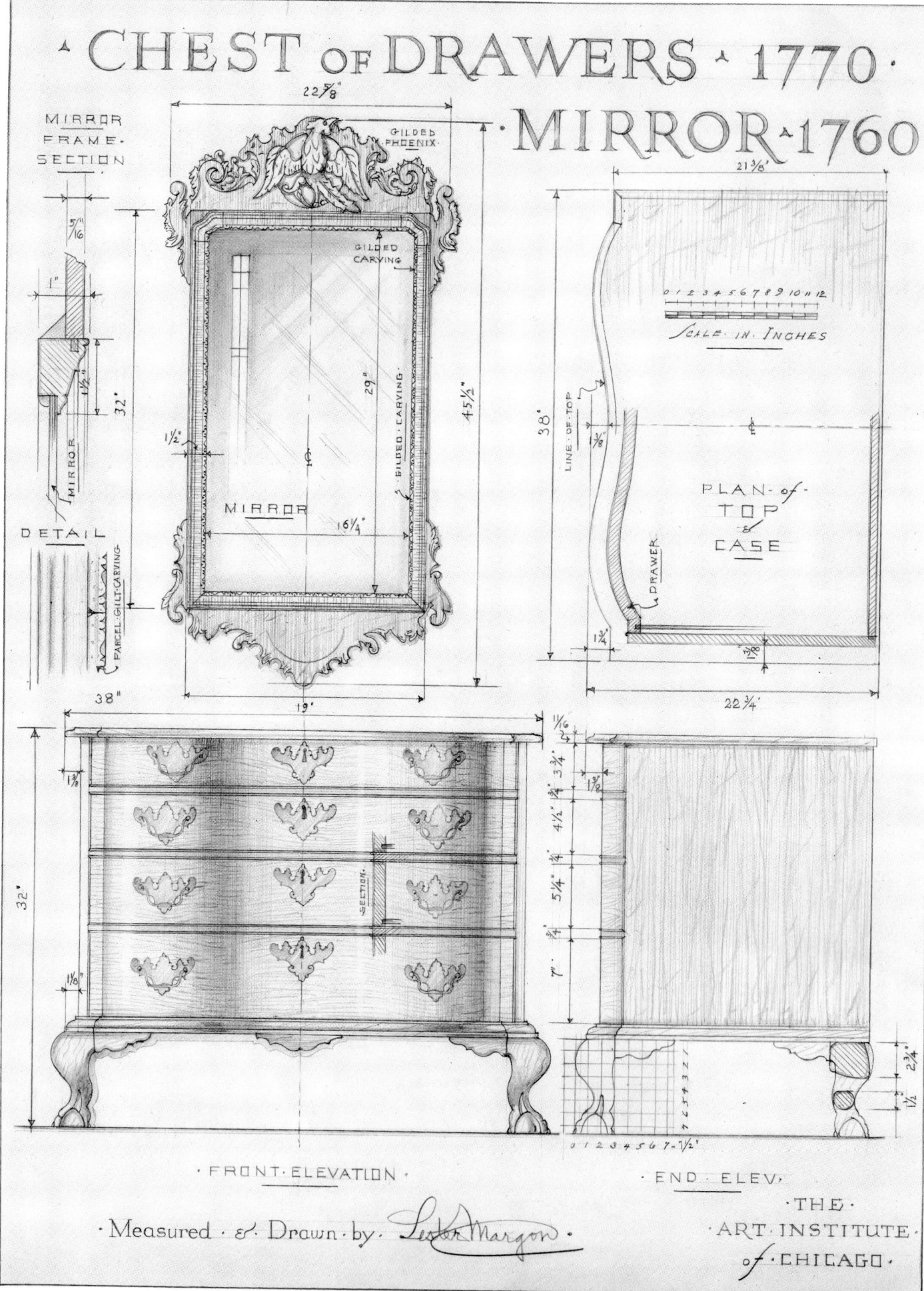

MIRROR
Art Institute of Chicago   Gift of Robert Allerton

This mirror is made of mahogany on pine, parcel gilt. The upright rectangular mirror frame is augmented at the top and at the bottom by cut-out arrangements. At the center of the top crest is an exceptionally fine carved phoenix which is gilded. The chest and the mirror indeed make a most felicitous combination that might grace the finest drawing room.

SHAPED CHEST OF DRAWERS
Art Institute of Chicago
The gift of the Antiquarian Society
through the Jessie Spalding Landon Fund

This mahogany chest of drawers is from New England, *circa* 1770. There is a serpentine front with ball-and-claw feet. It is of Chippendale inspiration. This indeed is a compact chest of drawers, bespeaking elegance which should please the most discriminating. To produce this serpentine effect it is necessary to build a sturdy core to receive the veneer. The cut-out brass pulls and the escutcheon plates are exclusive and were only used on the most expensive chests.

PANEL MIRROR
Art Institute of Chicago

There are mirrors and mirrors. Designers of all periods seem to have found in them opportunity for free expression. This mirror from New England is dated *circa* 1750. It was no doubt made to hang on "piers" between windows or doors. This design is in the Georgian manner, the double scroll top with gilded carved moldings. On the sides are long strings of leaves and flowers. It is difficult to decide if the bird is a phoenix or an eagle. The mirror is a gift of Mrs. Emily Crane Chadbourne.

"CONSTITUTION" MIRROR
Metropolitan Museum of Art

This Chippendale mahogany "Constitution" mirror is from New York, 1750-1780. It is a truly striking mirror of unusual design. The carved moldings are gilded, as are the swags and the top scroll ornaments. The crowning eagle is the center of interest and its position accentuates its importance. The cut-out panels at the top, bottom and at the sides are a bit unrestrained. However, taken as a whole, the mirror is prepossessing and in a right location could be most effective. Mirrors have a way of opening up a room into multitudinous phantasmagoria.

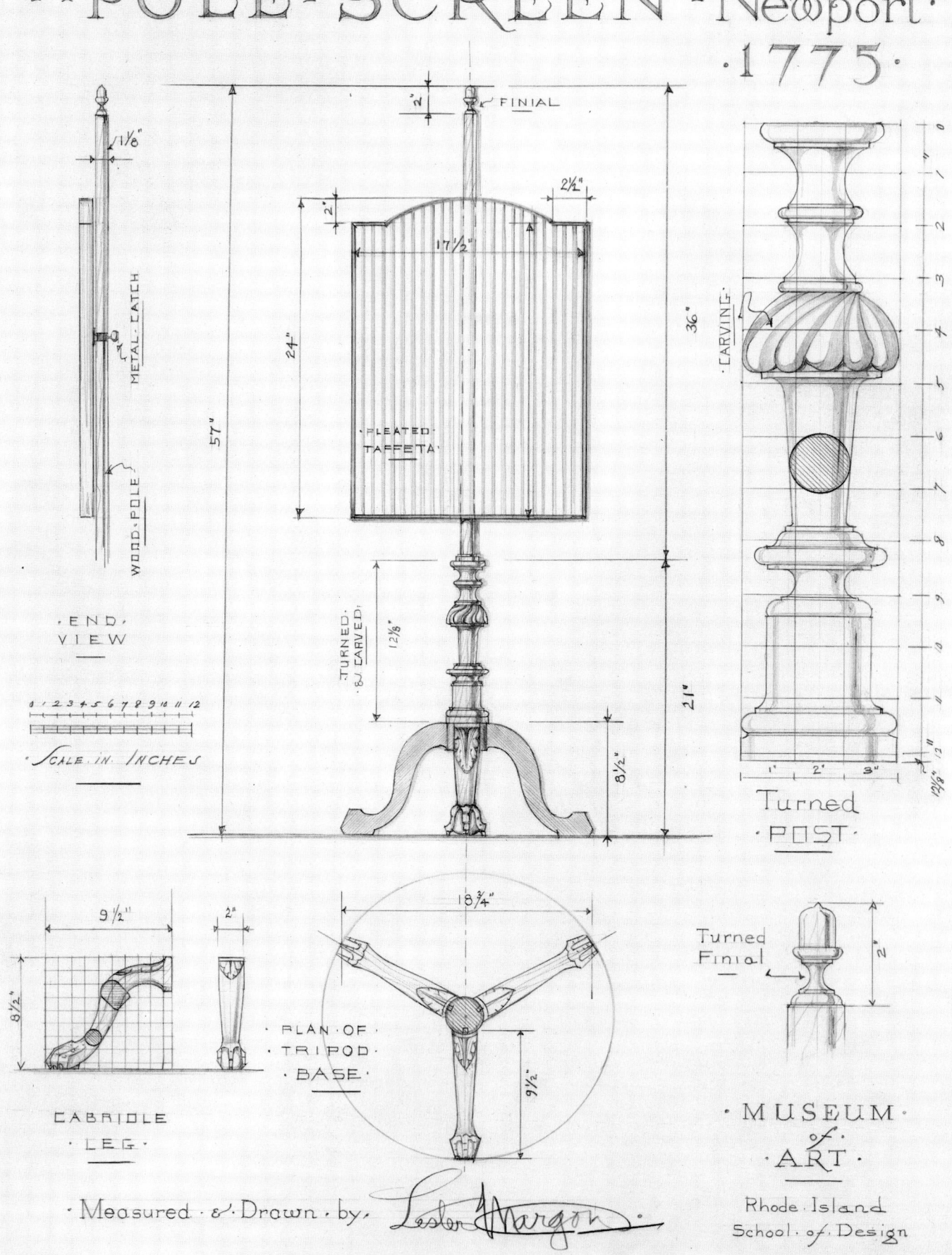

POLE SCREEN
Museum of Art, Rhode Island School of Design

This mahogany pole screen is of English design and is dated 1775. It is from Newport and is in the Pendleton Collection. The design is pure Chippendale, the tripod base featuring the carved cabriole legs with the ball-and-claw feet. The turned supporting post is very delightful, with just a bit of carving at the upper part. Of course the screen can be raised or lowered. The shaped screen panel is now covered in a pleated taffeta but probably in its original surroundings the panel held a piece of precious tapestry worked by the lady of the house. In the Georgian period these incidental pieces of furniture found great favor and ranged from the simplest designs to the most elaborate. They were part of the gracious setting found in the splendid drawing rooms of the period and are excellent examples of the period's furniture development. In fact, these little pieces of furniture were part of the stage setting against which Colonial life was enacted.

POLE SCREEN AND CANDLE HOLDER
Detroit Institute of Arts

This graceful mahogany pole screen, with a drop-front candle holder attached, is of Sheraton inspiration, *circa* 1775. The oval panel is made up of a series of triangular pieces of veneer divided by lines of satinwood with an oval insert in the center. The panel can be raised or lowered at will. The tripod base of unadorned cabriole legs fits the general design perfectly. The rather severe turned pedestal is just right. These incidental pieces of furniture were very popular at this time and could be found as part of many drawing-room settings.

GEORGIAN SCREEN
Victoria and Albert Museum

Pole screens were as popular in English drawing rooms of the early nineteenth century as they were in America. Note the stately formality of this model compared with the graciousness of the American prototypes. This model shows Adam inspiration and is completely gilded. Especially interesting is the fine embroidery panel in the oval frame. The carved pedestal is fine in detail. It is important to note that furniture design in England and America during this decade seemed to follow the same direction.

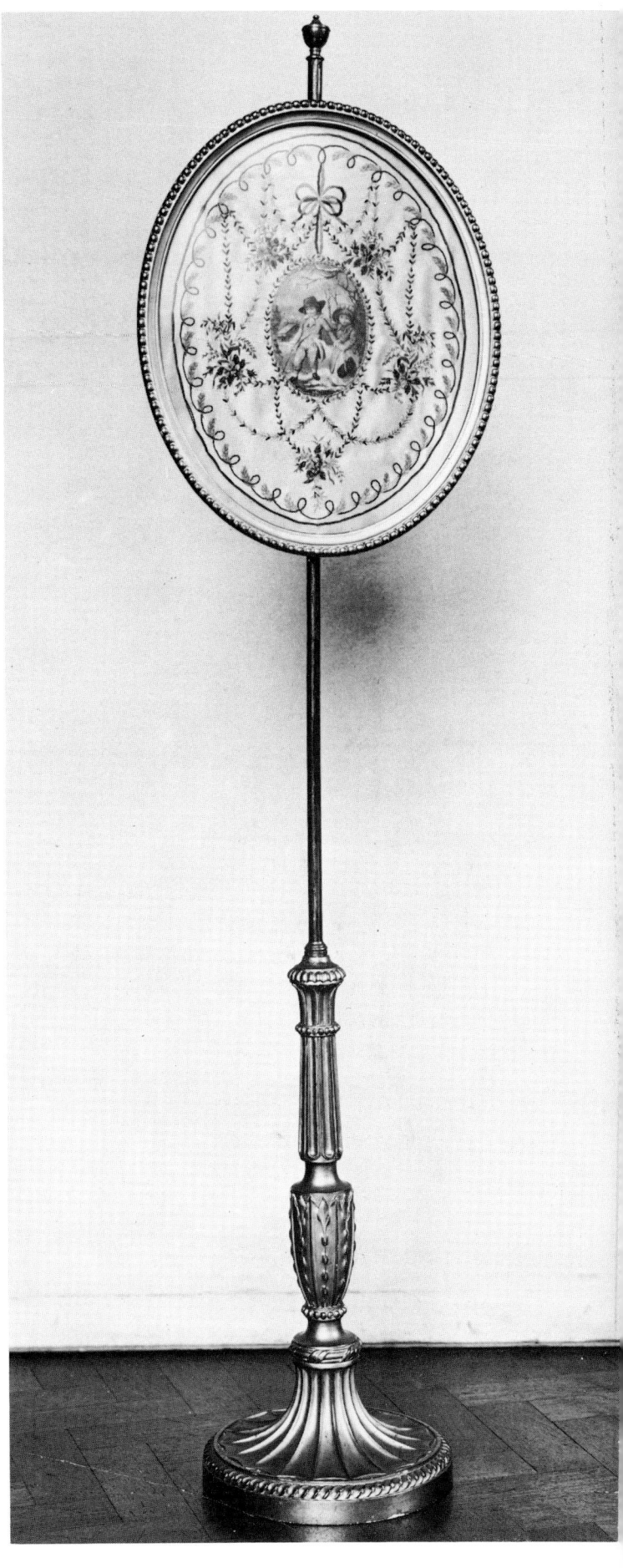

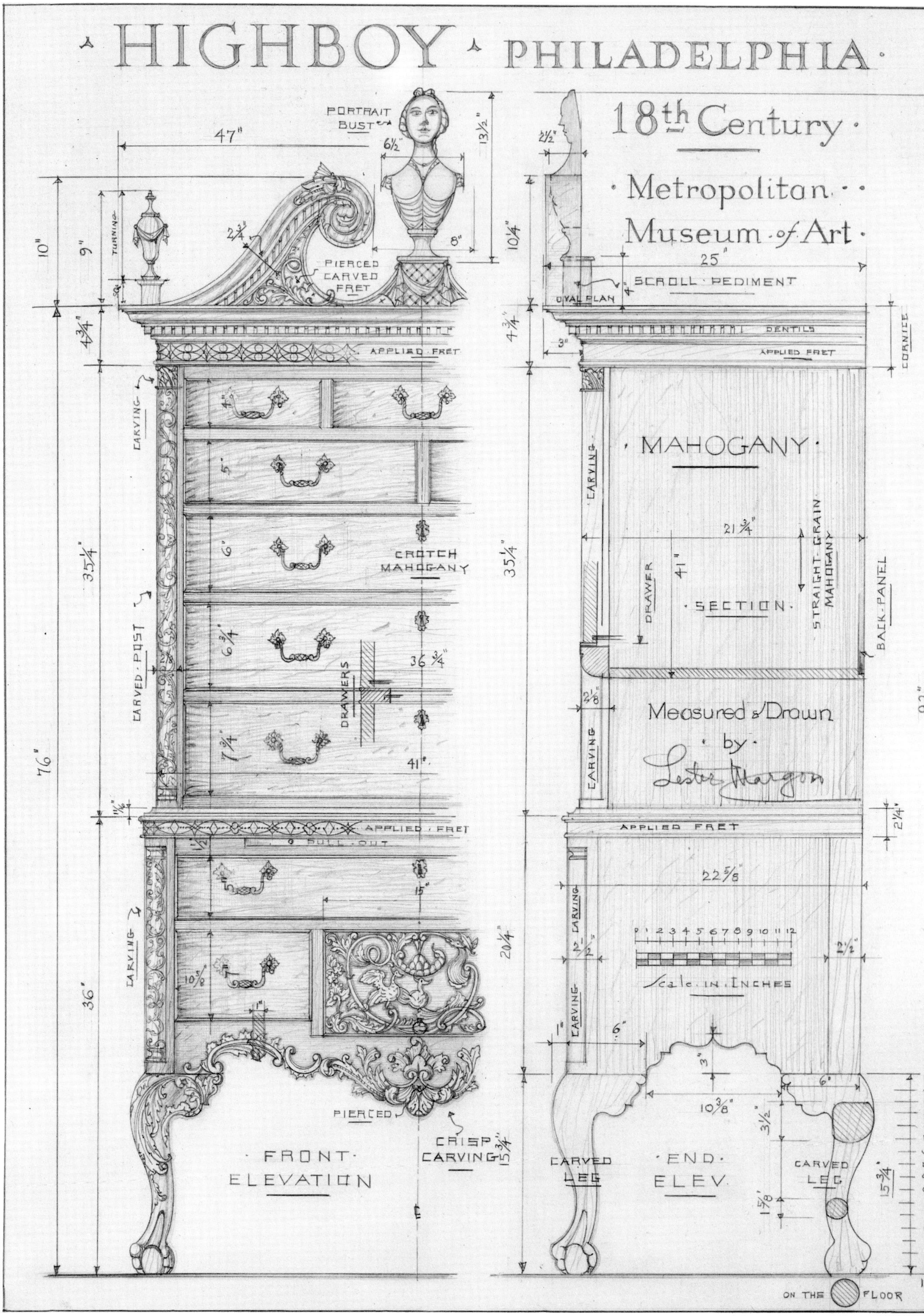

HIGHBOY · PHILADELPHIA

18th Century
Metropolitan Museum of Art

PORTRAIT BUST

- 47"
- 6½"
- 13½"
- 2¾"
- 8"
- 10"
- 9"
- TURNING
- PIERCED CARVED FRET
- 10¼"
- 2½"
- 25"
- SCROLL PEDIMENT
- OVAL PLAN
- 4¾"
- 3"
- DENTILS
- CORNICE
- APPLIED FRET
- 4¾"
- CARVING
- CARVED POST
- 35¼"
- CROTCH MAHOGANY
- 36¾"
- DRAWERS
- 7¼"
- 41"
- MAHOGANY
- 21¾"
- DRAWER
- 41"
- SECTION
- STRAIGHT GRAIN MAHOGANY
- BACK PANEL
- 35¼"
- 76"
- 93"
- 1½"
- APPLIED FRET
- PULL OUT
- 2⅛"
- CARVING
- 2¼"
- APPLIED FRET
- 22⅝"
- 15"
- 36"
- CARVING
- 10⅝"
- 20¼"
- 2½"
- Scale in Inches 0 1 2 3 4 5 6 7 8 9 10 11 12
- PIERCED
- CRISP CARVING
- 15¾"
- 1"
- 6"
- 3"
- 10⅜"
- 3½"
- 6"
- 1⅞"
- 15¾"
- 15¾"

FRONT ELEVATION

CARVED LEG · **END ELEV.** · **CARVED LEG**

ON THE FLOOR

Measured & Drawn by Lester Margon

PHILADELPHIA HIGHBOY

Metropolitan Museum of Art   Kennedy Fund 1918

Certainly the grandest pieces of furniture made in Colonial America are these Philadelphia highboys. This one, of mahogany, *circa* 1765, is of definite Chippendale inspiration, but there the similarity stops. The wealth and proficiency of detail, the glorious space-divisions and the brilliancy of the carving are beyond compare. The elegance of the double scroll top and the placement of the sculptured bust of a fair lady, the classicism of the urn finials at the top and the masterly way in which all portions of the design have been brought together harmoniously add up to quite a prodigious feat. These Philadelphia highboys are justly famous for the display of paramount artistry and skills. The selling price of these pieces today is astronomical. No book on Colonial American furniture would be complete without at least one inclusion of this type of highboy. The richness of detail and the masterly treatment of the carving are simply unequivocal. It beats by far anything that was being attempted in Europe at the time, and of this we can be justly proud.

POWEL HOUSE DRAWING ROOM
Metropolitan Museum of Art

This view of the drawing room in the Powel House shows the Philadelphia highboy in an appropriate setting. The background of the Chinoiserie painted wallpaper depicting the "boasted villas of Pekin" and the association with the Chippendale furniture give some idea of the magnificence of this famous house. This room was taken from a house that is still standing on South Third Street in Philadelphia. In pre-Revolutionary days these highboys were essentially necessary parlor pieces in which to put linens and accessories for entertaining. The crystal chandelier is especially brilliant.

POWEL HOUSE DRAWING ROOM
Metropolitan Museum of Art

This drawing room from the Powel House, Philadelphia, is dated 1768. It is one of the most splendid Colonial American rooms in existence. The Chinoiserie painted wallpaper, the Georgian carved mantelpiece and the painted paneling are all fine. The carved gilded mirror is excellent and all the furniture is of Chippendale inspiration. The elegance of this house is suggested by a letter from Powel's friend George Roberts, who wrote, "Indeed your house is so finely situated in the noblest spot in the city."

41

AMERICAN GALLERY
Museum of Fine Arts, Boston

This small group of Sheraton-inspired furniture is part of the American Gallery. The painted wallpaper was brought from China by Thomas Handasyd Perkins in 1805. The chair rail and the cornice are from the Dodd House, which formerly stood on Salem Street in Boston. The roll-top secretary is of unusual presence and the tripod occasional table has a top that can be raised or lowered. The frequent use of the peacock as a motif in Chinese decoration must have some spiritual significance.

CHEST ON CHEST
Philadelphia Museum of Art

This Chippendale-style mahogany chest on chest is attributed to Jonathan Gostelow of Philadelphia, *circa* 1775. He was one of the Philadelphia group which included Benjamin Randolph, Thomas Affleck, James Gillingham and Thomas Tufft. They produced a series of masterpieces that are beyond compare. The feature of this model is the double scroll at the top with the pierced fret and interrupted by that free form arrangement of oak leaves and acorns growing out of a basket. This is certainly the epitome of gracefulness. The crotch veneer is lively and flamelike. The detail of the cornice is profound.

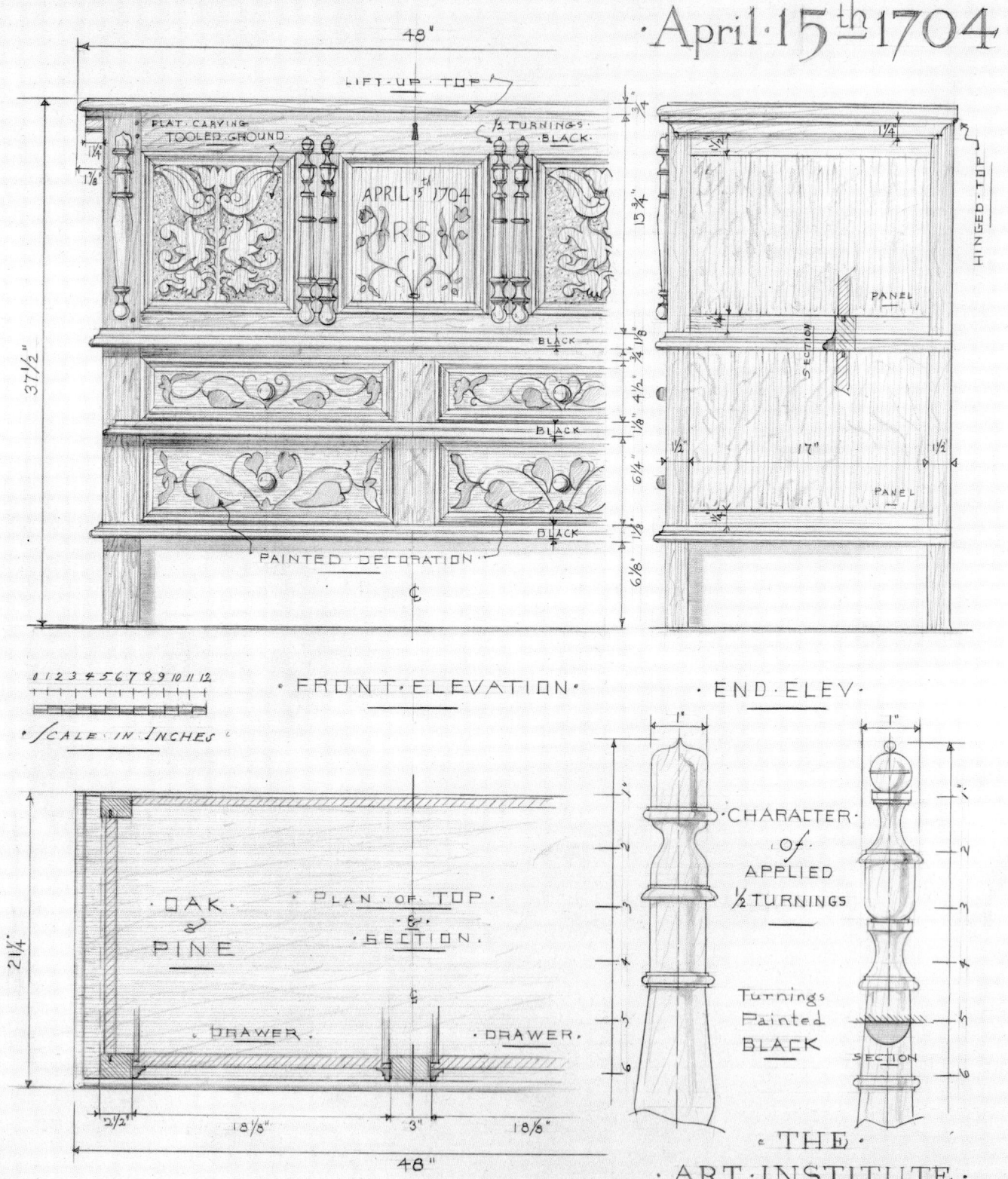

TULIP CHEST
The Art Institute of Chicago Purchased through the Wirt D. Walker Fund

This tulip chest of oak and pine is from Connecticut, *circa* 1704. It is one of the finest of the Colonial American early chests in design and character. The carving is sharp but shallow with the background hand-punched and scratched. The bold and finely turned half-applied turnings are ebonized and afford just the needed contrast. This chest is particularly outstanding because of the combination of carving and painting on the panels of the lower drawers. The top is a single board of pine, fastened to the molded oak cleats to prevent warping when the hinged top is raised. The center molding and the lower molding run around the sides but the center molding between the drawers appears only on the front. The top shaping and all the other moldings are painted black. As a rule in these chests the top, bottom and back as well as the drawer fronts are made of pine; the balance is oak. It is rare to find a piece of this character initialed and dated.

SUNFLOWER CHEST
Brooklyn Museum

This splendid example of a sunflower and tulip chest, made of oak and pine, is probably from Connecticut, *circa* 1675-1700. The hinged top is a single piece of pine, fastened to oak cleats to prevent warping. The panels are carved, boldly interspersed by half turnings painted black. The bosses and the dividing moldings are also ebonized. The side view is interesting, the way it is divided with two rectangular panels in the lower space. These sunflower chests are among the most original and typical Colonial American creations.

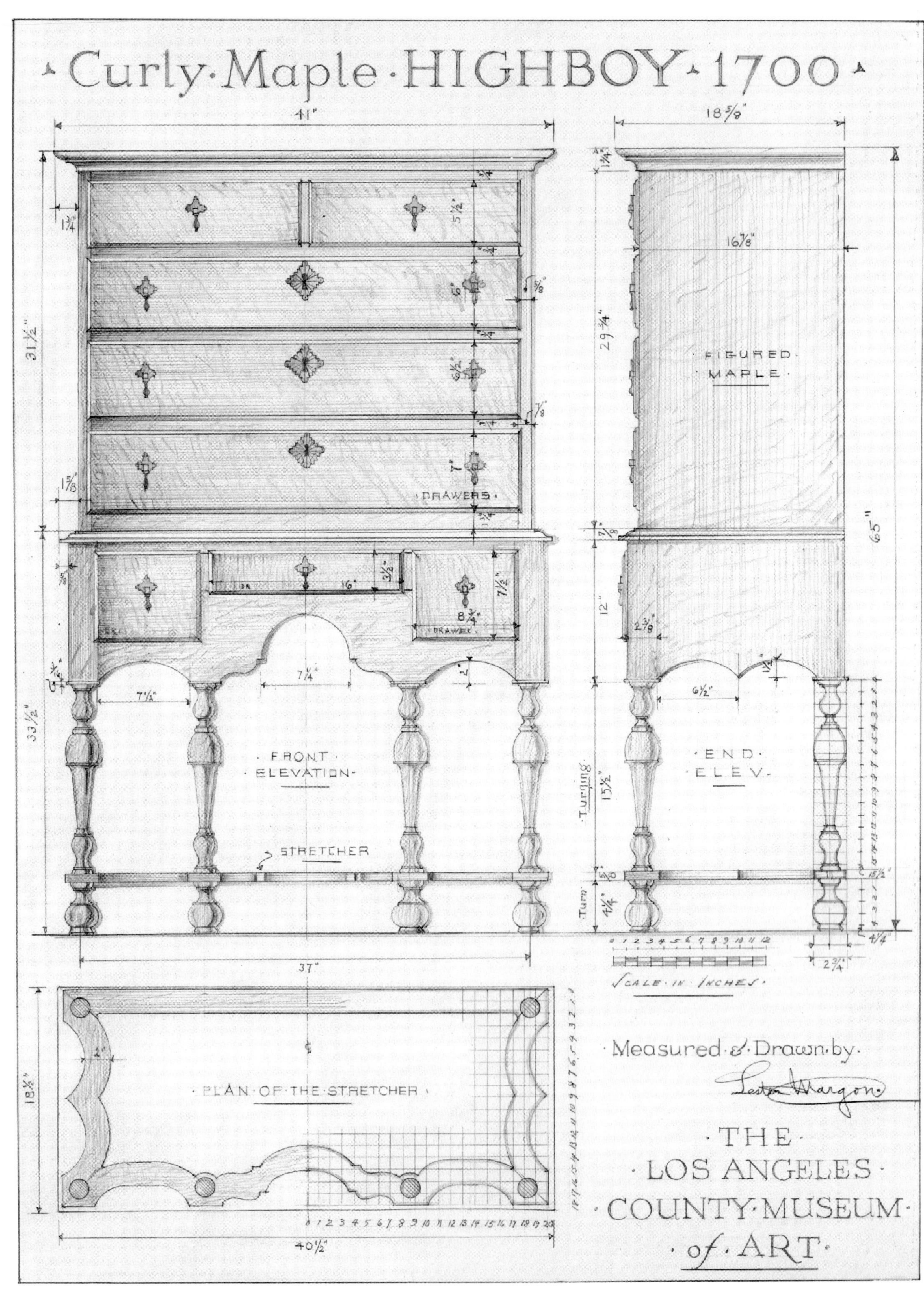

MAPLE HIGHBOY
The Los Angeles County Museum of Art   Gift of Alan Ross Smith

This magnificent highboy is made of curly maple with trumpet turned legs, from New England, *circa* 1700-1720, probably from Massachusetts. A highboy may be defined as a tall chest of drawers made in two sections, the lower section being a stand on legs. The origin of these highboys may be attributed to the desire to make a utilitarian chest that was readily accessible without bending down to open the lower drawers. Of William and Mary inspiration, this Colonial American model has six turned legs held in place by a shaped stretcher. There are bun turnings as feet. The trumpet turning may be called truly American because of its historic significance. The entire piece shows a restraint and refinements include the shaped lower apron. The selected curly maple used especially on the drawer fronts is spectacular and the finish of this piece resembles the color of dripping maple sap. Note how readily the lower portion could be made into a presentable lowboy. Undoubtedly the highboy form was developed from the setting of a chest of drawers on a stand and a new article of furniture was created.

47

WALNUT HIGHBOY
The Metropolitan Museum of Art

This crotch veneer walnut highboy dates from 1700-1720. The trumpet turnings are exceptional in their flare and beauty of line. The cut-out stretcher is well shaped and holds the legs in position. This is an excellent model, full of grace and dignity. The drawers are surrounded by a raised bead and bordered with a double herringbone inlay. In fact, these are the most dynamic trumpet legs that we have encountered.

HIGH CHEST
Brooklyn Museum

This high chest of walnut veneer is dated *circa* 1680. It is from New England. Of special interest is the crotch-walnut veneer used in the drawer panels as well as on the face of the chest. The drawers are divided by a double bead with borders of inlaid herringboning. The turned trumpet legs are remarkable by reason of the broad portion near the top. The shaped stretcher is fanciful and the elongated bun-feet fit well into the design. The one fault that we would have with this high chest is the meager crown cornice molding. It just does not appear adequate.

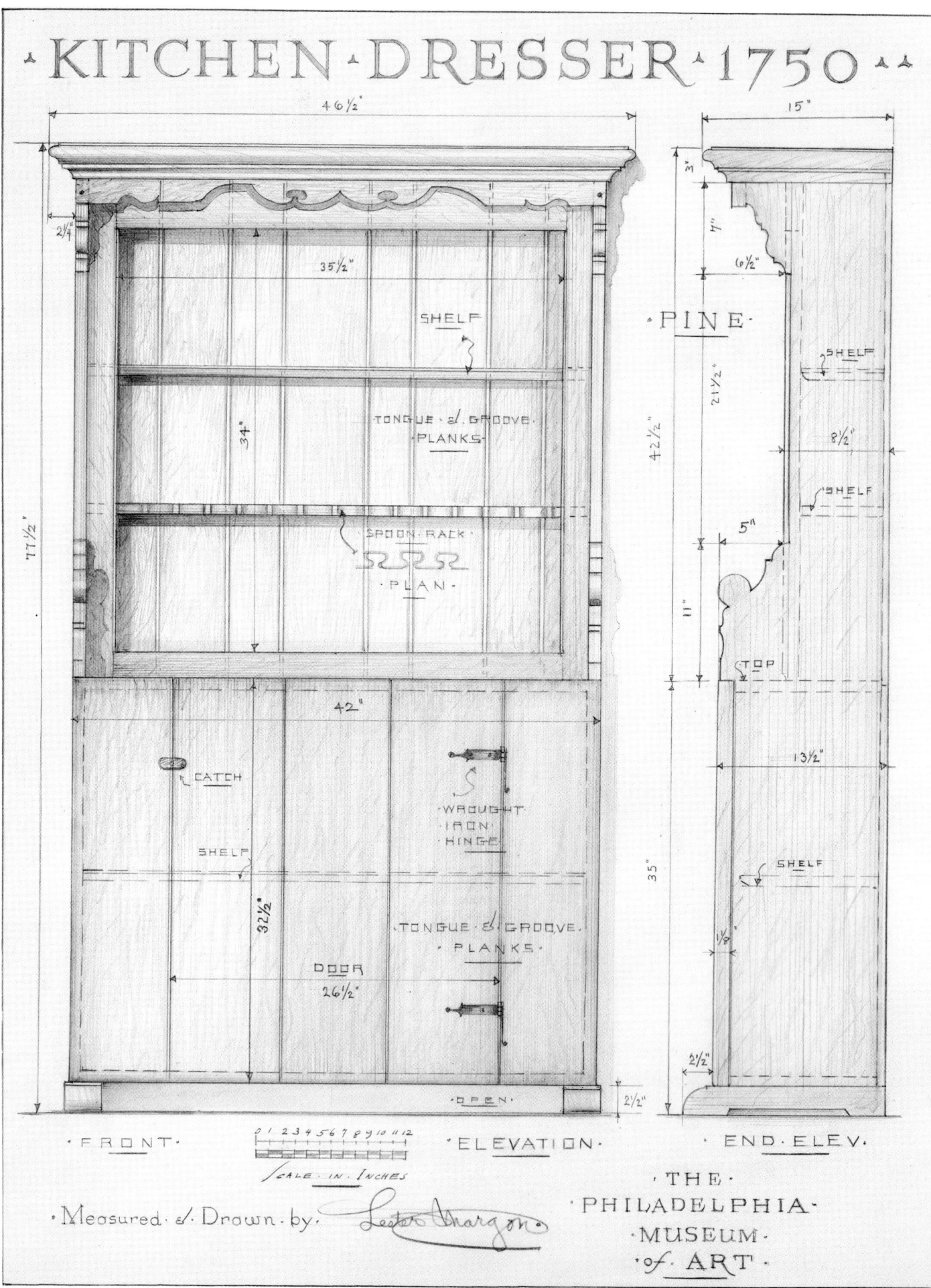

PINE DRESSER
Philadelphia Museum of Art

Few examples of Colonial American furniture embody the primitive charm and unique artistry of these Pennsylvania German examples. This pine kitchen dresser, *circa*, 1750, is shown in the restoration of the kitchen of the House of the Miller of Millbach. The single lower cupboard, faced with tongue-and-groove planks of random widths, is for storage of cooking utensils while the open Welsh cabinet-top displays some of the finest examples of ceramics. The design and colorings of this peasant pottery are beyond description. It must be seen to be appreciated. This is indeed a splendid piece, with excellent bracket details and wrought-iron hinges. This dresser is part of the collection of furniture presented by Mrs. Pierre S. Du Pont and Mr. and Mrs. Lamont Du Pont. Seen in this appropriate setting, we can get an excellent conception of the charm of these farmhouse kitchens with open fireplaces and the multitude of pots hanging about. In those days, the kitchen was the gathering place of the family, where all business and activities were conducted. It was indeed the forum for family discussions and decisions.

KITCHEN CORNER
Philadelphia Museum of Art

This is a view of the northwest corner of the kitchen from the House of the Miller of Millbach, Lebanon County, Pennsylvania, 1752. It clearly shows two cabinets or dressers with the open shelving above in what is known as Welsh cabinets. Here we see on display a choice grouping of the wondrous earthenware and pottery of these Pennsylvania Germans. The long table and benches, the wainscot chairs, are shown in detail elsewhere. Note the wrought-iron chandelier dangling from a beam and be sure to see the thickness of the walls and the setback windows.

PENNSYLVANIA GERMAN INTERIOR
Metropolitan Museum of Art

This gallery shows a Pennsylvania German interior, the furniture and the decoration of the eighteenth and the nineteenth centuries. The wooden mantelpiece is impressive in contrast with the plain plaster walls, broken only by a dado and wooden baseboard. The furniture, which is most interesting, includes a sawbuck and a trestle table, a hanging cabinet with a bold eagle set on top and a banister armchair. On the wall is a pipe rack, and do not overlook the very wonderful painted dower chest. Over the hearth is a musket to welcome any intruder.

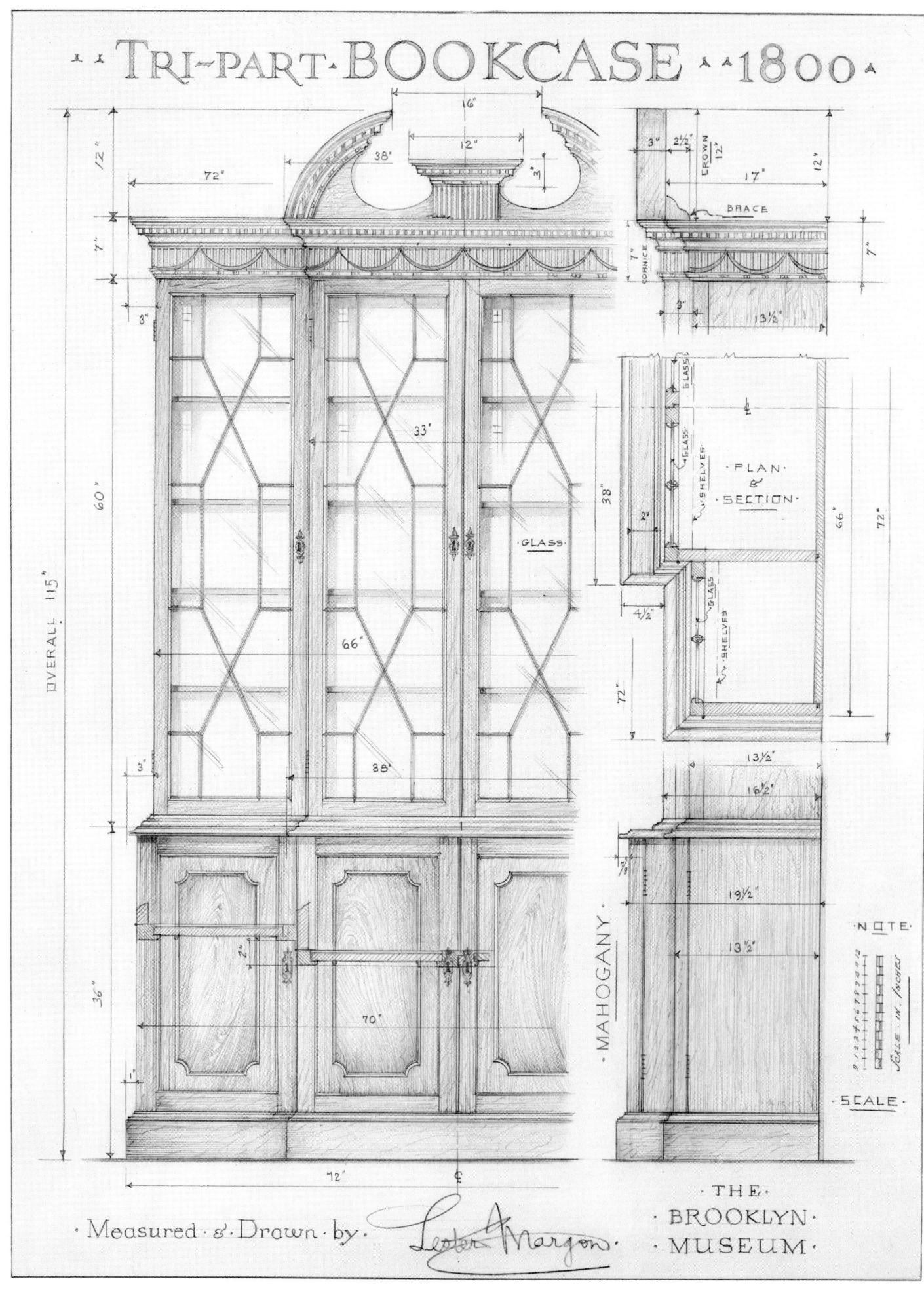

TRI-PART BOOKCASE
Brooklyn Museum

This very tall tri-part bookcase is made of a richly grained mahogany. It is in the Sheraton style – Southern – and is certainly of excellent design and stunning proportions. Its great height should easily meet the needs of a great number of volumes. The cabinets below are for very large books and portfolios, whereas the glass-door-enclosed area has numerous movable shelves. It is a breakfront, which adds to its elegance. The Georgian, almost Adam, detail and carving are academic. The broken circular pediment is penetrated by a sort of architectural pedestal arrangement which is quite in keeping. It is a bit pseudo-classic but quite effective. Of course the piece requires a tremendous room with a high ceiling to carry it off. Pieces like this go well in a manor house. The geometric arrangement of the glass door panels only tends to accentuate the height. Of course a piece like this has to be made in three parts to permit of transit and placement. This bookcase does hold much for inspiration and study. To produce such a huge piece of furniture and still maintain a sense of scale and proportion is indeed an achievement. The date is *circa* 1800.

SECRETARY BREAKFRONT
Philadelphia Museum of Art

This Sheraton American secretary breakfront is of mahogany with satinwood panels and inlays. It is dated 1800 and is from Massachusetts. This is indeed a splendid combination piece of a chest of drawers, a drop-front secretary compartment and cabinet top for books or the display of china or bric-a-brac. The arched treatment of the glass doors is most effective. The crotch matched veneers used are particularly flamboyant. The breakfront adds to the impressiveness of the piece.

SECRETARY & BOOKCASE
Detroit Institute of Arts

This Sheraton-type secretary, chest of drawers and bookcase is a representative piece of American artistry. It is as fine as anything produced on the continent at this time. The date is 1790-1800. It is from Salem, Massachusetts, and is made of mahogany with overlays of satinwood and crossbanding. The cathedral-shaped panels on the bookcase doors are impressive. The fold-over top affords a large writing surface. The eagle, perched on top, is ready to take off.

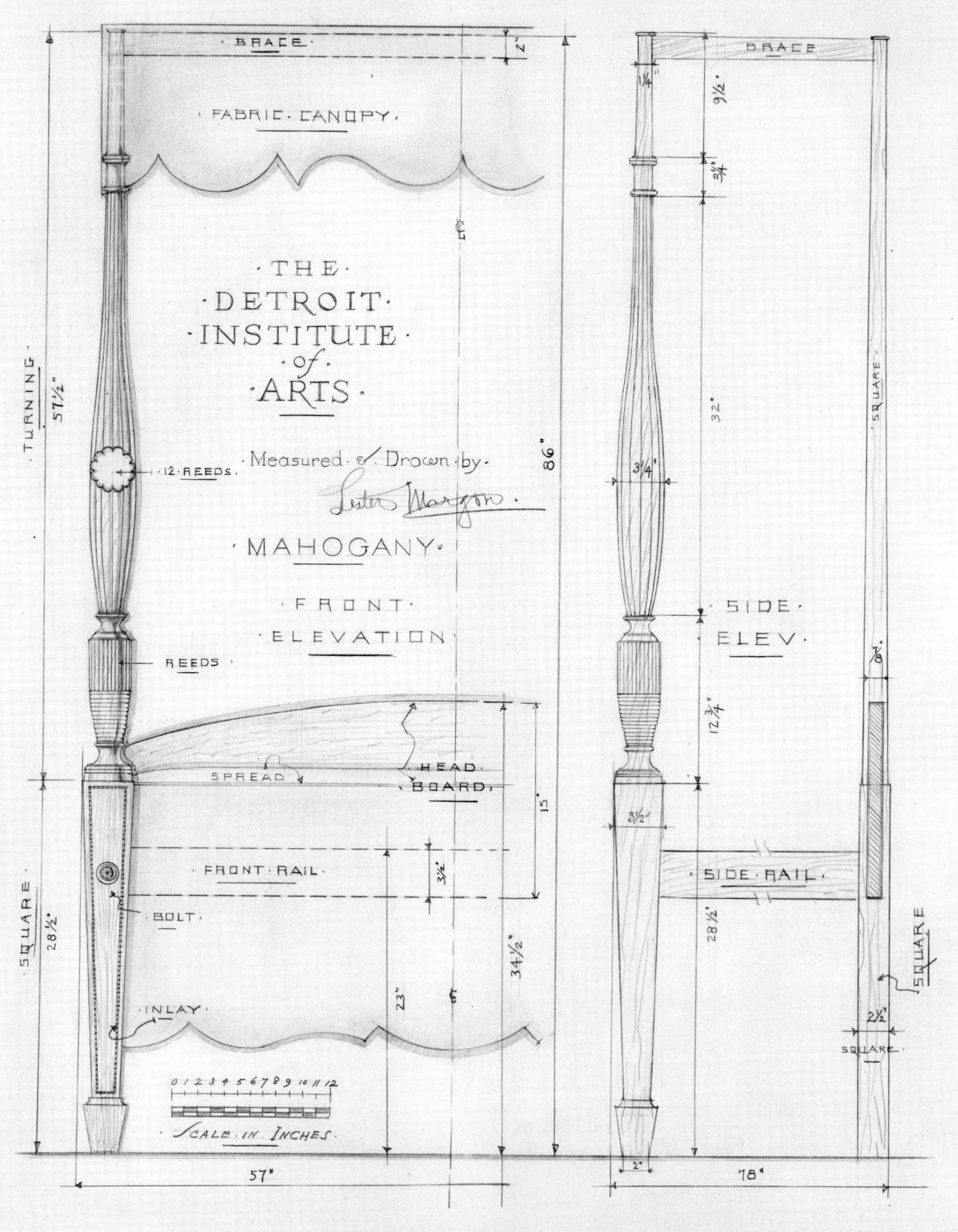

FOUR-POSTER BED
Detroit Institute of Arts

It is sometimes difficult to ascertain whether some of these four-poster beds should be classified as of Sheraton or Hepplewhite inspiration. There is so little difference. However, that need not worry us too much because the two styles often overlapped. The thing to interest us in this model is the superb rendering of the intricately turned front post. It is certainly a virtuoso performance. The interestingly shaped canopy shown, of Toile de Jouy, is held in place by an encircling wood tester. In these beds the turned front posts are the feature. Many of these beds had curtains to help keep out the drafts and to afford the occupants semi-privacy. On the posts, note, the fine reeding runs vertically, and horizontally on the urn portion. The simple tapered square legs with the spade foot create a pleasing contrast. The headboard is very simple. Let us put the date as *circa* 1785. It was not infrequent in those days for ladies to receive guests while they were in bed, and for that reason the bedspreads were often most elegant. Very often these beds were set on a raised platform in quite a regal manner.

FOUR-POSTER BED
Museum of Art, Rhode Island School of Design

This Chippendale-style four-poster bed in mahogany is dated 1775. The elegant cabriole legs with the claw-and-ball feet are distinctive. The turnings are a tie between Sheraton and Hepplewhite (these styles often overlap). The shaped canopy with matching bedspread is effective. The backboard is simple, just a slight curve at the center. These four-poster beds seem to be coming into vogue again but it requires a good-size room to carry it off. This model, set up in the Pendleton House, is in its correct setting.

Origins of the Colonial

LIST OF ILLUSTRATIONS

(Asterisks indicate photographs accompanied by measured drawings.)

DESK ON STAND*
    Metropolitan Museum of Art
SLANT-TOP DESK
    Old Sturbridge Village
DESK ON FRAME
    Art Institute of Chicago
PRESS CUPBOARD*
    Wadsworth Atheneum
IPSWICH ROOM
    Museum of Fine Arts, Boston
WAINSCOT CHAIR*
    Philadelphia Museum of Art
WAINSCOT CHAIR
    Victoria and Albert Museum
DUTCH TABLE*
    Metropolitan Museum of Art
DUTCH LOWBOY
    Metropolitan Museum of Art
DINING TABLE
    Brooklyn Museum
EARLY GATE-LEG TABLE
    Old Sturbridge Village
DROP-LEAF TABLE
    Metropolitan Museum of Art
BIBLE BOXES*
    Wadsworth Atheneum
SWISS CHEST
    Schlossmuseum, Berlin

OAK CHEST
    Victoria and Albert Museum
BIBLE BOX
    Philadelphia Museum of Art
TABLE BOX
    Art Institute of Chicago
BIBLE BOXES
    Metropolitan Museum of Art
TUDOR CHEST*
    Art Institute of Chicago
TALL CHEST OF DRAWERS
    Philadelphia Museum of Art
PAINTED CHEST*
    Wadsworth Atheneum
PAINTED CHEST
    Metropolitan Museum of Art
PAINTED TALL CHEST
    Nordiska Museum, Stockholm
BANISTER-BACK ARMCHAIR*
    Art Institute of Chicago
BREWSTER SLAT-BACK CHAIR
    Art Institute of Chicago
LADDER-BACK CHAIR
    Wadsworth Atheneum
VASE-BACK SIDE CHAIR
    Los Angeles County Museum of Art

2
ORIGINS OF THE COLONIAL

Our interest and concern in Colonial American furniture are natural because it is one of our greatest heritages from the past. It is so important to us because we are Americans and we have reason to be proud of the furniture produced by these early craftsmen. At the beginning, much of the furniture that they managed to put together was crude and bulky, expressing their strength and virility, with little thought given to design or proportions. Although working under terrific handicaps and disheartening privations, it was not too long before they were producing furniture that often compared favorably with the contemporary European products. Certainly it was not as elaborate or as complex in the profusion of the details, moldings, carvings and the like. Despite these shortcomings their furniture had a quality all its own. These qualities will be taken up later in this synthesis.

The term "Colonial" originally designated the thirteen British colonies stretching along the eastern shore of North America in what is now known as the United States. These colonies remained subservient to the mother country until 1776. However, the term "Colonial" has been extended to include all furniture designed and made here from 1620 to 1840 and some even extend the date to 1860. This is a purely arbitrary inclusion, for practical purposes, and has no real historic significance.

It is a well-known fact that approximately fifty per cent of the settlers who came to these shores were English. The two earliest settlements were at Jamestown in Virginia in 1607 and that of the Puritans in Massachusetts in 1620. They were soon augmented by the Dutch in New York's Hudson Valley, the French in Louisiana and the German settlers in Pennsylvania, called the Pennsylvania Dutch instead of, rightfully, the Pennsylvania Germans. The Swedes preferred the region around Delaware, while the Spaniards found Florida more to their liking, probably because the climate resembled more closely that of their native land. Right from the start we had a varied and conglomerate group of settlers, a veritable melting pot.

No doubt there were many reasons why they ventured forth to a strange land to make new homes and a new life. Among these reasons were to seek freedom from religious and political persecution. Many no doubt saw this opportunity to escape from social entanglements, but above all there was that inescapable urge to seek adventure in a foreign land. No matter how fair conditions may be where we are, many of us are readily lured by the fata morgana to venture forth into unknown regions, even if it means hardships and privations. These settlers were a sturdy lot who, unhappy and dissatisfied in their native habitat, sought relief in a faraway land. They included workers, farmers, tradespeople, professionals, joiners, carpenters and builders. Among them of course were soldiers of fortune, apprentices eager to learn a craft, adventurers, maidens seeking better marital opportunities and, as always, ne'er-do-wells and criminals who took this chance to get out of the country to avoid arrest and prosecution. On the other hand, there were men of high estate, young men of the nobility who came here well endowed and soon became the early landowners of Virginia with grants from the Crown. The Pilgrims who settled farther north around Massachusetts were of a more sturdy, hard-working element who sought a better life and were willing to work for it. They were for the most part persons of the commonality who sought relief from the political malevolence of James I and Charles I of England. Later came the influx of the Irish, Italian, Russian and Balkan emigrants, but their influence was negligible on the development of Colonial American furniture.

Amongst the first settlers in Jamestown there undoubtedly were a few experienced journeymen and even some cabinetmakers, but at the beginning there were too many fundamental things to be done for them to practice their trades. That would come later when matters settled down. The vastly different conditions which they found here made them soon realize that they could not practice their craft as heretofore. While it is true that most of the furniture styles originated in England, they did not find fruition over here. Their influence was only secondary and the results proved vastly different. Therefore in considering the design of Colonial American furniture, even from its earliest conception, many

Origins of the Colonial

people are inclined to suggest that it was little more than a cruder interpretation of the styles then prevalent in the Old World. This thoroughly erroneous conclusion tends to libel those early American woodworkers as uninspired copyists. This is farthest away from the truth of the matter. Even if they had attempted to copy the foreign models brought into this country from England and the Continent, it would have been an impossible undertaking due to the unavailability of the correct woods, their lack of materials, tools and skills.

The fact of the matter is that these settler-craftsmen had to pursue the hard road of failure, poverty and ofttimes privation and despair in an effort to further their craft. They struggled for a livelihood in a strange and hostile country, overcoming obstacles and indigence. The majority of the workers learned their trades here. Not only did many of them develop into excellent craftsmen, but all through the Colonies they showed a definite creative potentiality that not only tended to make their furniture individual but often surpassing the European prototypes. Names here are not important. We have preserved in the museums countless examples of their early work that bespeaks its excellence.

With a certain amount of European furniture being brought into this country by new settlers and prospecting businessmen, coupled with the ever-increasing mercantile trade from various countries, it was unavoidable that these importations should have a certain influence on the woodworkers over here. However, the radically different local demands had to be met. For chests, lowboys, highboys and cabinets affording the needed storage space, there was great demand. Also needed were cupboards to hold precious china and linens, shelving to put away the pots and pans, boxes in which to store Bibles, trundle beds for the children to sleep in.

The differences in climate, the hot summers and the frigid winters — all these conditions had to be coped with, and strangely enough they proved to be a benefaction instead of a deterrent. The woodworkers were faced with so many challenges that had to be solved. They had to find new and more expedient methods of doing things to achieve the desired results. What was more important, they had to use the woods close at hand and native to the various localities, such as pine, cherry, maple and birch. There was no calling up the lumberyard and ordering so many feet of this and that. The trees had to be felled and the boards often cut by hand. Soon the Colonies grew and prospered and hard woods such as oak and walnut were made available. Soon the varieties of woods became abundant and what they did not have was brought in.

In the matter of furniture design, a lot of the foreign extraneous matter had to be eliminated, much of the gingerbread discarded, applied carvings done away with and inlay and painted decorations abandoned. These deletions fortunately only tended to emphasize the beauty of line, the fineness of the proportions, and emphasize the renascent silhouette. These are the features that we find so matchless in Colonial American furniture. To illustrate the point, if it were possible, let us take a William and Mary highboy and an American highboy of the same approximate date and set them side by side. Let us compare.

The English model is made of walnut, the drawer-fronts are raised and framed with borders of herringbone inlay surrounding the burl panels. A heavy protruding cornice of many members crowns the top. The upper structure has two small drawers toward the summit and three full-length drawers beneath. The extended lower structure has three drawers, two square ones at the sides and one shallower drawer at the center to permit of the shaped apron. The highboy is supported by four cabriole legs of drastic S curvatures. The drawer-pulls and escutcheon plates are completely covered with intricate engraving.

The American highboy was made in Massachusetts, of solid maple. The drawer-fronts are of selected curly maple surrounded by quarter-round edges to give the needed contrast with the body framework. The particular cornice has been greatly reduced and simplified, using only a bold "O-G" crown molding of a few members. The cabriole legs have been straightened, affording a much better support for the rather heavy carcass. The pulls and the escutcheon plates are also of brass in similar outline but perfectly plain, without a lot of curlicues or elaboration. Not only have the general proportions been maintained but the lower shaped apron has been dropped to welcome an incised fan motif. The entire aspect of the Colonial model is simpler and more prepossessing. There has been no artifice employed to detract and no undue embellishments permitted to distract. The American highboy is honest, straightforward and sun-clear. It sings. The piece is inviting, sturdy and wholesome. The English prototype appears overloaded, as though the designer tried to put everything he knew into it.

In a highboy especially the intent and purpose should be to build a piece of furniture that is utilitarian in the most compatible manner. It need not necessarily be a masterpiece or a showpiece of elaboration. The far superior solution is evident in the Colonial American example. Here the cabinetmaker succeeded in getting rid of all the foreign incumbrances that no doubt plagued his fresher conception. He appreciated the truism

Origins of the Colonial

that simplicity is the better part of virtue. Say what you must, but speak clearly and distinctly. Fancy phrases and unwarranted complexities only tend to defeat the purpose of concise expression. Thus reducing the design of the American highboy to the least common denominator made it come out the victor. That is how the American style in furniture design came into being and why it has prospered.

Particularly in England during the eighteenth century many furniture manuals were published. These included works by Jones, Copeland, Langley and Swan. In 1754 Thomas Chippendale brought out his *The Gentleman and Cabinet-Maker's Director* and in 1788 the wife of George Hepplewhite published posthumously his work entitled *The Cabinet-makers' and Upholsterers' Guide*. These volumes soon found their way to these shores and possibly had some influence on the current output. Little effort, however, was made to copy these designs, as they were a bit too complicated and sophisticated for local digestion.

Chippendale was a philanderer. He had no scruples and knew no bounds. He usurped whatever he could lay his hands upon, used it for his purpose and claimed all as his own. During his active years he certainly produced a vast, incongruous and flamboyant aggregation of furniture which incorporated Gothic tracery, bamboo motifs, the Chinoiserie, prolific ribbon extravaganzas, takings from Louis XV unsymmetrical vagaries to the untamed Rococo manipulations. All these attributes he fashioned to suit his purpose without regard to reason or causation. He was not satisfied to use one or two design elements on a single piece but he had a penchant for jumbling varied, different motivations together in a free-for-all arrangement. Chippendale was clever but we question his rationality.

For the Colonial cabinetmaker all this tomfoolery was out of bounds. He did not succumb to its wiles. All this was too capricious and arbitrary to suit his rather sedate taste; he was slow to accept or even adapt these vagaries and when he did use excerpts from this amalgamation it was in a much modified and restrained manner. This was very evident in the classical approach of the New York cabinetmaker Duncan Phyfe, who was more inclined to favor the symmetrical eurythmics of Thomas Sheraton. It is worthy of note that the Colonial designers consciously avoided the eccentric and bizarre in their work. The tendency was always toward simplification, clarification and clear thinking. What was emphasized was purity of line, refinement in detail, the careful selection and assembling of woods and, above all, excellence of proportions and valid construction. Come to think of it, are not these the very same qualities that persist to this day as being the manifest requisites for all good design and cabinetwork? In England the eighteenth century was called "The Golden Age" in furniture design, with such celebrated designers as Chippendale, Hepplewhite, Sheraton and Robert Adam in the foray. While they all worked in different directions, they managed to accelerate the progress of good design.

Strange to say, the works of this constellation of talents did not have immediate effects in this country and it took a while before their influence was transmitted and showed up in our work. Again, when these excrescences became evident it was in a much modified and quite different result. The sweep of the prairie, the smell of rich swaying fields of wheat, the music of babbling brooks and the glory of the sun circumventing the mountains, all had their conducive effect on the rational thinking of the Colonial designers. The extravagances, debauchery and profligacy of the Old World could produce little reverberation here. Having minimum tradition to restrict them, they were free to create new images that reflected the unfettered life here. Uninhibited, these designers sought fresh outlets for their creative prognostications.

Here then is the secret of these Colonial Furniture Treasures of which we may be justly proud. Their glory consisted in the position that there never was the slightest desire or inclination to copy or produce facsimile reproductions of European furniture styles. The American furniture designers and cabinetmakers were determined to fashion furniture that fulfilled the needs and embodied the consciousness and the culture that were being promulgated here. We are indeed indebted to these early craftsmen for their courage, foresight, independence and valor in designing and building furniture that so completely embodied the spirit of the times in which it was made. This surely is our greatest heritage because their approach and the results are so typically American. We do understand this furniture and can dwell with it in peace and contentment. It would be well for all of us to revere and nurture this very important contribution to Americana.

Origins of the Colonial

After the settlement at Jamestown and the landing of the Mayflower the eastern seacoast of the North American continent, of what is now the United States, was thrown open to settlement. They came from all over Europe, from England, Scotland, Holland, Germany, Sweden and later from Italy and Ireland. They made their way here to escape from religious and political persecution. Here they looked to a better life where liberty was indicated. Little did they know of the hardships that were to follow, the infinite sacrifices that would have to be made, the relentless fight against the elements and the savagery of the Indians. That the fight was worth the while is indicated in the continued flow of immigrants that came here from all sections of the globe.

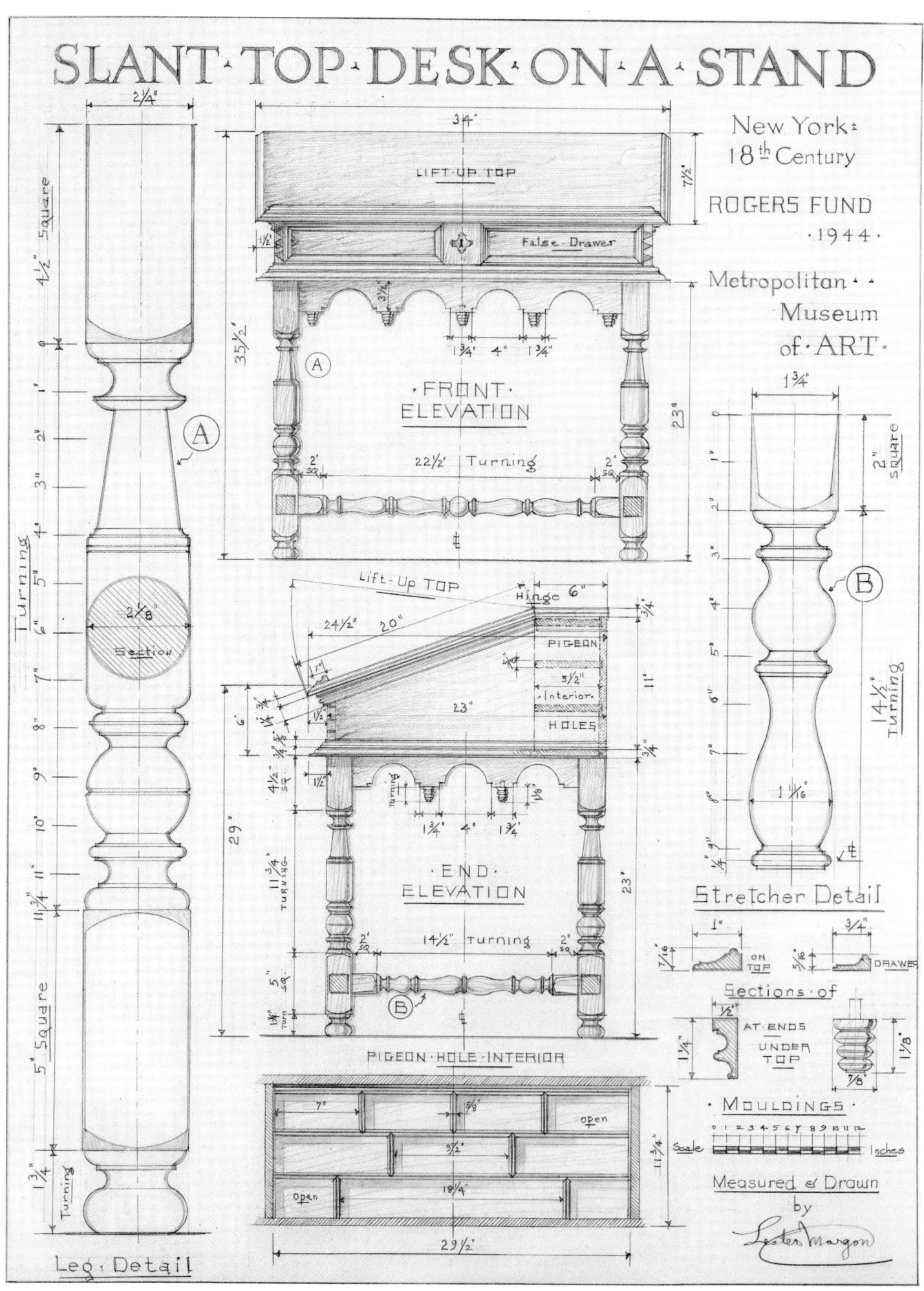

DESK ON A STAND
Metropolitan Museum of Art   Rogers Fund 1944

There are some forms in Colonial American furniture that are definitely related to the locality. This is the case with this red gumwood desk on a frame from New York, *circa* 1700. It is one of the most elaborate and sophisticated designs of its type, with the series of arches in the apron and punctuated by turned drop finials. The urn-shaped turned legs are excellent but appear a bit too formal for the desk, while the turned stretchers are intricate. Lift up the slanted top and note the interior at the rear. It is a series of varied-sized pigeonholes. All the moldings are finely delineated and, taken all in all, the desk is quite a formidable creation. The use of gumwood in this instance is unusual but then much depended upon the finish, which resembled walnut. New York, even at that time, was the coming metropolis and no doubt this desk was made to fit into a particular setting. In it we get a feeling of the approaching elegancies of the English trend to classical forms. Despite its evident solidity there is still a very definite colloquial feeling in this desk.

SLANT-TOP DESK
Old Sturbridge Village

This desk on a frame or desk on a stand, whichever you prefer, is from Old Sturbridge Village, that wonderful congregation of old houses brought from the surrounding countryside and full of choice treasures in furniture and implements from the early Colonial days. It is a delightful place to visit, showing how the people of New England lived, worked and prospered. This desk dates from *circa* 1700-1725 and is made of maple. The slant top is held in place by wrought-iron hinges.

DESK ON A FRAME
Art Institute of Chicago

This is a very simple early model of a desk on a stand and dates from 1690-1720. The woods used are pine and maple. It could have been made in almost any of the Colonies. Of special interest here are the pull-outs at the sides of the front apron. The top is hinged at the front and opens forwardly, using the pull-outs as the supports, thus affording a large writing surface; this is most unusual. The desk was purchased through the Wirt D. Walker Fund.

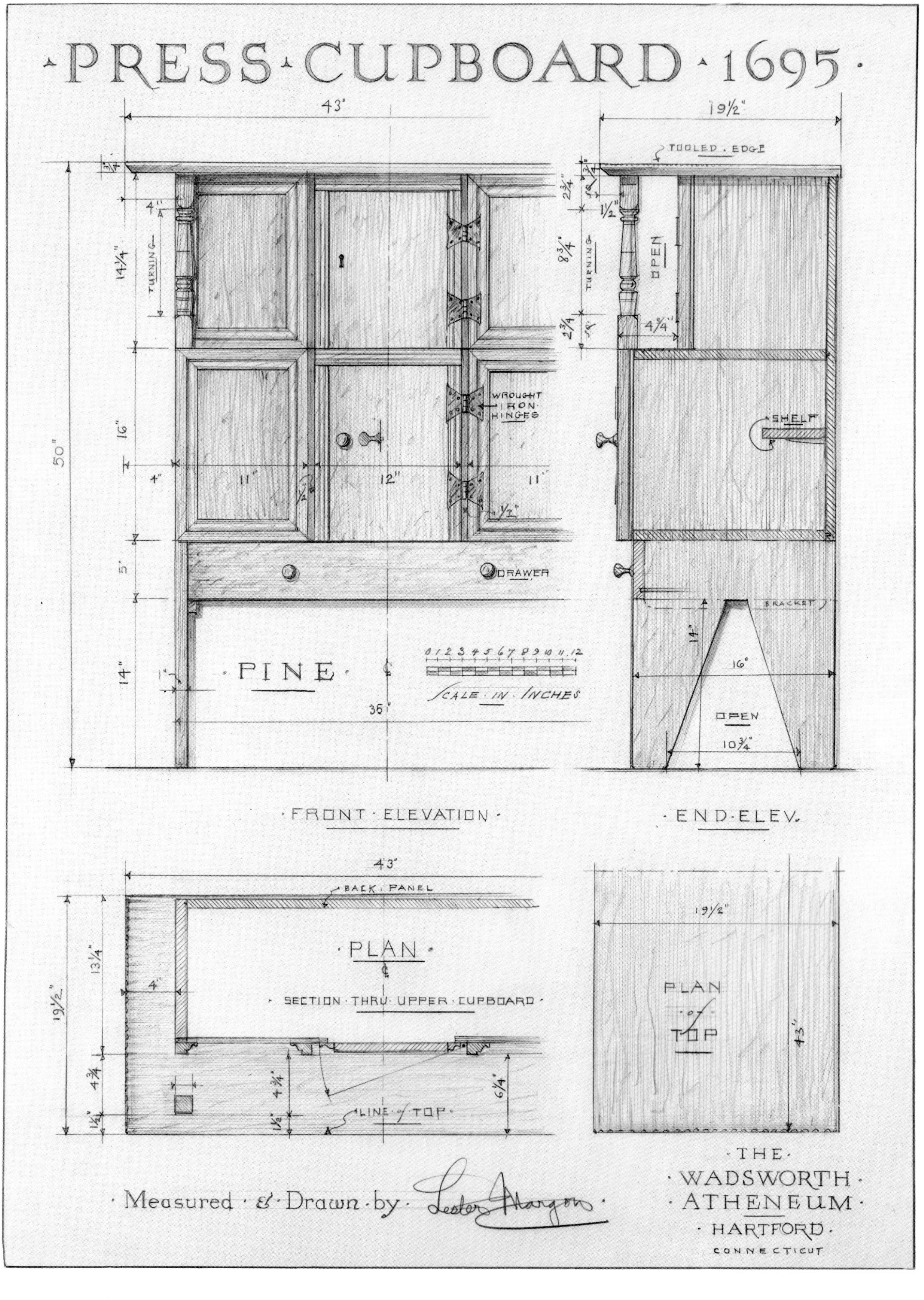

PRESS·CUPBOARD·1695

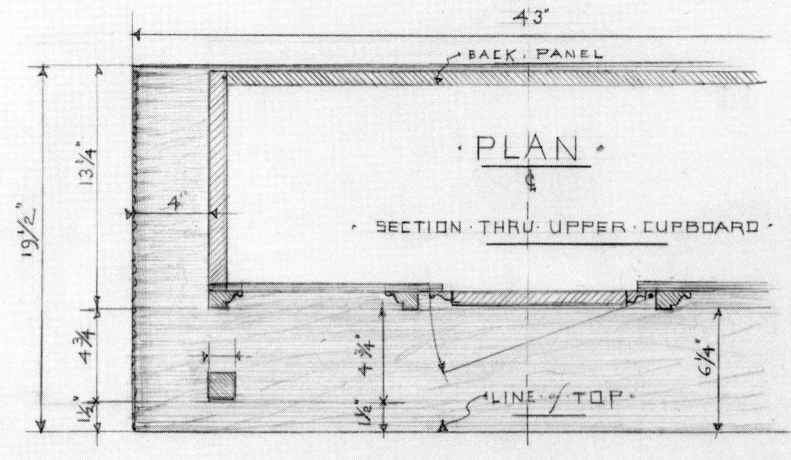

·FRONT·ELEVATION·

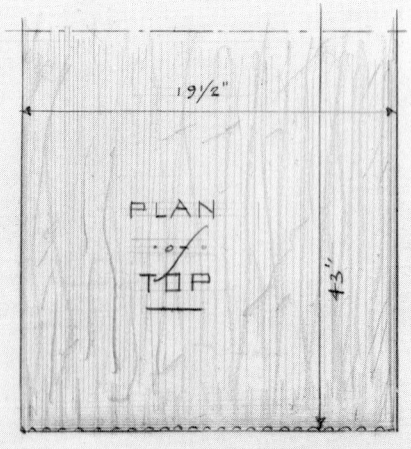

·END·ELEV·

Measured & Drawn by Lester Margon

·THE·WADSWORTH·ATHENEUM· ·HARTFORD· CONNECTICUT

IPSWICH ROOM
Museum of Fine Arts, Boston

This gallery originally was the entire second floor of a house that stood at the corner of High and Manning Streets in Ipswich. The timbers were carefully removed and reassembled in the same order. The frame is the longest of its kind known: forty-nine feet, three inches. This house dates from *circa* 1675. The furniture and other objects shown are included through the courtesy of a group of collectors known as "The Trestle Board." The room was purchased through The John Lowell Gardner Fund, 1925.

PRESS CUPBOARD
Wadsworth Atheneum

The Reverend Dr. Wallace Nutting turned to writing and photography because of ill health. He became interested in Colonial American furniture and collected hundreds of pieces for publication in his *Furniture Treasury*. He believed that objects which our ancestors made and used enriched our lives and afforded an appreciation of the past in retrospect. Mr. J. Pierpont Morgan selected some of the better pieces in his collection and presented them to the Wadsworth Atheneum. This press cupboard of pine with ash pillars, *circa* 1695, comes from southern New Hampshire. It may be described as a poor man's court cupboard. The crudity of this piece from New England is shown in contrast to the more elaborate cupboards of a later date which had reference to the royalty and the judiciary. However it is this crudity that makes this press cupboard so interesting. Note the long panel ends and the naïve way the base has been cut out. The edges of the top have been gouged to create a sort of pattern — very unusual. These press cupboards were probably used to hold clothing, linens and the like. Whether they were actually used as clothes presses is doubtful.

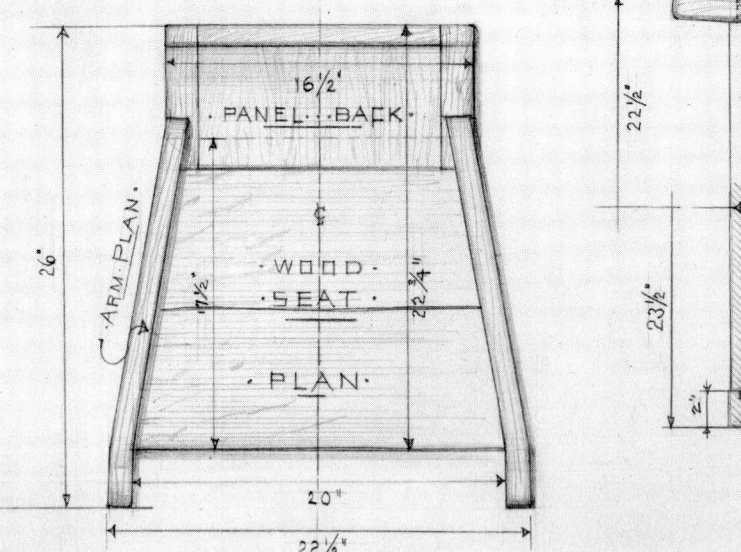

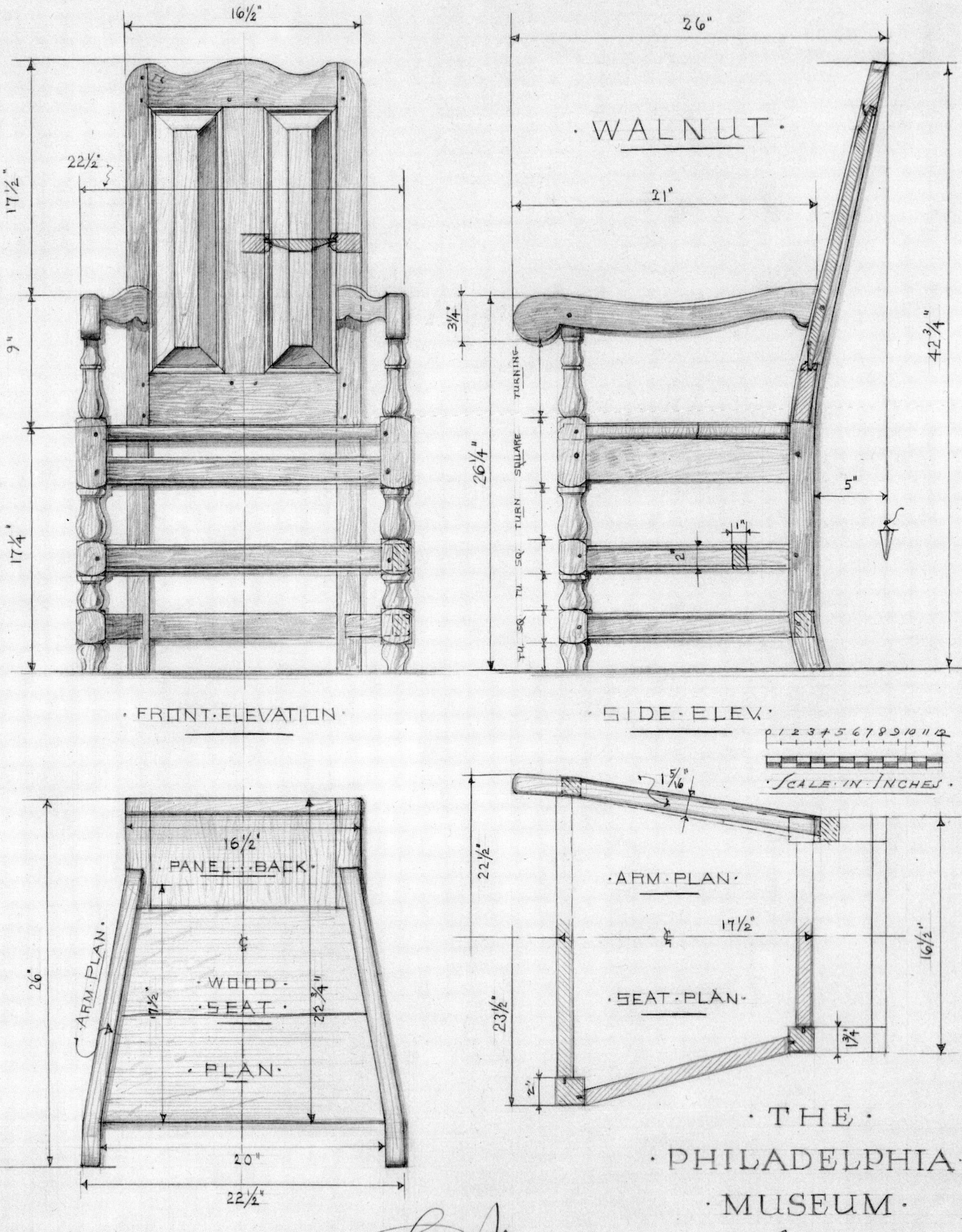

WAINSCOT CHAIR
Philadelphia Museum of Art

Wainscot chairs were for the main part made of oak and followed English models. They were heavy and not easy to move about. The name "wainscot chair" comes from the fact that similar wood paneling was used on the wainscot in taverns and manor halls in England. It happens that this model is of walnut and dates from *circa* 1725. It was made by the Pennsylvania German craftsmen but is not native to their style of work. This chair is a conservative type with just two panels in the back, a shaped arm and quite ordinary turnings and plain stretchers. Many wainscot chairs were most elaborately carved and ornamented. While most of them had wooden seats and were later supplied with loose cushions, some were adequately upholstered. They are always masculine in character and appearance and not particularly gracious or comfortable. In a den or library they would be most appropriate. The date for the wainscot chair in England is 1650, so this model is frankly an adaptation of the type and is not a native product. Records show that many of these chairs were imported from England to Virginia.

WAINSCOT CHAIR
Victoria and Albert Museum

Since Colonial American furniture was influenced so strongly by the imports from England, it is important to compare the foreign models with the work done here. Therefore we have selected a few examples for study and investigation. Here we see an English oak armchair from the seventeenth century, carved with floral scrollwork within a roundheaded arch showing Jacobean influence, showing how elaborate these wainscot chairs had become. All the detail of the carving had historical significance.

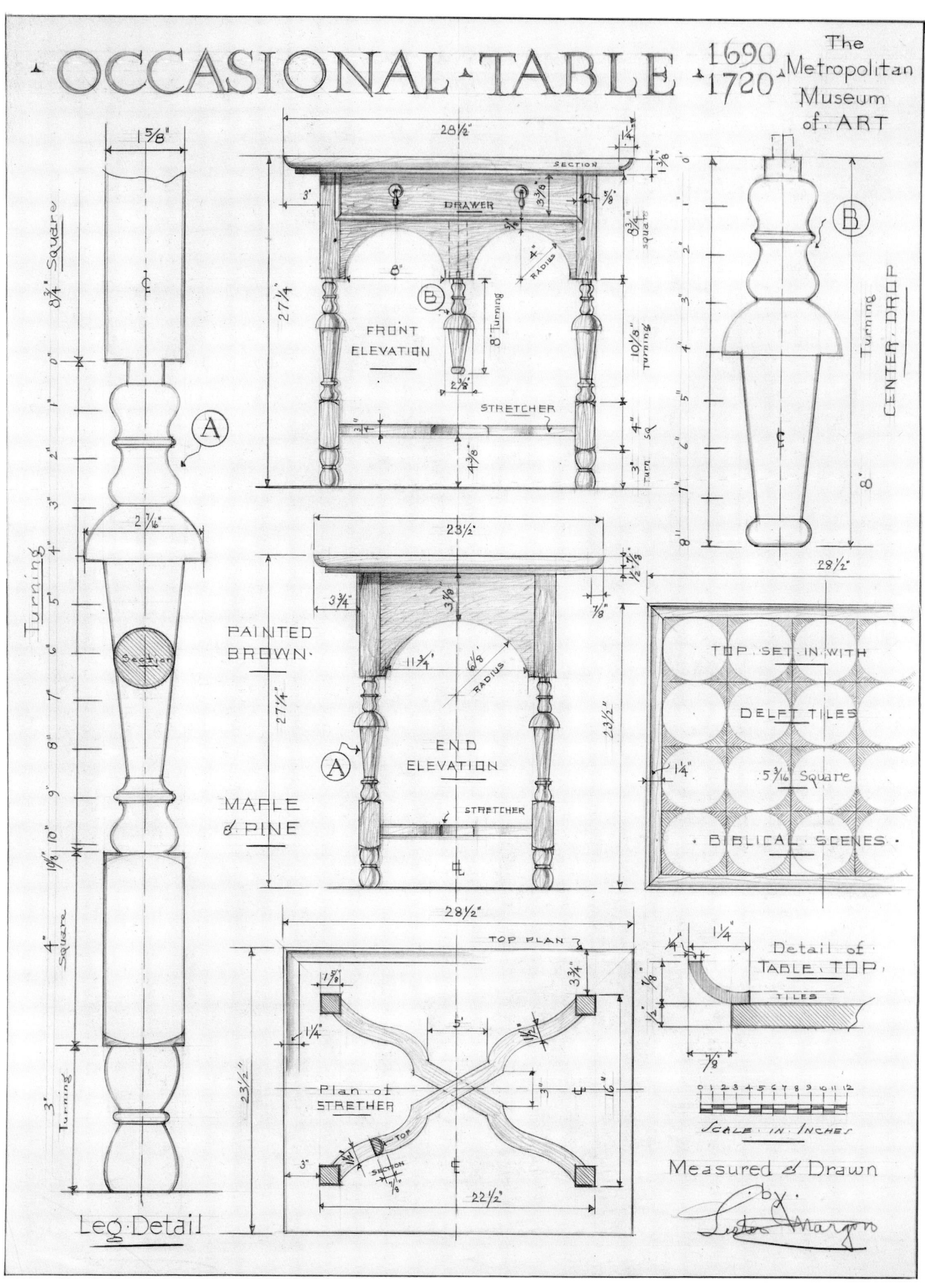

OCCASIONAL TABLE
Metropolitan Museum of Art   Gift of Mrs. Russell Sage 1909

The Dutch settlers in New Amsterdam brought with them the cultural influences and traditions from the Netherlands. This is very evident in the design and treatment of this occasional table, 1690-1720, made of maple and pine. The table is painted a chocolate brown. Note that the table top is inlaid with blue and white Delft tiles depicting Biblical scenes. The turnings of the legs seem to be a Dutch interpretation of the William and Mary style but the placing of such a large center drop turning is certainly most unorthodox. The crossed stretcher is usual but the whole effect of the table is a sense of heaviness. Without knowing, we would immediately classify it as Dutch. No doubt this was the sort of furniture they were accustomed to and they tried to remake it in the New World. In England at this time, pieces of this type were generally made in walnut. It is interesting to note how national traits and tendencies persist and how difficult it is to abandon them. The tile top is most effective and the Biblical legend portrayed denotes the sensibilities of the maker.

DUTCH LOWBOY
Metropolitan Museum of Art

This rather quaint model of a lowboy with a marble top appears to us to be definitely of Dutch origin. The legs, an unusual combination of turnings and a six-sides portion, are a bit heavy. The cross-stretcher has a rounded facing and is subjected to the placing of a disk right at the crossroad. This is one of those pieces we find difficult to classify due to lack of definite information. However we will venture to call it Dutch because of its apparent awkwardness.

DINING TABLE
Brooklyn Museum

This rather complicated arrangement of turned legs and stretchers is the base for this oval-top drop-leaf dining table in mahogany. The date is *circa* 1700. This is the type of dining table that was popular at this time and could be found in many of the Colonists' homes. The drop leaves were supported by wings that folded into the stretchers when not in use. The designer was not content to use only the array of turnings but added the newly discovered Spanish foot. One of the reasons for the popularity of this table was that when opened it was sufficiently large to seat a good-sized family.

EARLY GATE-LEG TABLE
Old Sturbridge Village

In the living room of the Fresno House in Old Sturbridge Village is this early Colonial American gate-leg table with hinged extension supports, *circa* 1670. It is a fine country piece, made of maple with cherry legs. The top opens into a pleasing oval. The turnings are simple and adequate. The extensions at the bottom produce a base when the table is closed. The location is New England. The furniture collection at Old Sturbridge Village covers the period from 1670 to 1830. It shows "middling," "common" and "best" furniture.

DROP-LEAF TABLE
Metropolitan Museum of Art

This trestle-type gate-leg table made its appearance early in the Colonies. When closed it looks like a narrow console that can be set against the wall. When opened it becomes a good-size dining or utility table. The gate-legs are pivoted to the central frame and when opened the leaves are supported. The turnings in this table are a little out of the ordinary. The one drawer is for the cutlery that is used daily. These tables still maintain their popularity but appear especially well suited to the Colonial American tradition.

Circa 1670 · BIBLE BOXES

- FRONT ELEVATION -

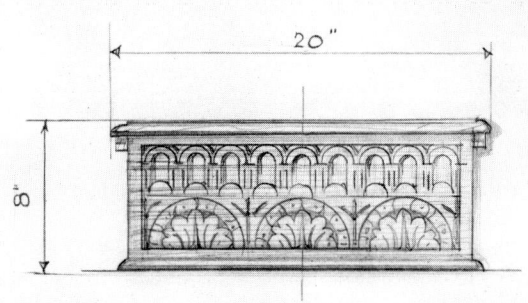
- FRONT ELEV -

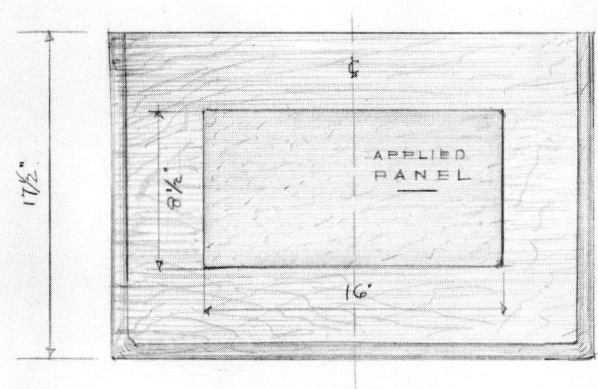
- TOP PLAN -

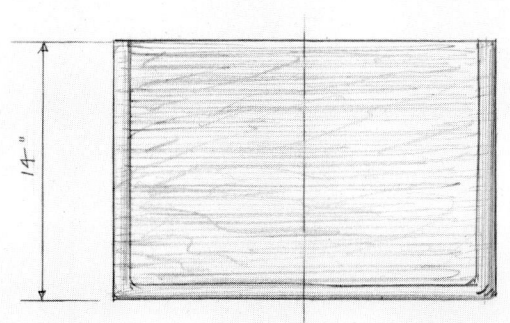
- TOP PLAN -

- END ELEV -

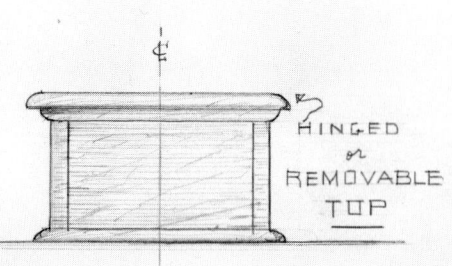
- END ELEV -

· OAK ·

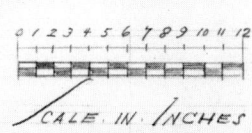
Scale in Inches

Measured & Drawn by Lester Margon

· THE WADSWORTH ATHENEUM ·
· HARTFORD CONNECTICUT ·

BIBLE BOXES
Wadsworth Atheneum

Bible boxes were the most treasured possession of the early settlers throughout Colonial America. Many of them were made of oak, *circa* 1670. Safekeeping of the family Bibles being of the utmost importance, many of the boxes had locks to preserve them from the ravages of time and the possibility of theft. The making of these boxes was always a labor of love and they often were richly carved and ornamented. What beauty and what sentiment were expressed in these crude carvings! The Hadley-type box shown in the upper drawing is from Lyme County, New Hampshire, and is a combination of pine and oak. The carving is deep and expressively done. Here we see the image of a strange conventionalized plant growth, with its roots firmly pressed into the earth and with blossoms reaching into the heavens. The lower Lunette model has the crude, bold carving of the circled acanthus with the repeat pattern gouged out above. Some of these boxes had slanted hinged tops and were used as table-writing desks, with the interiors partitioned off according to the needs. These boxes are most decorative and are much sought after today.

OAK CHEST
Victoria and Albert Museum

This fine example of a carved oak chest with a flat tracery design and pilasters of full acanthus leaves, bordered by a guilloche, is typical of the English version of the small chest. Dating from 1640, it is proudly inscribed with the name of its owner — Elezabeth Lovell. Note that in this chest the carving is of a higher finished order than on the American chests of the period because no doubt they had the skills and the tools to do this fine work.

SWISS CHEST
Schlossmuseum, Berlin

Peasant art interests us tremendously because it speaks a universal language. This chest dated 1641 shows a type of incised carving that was similar in technique and design throughout all Europe at that time. Since so many of the American colonists came from these parts of Europe, it is only natural to expect that their artistic expression would be similar to the work produced in their native lands. These chests all tell the same story of love and devotion.

ANOTHER BIBLE BOX
Philadelphia Museum of Art

This Bible box dates from 1690, from the vicinity of Massachusetts. We know this by the circumspect and proper alignment of the design. Generally made of oak and pine, the softer wood permitted of easier manipulation. The design is ingenious, a combination of rosette and leaf formations. What beauty and sentiment found expression in these little treasure boxes! They are like a song sung with tender feeling.

TABLE BOX
The Art Institute of Chicago

Call them what you will — Bible boxes, writing desks — we prefer to call them treasure boxes. Because of the varied and prolific carving, their intent and invention, their freedom from all rules and regulations, they are a delight to behold. This one, made of oak, is probably from Pennsylvania, *circa* 1690-1700. Note how cleverly the tulip has been included in the carving. The initials MP proclaim the identity of the proud owner. This box was purchased through the Wirt D. Walker Fund.

BIBLE BOXES
Metropolitan Museum of Art

The variety of these Bible boxes is infinite. The display of the homely artistry of these Pennsylvania German folk is likewise infinite. They are crudely done but tremendously compensating. They clearly show that these early craftsmen had a sense of the appropriate and a feeling for color and decoration. The two boxes illustrated are more conventional than usual yet the fine sense for design and placement is evident. The painted chest is shown separately in a better photograph.

BEHOLD – ANOTHER BOX
Wadsworth Atheneum

Bible boxes, small boxes for the safekeeping of personal articles, were used throughout the Colonies from the earliest times. This one from the South is of pine, as can be plainly seen, *circa* 1690. It again shows the skill and creativity of these peasant carvers who were bent on putting their dreams into reality. Note the hilarious onslaught of the dogs and the straightening effect of the Egyptian rosettes. Without any rhyme or reason, it was all just a bit of gleeful decoration.

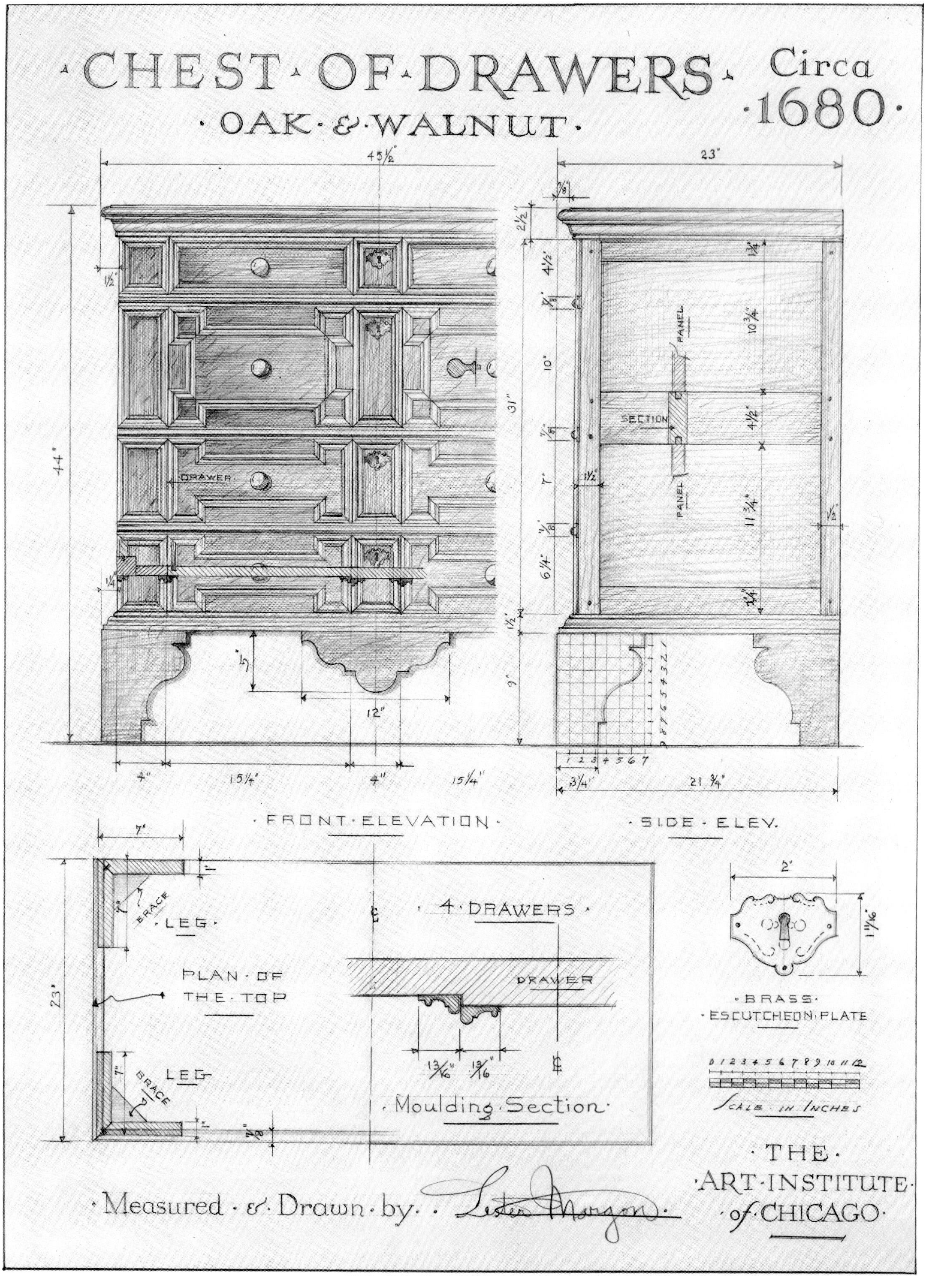

CHEST·OF·DRAWERS· Circa ·1680·
·OAK·&·WALNUT·

·FRONT·ELEVATION· · SIDE·ELEV·

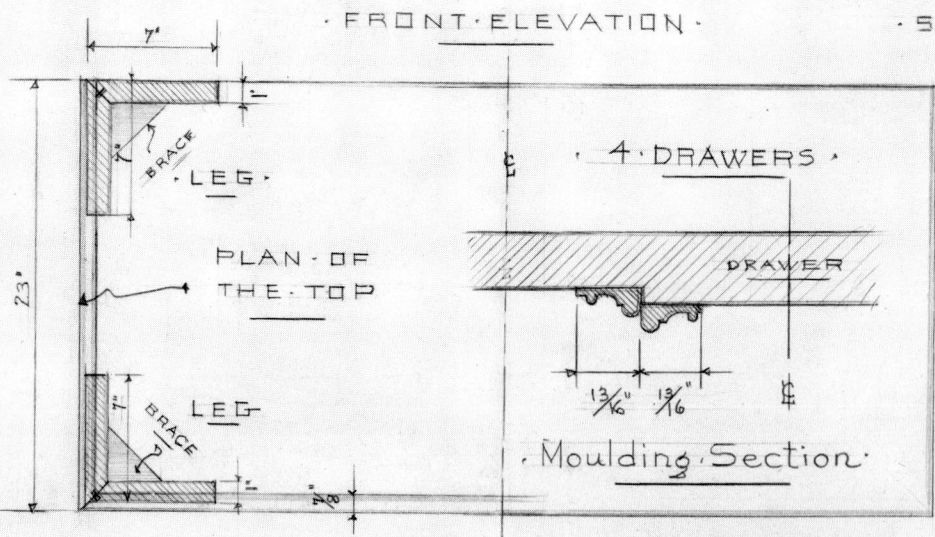

·PLAN·OF·THE·TOP· ·Moulding Section·

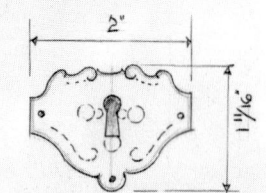

·BRASS·ESCUTCHEON·PLATE·

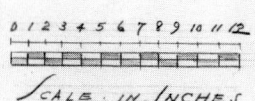

·SCALE·IN·INCHES·

·Measured·&·Drawn·by·· Lester Morgan

·THE·ART·INSTITUTE·of·CHICAGO·

CHEST OF DRAWERS
The Art Institute of Chicago   Gift of Mrs. Emily Crane Chadbourne

This Pilgrim Century chest of four long drawers is made of oak and walnut, *circa* 1680, and comes from Pennsylvania. The piece exemplifies the care and the ability of these early Colonial craftsmen to produce the varied geometric patterns on the drawer fronts. The effect is rich and rewarding. Each drawer front is different and the effect produced is that of a series of set-in panels. Of special interest are the unusually high cut-out legs and the center pendant. This is certainly unique and different. It may not be exactly according to Hoyle, but that makes it interesting. The turned knobs and the cut-out escutcheon plates are distinctive. This is a chest to remember; you may never see its like again. Of course it is of Jacobean inspiration and no doubt many chests of this character were brought into this country from England. There is a certain sense of originality, however, about our chest and the effect is not unlike a rich mosaic in pattern. It is always a delight to come across a piece of furniture that breaks the rules.

TALL CHEST OF DRAWERS
Philadelphia Museum of Art

This Pennsylvania tall chest of drawers is walnut, dating from the middle of the eighteenth century. There are four long drawers of various depths, two smaller drawers above and near the top, three still smaller arched drawers. It is a beauty, especially where storage space is at a premium. On the sides there are long panels. These bracket legs are straight, with curlicues. The color of the walnut is that of deep amber. This chest was given to the Museum by J. Stogdell Stokes and has found a fitting background in a room from the House of the Miller of Millbach.

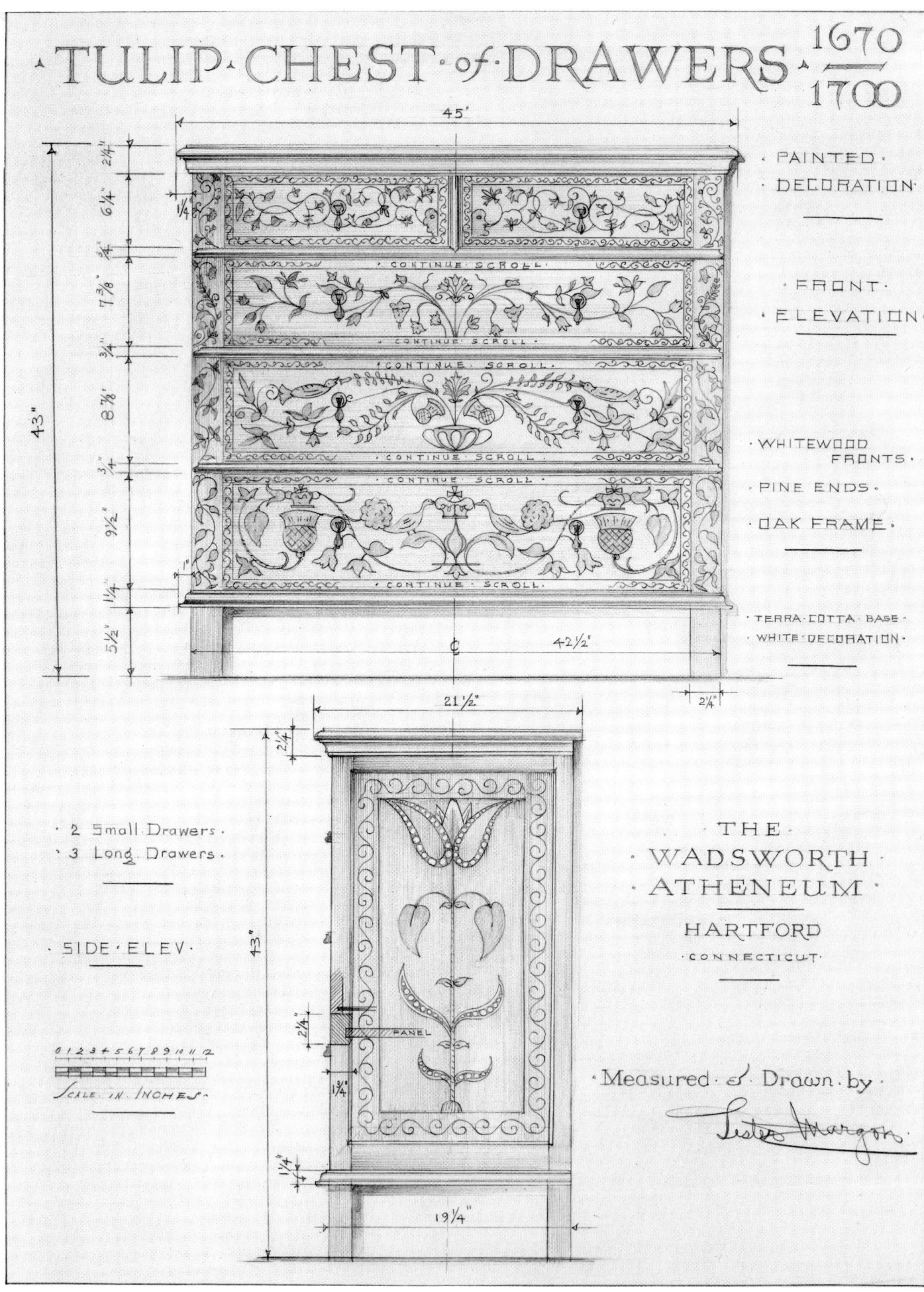

PAINTED CHEST OF DRAWERS
The Wadsworth Atheneum

Also from the Wallace Nutting Collection is this chest of drawers. This is possibly the most elaborate and gorgeous painted chest in the annals of Colonial American furniture. It comes from central-southern Connecticut, *circa* 1670-1700. The piece has white wood fronts, pine ends and an oak top and frame. The inspiration for the decoration probably came from Holland, with the tulip plainly identified in huge scale painted on the sides. The ground is painted a chocolate brown and the linear arrangements are in white, while the flowers vary in tones of reds and terra cotta.

This chest is without doubt the ultimate in decoration and yet when viewed as a whole, it presents a picture of classic splendor. The decoration is not only beautiful in line and artful in execution, but it has a freedom and a flair that only the uninitiated could produce. There is present a fine sense of rhythm and expresses the peace and contentment of these peasant people. It may be farfetched to suggest that this painted decoration resembles in its ecstacy the decorations found on the walls of Pompeii but it does bespeak the joy of living.

PAINTED CHEST
Metropolitan Museum of Art

This painted and decorated chest is from Guilford, Connecticut, *circa* 1705. It is made of oak and pine and there is one long drawer. A deep chest at the upper section has a hinged top. The surface is painted brown in a mottled effect. The upper side panels are decorated with a tulip arrangement and the center panel has a wreath with the date and the owner's initials. The free floral treatment of the decoration on the lower drawer is delightful. This chest is the gift of Mrs. Russell Sage, 1909.

PAINTED TALL CHEST
Nordiska Museum, Stockholm

All throughout Europe during the first half of the seventeenth century there was religious unrest with the subsequent suppression. The peasants rebelled and many sought religious freedom in the New World. Like all primitive peoples they found expression for their suppressed desires in painting religious subjects on the expanses of their furniture. This was true of the Pennsylvania Germans but it did not apply only to them. This high painted chest from Sweden is a fine example. Note the profusion of painted flowers on the lower drawer fronts.

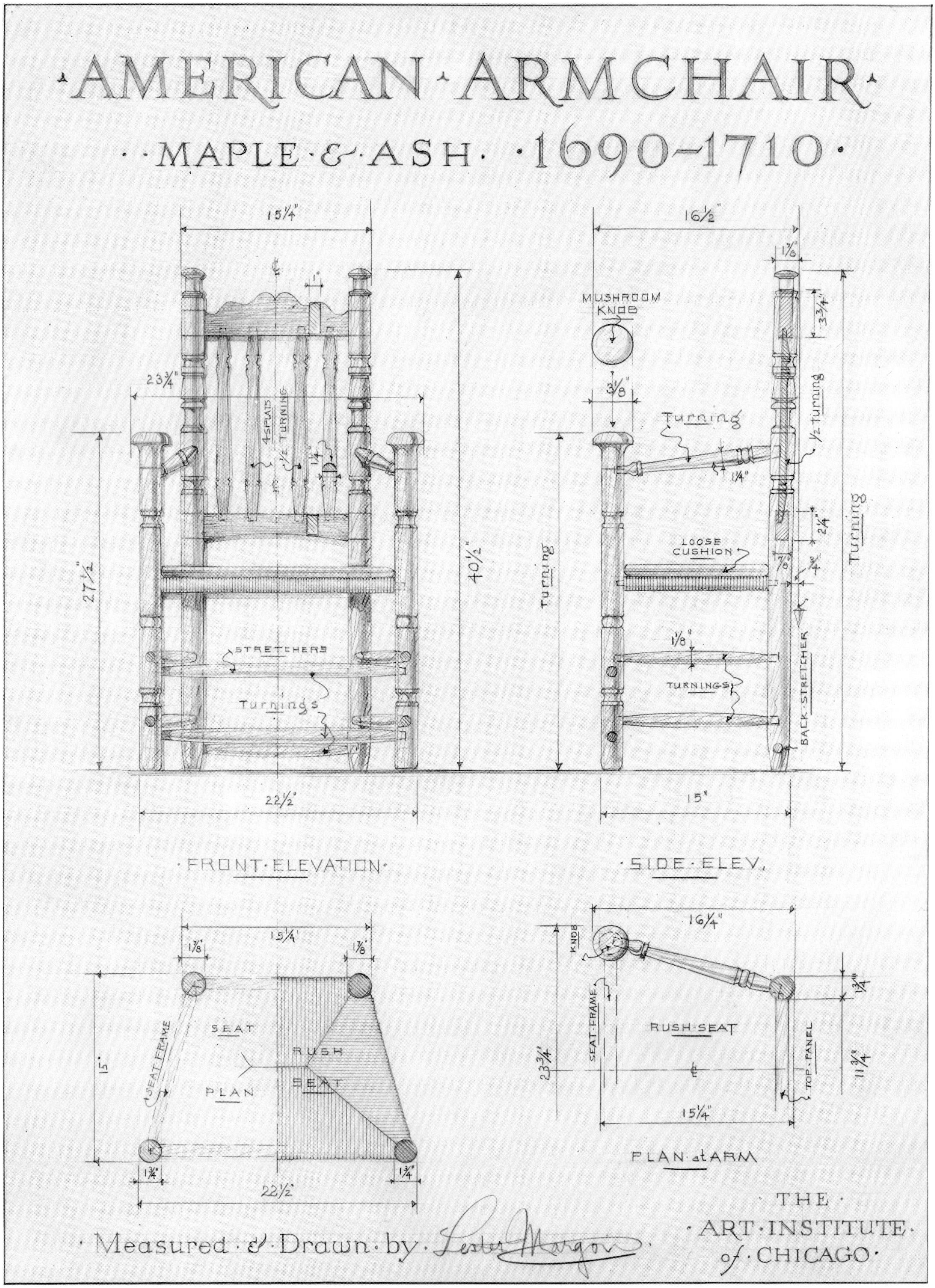

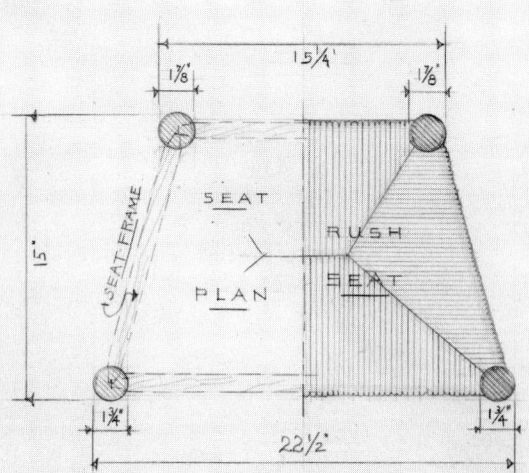

BANISTER-BACK ARMCHAIR
The Art Institute of Chicago
Alfred T. Carton (Purchase) Fund

This Pilgrim banister-back armchair, made of maple and ash, comes from New England, *circa* 1690-1710. It is a chair of good proportions. The back post turnings are rather rich in detail and the front post with the mushroom handle is typical. The rake of the arm and the plain turned stretchers complete the make-up of this chair. The split banisters are used in the panel of the back to permit of greater sitting comfort. There is a rush seat, and a knife pad has been added. It is said that one of these chairs was brought over in the Mayflower by a Pilgrim Father named Carver, hence his name is sometimes used to designate this type of chair. These banister chairs had good turnings and sophisticated lines. They generally were made of maple and were very popular at the time, especially in country areas. The design of the cut-out cresting gives a pleasant aspect to this chair. The split turnings were made by splitting turnings in half and then inserting them into the back rails with the flat part toward the front.

BREWSTER SLAT-BACK CHAIR
Art Institute of Chicago

This rather unusual combination of a Brewster and a slat-back chair comes from Connecticut or New York and is dated *circa* 1680-1700. Made of maple and ash and painted black, it is the only one of a kind that has come to our attention. The front and back posts are definitely of a Brewster-type chair and the curved shaped slats are certainly those of a slat-back chair. The combination being a bit uncertain, it is difficult to classify this unique chair. It is a museum purchase of the Sewell L. Avery Fund.

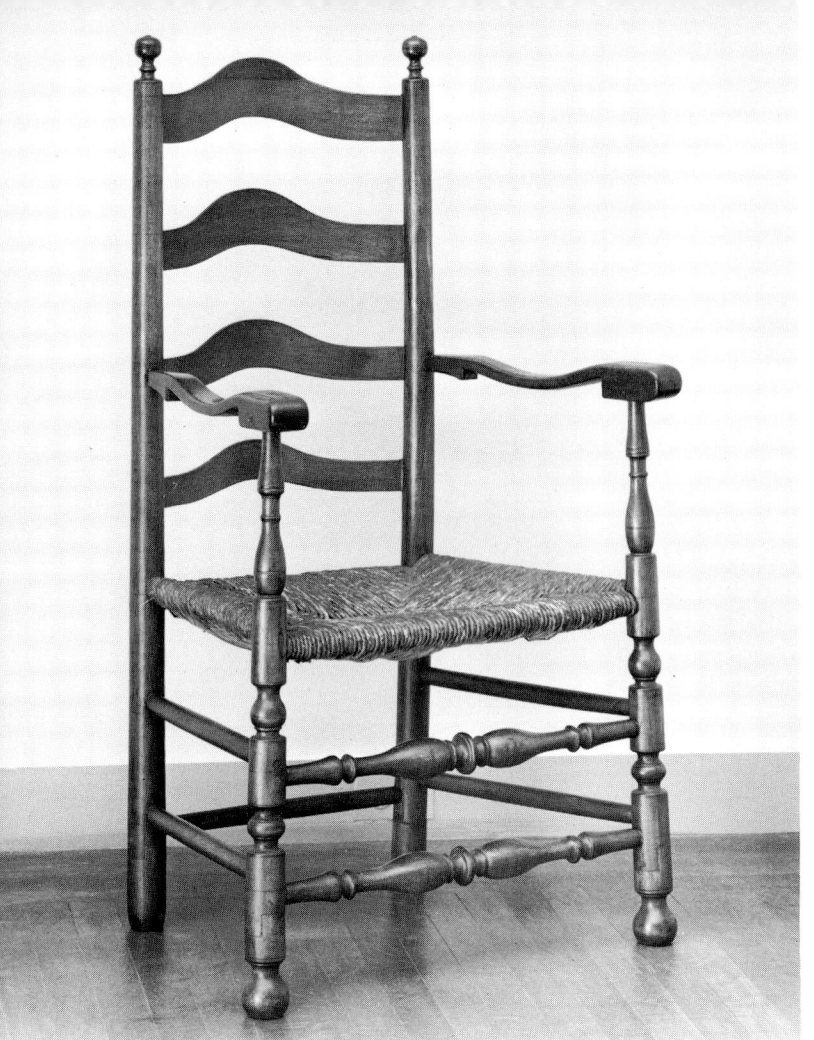

LADDER-BACK CHAIR
Wadsworth Atheneum

We are again indebted to the good selection of Wallace Nutting for this superb example of a ladder-back armchair. It embodies all the notable and distinctive features of these Early American chairs. It is a type found predominantly throughout Connecticut, *circa* 1725-1750. This particular chair mightily resembles a chair owned and used by William Penn which was brought over from England. The use of a rush seat, the gracious slope of the arms and the beauty of the bent slats — they are all different — make this an important model.

VASE-BACK SIDE CHAIR
The Los Angeles County Museum of Art

This Colonial American vase-back side chair with the yoke-shaped cresting rail, front legs with pad feet and woven rush seat is from New York, *circa* 1730-1750. This type of chair was found in the Hudson River Valley and on Long Island. Such a straight-back chair with turned stretchers may be characteristic of the rather straitlaced people of that community. In this type of chair one must sit up straight and look directly forward. It is from the Kenneth B. Pattison Collection.

Pre-Revolutionary Days

LIST OF ILLUSTRATIONS

(Asterisks indicate photographs accompanied by measured drawings.)

QUEEN ANNE CHAIR*
   Museum of Art, Rhode Island
   School of Design
TIGER-STRIPED HIGHBOY*
   Art Institute of Chicago
PHILADELPHIA HIGHBOY
   Metropolitan Museum of Art
HIGH CHEST OF DRAWERS
   Museum of Art, Rhode Island
   School of Design
WING CHAIR*
   Detroit Institute of Arts
CRADLE*
   Philadelphia Museum of Art
CRADLE
   Wadsworth Atheneum
CRADLE
   Brooklyn Museum
WINDSOR CHAIR*
   Art Institute of Chicago
FAN-BACK WINDSOR CHAIR
   Art Institute of Chicago
WRITING-ARM WINDSOR CHAIR
   Metropolitan Museum of Art
CELLARETTE*
   Brooklyn Museum
CONSOLE TABLE
   Philadelphia Museum of Art
SERVING TABLE
   Brooklyn Museum

ROUNDABOUT CHAIR*
   Brooklyn Museum
BRIC-A-BRAC CABINET
   Victoria and Albert Museum
CHIPPENDALE SCONCE
   Victoria and Albert Museum
TIP-TOP TABLE*
   Brooklyn Museum
TRIPOD TABLE
   Los Angeles County Museum of Art
DE LUXE TRIPOD TABLE
   Museum of Art, Rhode Island
   School of Design
CARD TABLE*
   Metropolitan Museum of Art
VERPLANCK ROOM
   Metropolitan Museum of Art
TALL CLOCK*
   Wadsworth Atheneum
BURNAP TALL CLOCK
   Wadsworth Atheneum
LOWBOY AND MIRROR*
   Los Angeles County Museum of Art
PHILADELPHIA LOWBOY
   Metropolitan Museum of Art
PHILADELPHIA LOWBOY
   Museum of Art, Rhode Island
   School of Design

3
PRE-REVOLUTIONARY DAYS

If all the people who were supposed to have landed at Plymouth Rock on the good ship *Mayflower* could have been counted, their number would be legion — so many, in fact, that the little vessel never could have left port. Likewise, if all the furniture and household utensils supposed to have been brought over by the Pilgrims in this little ship could be collected they would have filled a multitude of warehouses. As time goes on we are inclined to exaggerate and blow up beyond all proportions events which we like to believe are memorable. Therefore all this effort to align ourselves with the past should be taken with much forebearance.

Another bit of legendary fancy which we all enjoy and succumb to is the belief that "Washington slept here." No doubt the Father of His Country, during his lifetime and travels, did rest his weary bones in many a cot and four-poster in various parts of the country, but that such accurate memorabilia of his insensibility should have been kept so painstakingly is altogether surprising. Likewise, so much furniture is claimed to have been housed at Monticello, the residence planned, built and occupied by Thomas Jefferson in Virginia, that it would fill the capacity of many houses of that size. It is altogether fascinating and contributes to the make-up of many intriguing legends, but we cannot accept as gospel truth folklore that at best requires verification and clarification.

We understand that during the early settlements throughout the expanse of the Colonies, the furniture made was of the heavy and crude type and no doubt resembled that which reminded the settlers of their former homes. It did, however, coincide with the strong and rugged type of people who came to this country and strove to get a foothold in the New World. At the start these folks were not particularly interested in beauty. That would come later. They were more concerned with the procurement of the basic necessities for their homes. Most of the furniture produced was purely structural and functional. As conditions improved, some thought was given to better proportions in the fashioning of their household requisites. Naturally this was a slow and gradual development, of which they were not particularly conscious at the time.

In the house too little thought or attention was given to the architectural niceties and embellishments. The buildings were constructed entirely of wood and were intended to serve as a protection from adverse weather, a stockade against the prowling wildlife and a bulwark against thieving, pillage and murder by the hostile tribes of Indians. Their houses were not alone places in which to dwell but had to serve as ramparts against the marauders. Many of the earliest structures were of the log-cabin type, the placing of tree trunks, one above the other, fastening them together with bits of metal and filling the cracks with mud or clay to make them fairly weather-resistant. All these early structures were not only crude but could not be considered architectural in any degree. Gradually the houses acquired design elements and structural propensities as better materials became available and the Colonies prospered. Some stone houses were put together by the Dutch in New Amsterdam but they tended to fall apart due to lack of cement. Later bricks were imported from Holland and rows of little attached red-brick houses appeared facing the shoreline and, in their way, presupposing the skyline of New York.

So much for the earliest houses of the Colonists. This is not our thesis except that it is necessary to understand the living and housing conditions if we are to consider the furniture that went into the houses. Here were definite needs that had to be met. Especially there was the demand for chests with tops that lifted up, cupboards with many shelves for much storage space, desks of all descriptions, highboys and lowboys, dressers and bureaux; all required for the storage of their essentials. There was demand for tables of all sizes and descriptions, including drop-leaf, trestle, dining and kitchen tables. This was coupled with the need for beds, panel-backs, four-posters, trundle beds and cradles. Beneath many of the beds were pull-out compartments for storage. There were chests for blankets.

Later came the need for the less essential articles of furniture in the homes, such as clocks, mirrors, china cabinets, bookcases, candle-

Pre-Revolutionary Days

stands, screens, occasional tables, dressing tables, consoles, dough boxes and, most of all, boxes for the safekeeping of their most treasured possession — the Bible. These boxes were often elaborately carved and decorated with initials or monograms of the owner. The carving consisted mostly of the jackknife type, done by indigent fellows and amateurs to fill in the long, cold winter nights. Despite their lackadaisical procedure, some of this carving is exceptionally good, expressing the deep sense of reverence in this labor of love.

The difficulty in securing choice woods continued and mahogany was at a premium until the early part of the eighteenth century, when it was brought in from Cuba and Santo Domingo. The furniture made tended to be somewhat smaller than the European prototypes, due to the fact that the rooms in Colonial houses were smaller and the ceilings lower. What ornament was used was confined to turnings, cut-outs, strapwork, applied moldings and some paneling. Carpets were mostly handwoven from rags — what we still call Colonial rag rugs.

Since chairs are probably the most necessary and important pieces of furniture in the home, the Colonial designer gave much thought and study to this problem during the seventeenth and eighteenth centuries. If we regard chairs in their chronological order, the history of furniture design will be revealed. From most ancient times the chair was the symbol of authority. It was reserved for the celestial hierarchy, the aristocracy and personages of importance. The multitude could stand or sit on benches. However, one of the main chores for the designer is to build chairs to fit the sitter. The style and size of chairs are dictated by the persons who use them. For instance, a lady wearing a hoop skirt will require greater seating area than her sister with a straight skirt. A man of corpulent proportions will require a larger chair than the man who resembles a string-bean. These are extreme cases, and the designer delineates chairs to fit the average person in moderate attire.

There was the wainscot chair, with panel back and shaped arms, made of heavy oak after the English models about 1650. The name was derived from the panels being used for wainscots in taverns of the period. Some were plain and austere while others were elaborately carved and ornamented. Then followed the Carver and Brewster type chairs, made entirely of turnings, posts and spindles. They were named after two of the Pilgrim Fathers who were supposed to have brought examples of these chairs with them on the *Mayflower*. Be that as it may, these chairs were very popular. Along came a third chair called the Banister, with split turnings in the back panel. Split turnings were found to afford better seating comfort than did full turnings when leaned against. The fourth chair, the Ladder Back, consisting of numerous shaped and bent slats in the back, had rush seats held in place by front, side and back stretchers. These ladder-back chairs were particularly associated with Connecticut and were made about 1740.

One of the most truly Colonial American products was the Windsor Chair, which reached its finest development here. It was supposed to have originated in a small town in England called Windsor. The date of its origin is undetermined. In the Colonies, with Philadelphia as the main source of supply, *circa* 1760, these chairs were manufactured in great quantity. One of the most interesting of the Windsor chairs was known as the Fan Back, with a deeply concave top rail, which extended beyond the spindles and was designated as "ears." The ends were carved in a volute pattern which gave the back the needed grace and balance. The back posts, the arm supports and the legs were of heavier "tulip" turnings. A two-inch block of wood was required for the saddle-seat, which was shaped, gouged out, chamfered and cut back at the front to give the needed sense of lightness. The heavier legs were set back considerably under the seat with a big rake, thus creating a broad base for the chair. There were innumerable types of these Windsor chairs, including the hoop, fan, comb, the loop and those with low backs. The New England farm armchair had the central horizontal bend continuing and forming the arms. There was a type known as the double-decker and many Windsor chairs had a double spindle bracing at the back for greater support. Another type had a broad extended surface on the right arm used for writing, and some had one or two drawers attached below the seat. Rockers were introduced at a later date by cutting short the legs of chairs and inserting the runners. Many Windsor chairs were painted but they were seldom decorated.

There were so many types of chairs being developed in Colonial America that it will suffice to mention only a few. There was the Fiddle Back chair, 1715, and the Queen Anne type, made about 1725. Later the early Chippendale and Sheraton designs made their appearance. The Chippendale chairs were important because they introduced the cabriole legs, which is a form of a double "cyma curve." Then followed the chairs attributed to Duncan Phyfe. If we seem to put undo emphasis on chairs it is because they are so important.

It was at this time that details of the Classical Revival became evident. The work of the Italian architect Palladio became known and the prevailing styles from France, England and Italy found favor. Native

Pre-Revolutionary Days

designers adapted these foreign influences to their advantage, always adding that Colonial touch that differentiated their output. It was impossible to ignore the European predisposition because the two continents were becoming so very closely associated. The demand for this type of furniture could not be evaded.

As the Colonies prospered furniture took a sudden advance about 1750. Even in the smaller towns there were capable craftsmen who did fine work. In the cities like New York, Boston, Philadelphia, Newport, Salem and Baltimore there was an increasing number of wealthy people who appreciated good design in furniture and were willing to pay for it. Splendid houses were being built and there was a genuine need for furniture that would fit graciously into these new and elegant surroundings. The increasing worldliness of the people induced by travel, these rich landowners and gentry from the South and the mercantile giants from the North, stimulated the demand for bigger and finer houses and for equally splendid furniture. As the prosperity of the Colonists increased, coupled with the persistent determination of Royal Government officials not to be outdone, the sky seemed to be the limit in the demand for display and ostentation in furnishings. These demands were met with fitting enthusiasm by the designers and cabinetmakers who turned out better and more glowing and spectacular creations. Style in furniture became the credo of the times. Increasing numbers of the Dutch in New York were amassing great fortunes; monied Quakers from Pennsylvania and affluent cotton field proprietors from the South, all added to the glowing prosperity. That bolstered demands for the finest woods and the world was searched to fill this demand for furniture. The country continued to grow and prosper and the citizenry assumed a sense of self-sufficiency that was compelling. The people had faith in their native craftsmen, with the result that much of the furniture produced at this time was outstanding in design and manufacture.

It was then that new pieces of furniture found favor in the fostering of greater social activities. Such pieces as shaped china cabinets, carved consoles, rolltop desks, cabinets with tambour fronts, Pembroke tables, full-length mirrors, great breakfronts with paneled glass doors and the lower section for storage; these were just a few of the innovations and improvisations in the furniture field. Small rectangular tables were made especially for tea service. About 1730 these tables became a necessity for the drawing room, where the serving of this new beverage became a ritual. These tables were generally fitted with a rim on the top to prevent the precious cups and saucers from falling off, giving the tops a traylike appearance. Under the top was a plain surface with a shaped apron below. The slender cabriole leg was the most featured.

Discretion was thrown to the winds and sophistry and pomposity prevailed. Much of this furniture, just prior to the Revolution, was formal, opulent, sophisticated and not always in good taste. The wide introduction of upholstery on seating pieces, chairs, lounges, settees and chaise longues, gradually became so lush that luxury superseded discretion. With indulgence getting the upper hand, it was readily easy to predict that the country was headed for an upheaval. Sometimes this can be a good sign.

The modest clapboard houses with wooden frames, as well as the attached red-brick dwellings in the cities, gave way to resplendent Georgian homes of stone and of brick with Classical woodwork, leaded glass and wrought-iron scrollwork. The rooms became larger and the ceilings higher, while imported crystal chandeliers added just the finishing touch of brilliancy to the reception halls and the galleries. Again, we are considering the interior design of the dwellings because this is the background that inevitably influenced the type of furniture to be placed therein. These pre-Revolutionary times were prognostic and exciting. A new era was in the making. The Colonists were coming into their own.

The Georgian style was pre-eminent. Rooms were fashioned with ornamental pilasters, free-standing columns, the complete Orders of Architecture were used. The influence of Robert Adam was overwhelming. Attention was given to the architectural details of doors, windows and openings. Mantelpieces assumed a prominence and an elegance never attempted before. Complete walls were treated as decorative entities and broken up by panels according to the whim and the knowledge of the architect. In some cases entire walls were covered with paneling while others were painted, of plaster with a wood wainscot. Color was used profusely; walls were painted white, yellow, green, blue and even red. With the increasing trade with the Orient, handpainted scenic wallpapers became available and soon became the rage. One of the walls would be covered with the colorful paper and the other walls painted or paneled. The effect was often quite prepossessing, as may be seen in the Salon from the Samuel Powel house from Philadelphia, 1769, now on view in the American Wing of the Metropolitan Museum of Art. The furniture is in the Chippendale style of bold and simple design carved with a variety of detail. This house was very prominent in historic channels, for when Lord Howe evacuated the city General George Washington made his headquarters there.

Pre-Revolutionary Days

In less proficient hands, some of these rooms suffered badly. They had no sense of proportion or scale, were put together haphazardly and irrelevantly, without regard of purpose or intent. Many of the rooms in the smaller houses just used a cornice, a dado and a baseboard with painted plaster between. Due to the lack of central heating, almost every room had a fireplace, often placed diagonally in a corner but always made a feature of the room. Even in the bedrooms mantelpieces predominated. Portraits were very popular investments, hung over a shelf and generously framed. Often the paintings were set into architectural decorative panels and became part and parcel of the interior design.

At first only the wealthy landowners and business tycoons could afford these grandiose residences but soon the prosperous farmers and smaller landowners as well as tradespeople were not to be outdone and built quite elegant smaller houses. To this day some of these less pretentious homes throughout the countryside are positive gems of good taste, avoiding undo ostentation and displaying a discreet knowledge and respect for the appropriate. In many of these inviting interiors we can readily see and understand how design-conscious the country had become. The people ordered their furniture fully conscious of the utilitarian requirements as well as the design proficiency. It was a time when all through the country people were taking pride in their homes and furnishings.

Along with the prosperity and affluence came tenseness and unrest. The atmosphere was full of dissension. The Colonists were slowly and surely becoming enraged at the surly insolence of George III of England. His pressures and the relentless edict of taxation without representation were becoming intolerable. The minor indignities showered upon objectors fired the ire of the populace. It was becoming more than they could endure. Subsequent indignities and acts of suppression only added offense to injury. Insurrection was becoming broadcast and subsequent events only added flames to the fire. Once ignited, the desire for freedom from the mother country spread over the colonies like a destructive conflagration. The yoke of oppression was intolerable and must be done away with. There was no turning back. The populace was determined to be free. The result culminated in the American Revolution, with General George Washington as the commander-in-chief and later the first president. The United States of America was born, to take its place among the nations of the world.

Pre-Revolutionary Days

Up to and preceding the Revolution the Colonists were in a continuous state of settlement, development and achievement. There was little time for procrastination or soul-searching. Prosperity was the keynote and the incentive to build a new country was paramount. Only when their enthusiasm and accomplishments seemed to be thwarted by the oppressive measures enacted by the mother country did they experience unrest and prostration. There arose, simultaneously throughout the country, a desire to unite and protest against what they considered unjust and discriminatory. Fortunately, there appeared leaders who possessed the ability to unite this unrest into defiance which culminated in the Revolution and freedom from oppression.

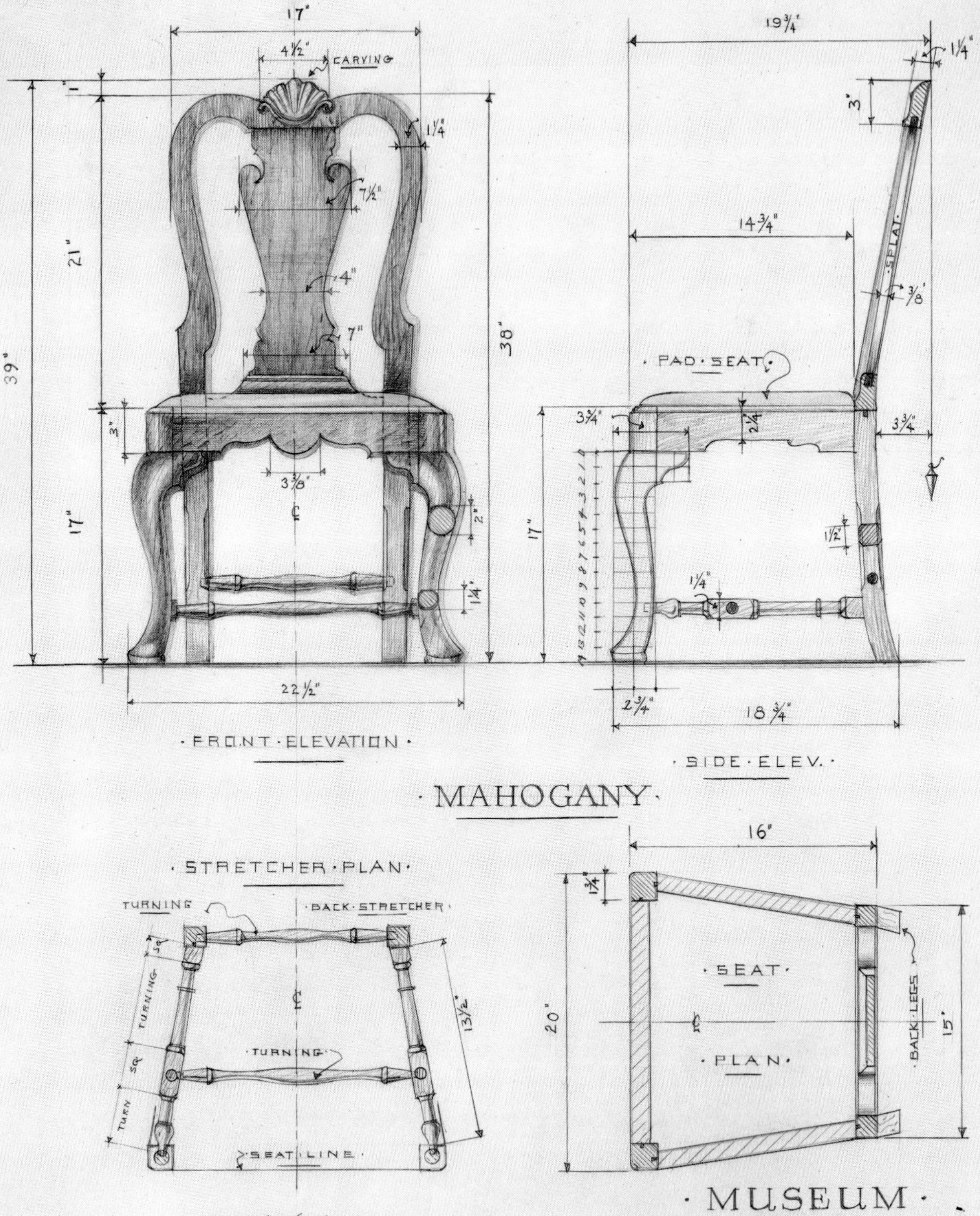

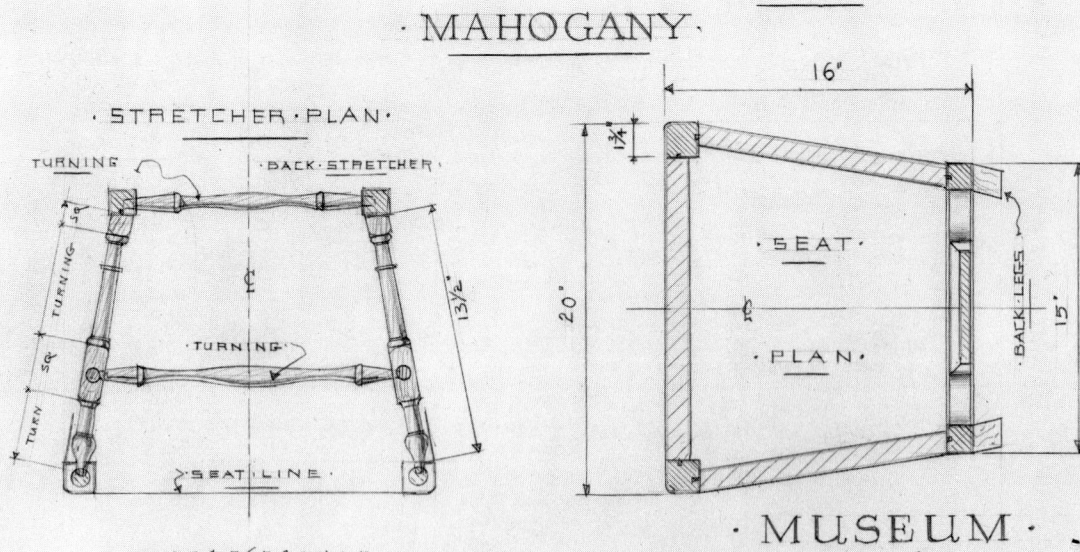

QUEEN ANNE CHAIR
Museum of Art, Rhode Island School of Design   *Estate of Robert Simmons Phillip*

This mahogany side chair from Newport, Rhode Island, *circa* 1720, is in the Queen Anne tradition. In elegance it rivals the products of the Philadelphia cabinetmakers at that time. This is truly a beautiful model, with a straight seat, just rounded at the front corners. The unadorned cabriole legs are satisfactory and the turned stretchers produce a sense of stability. The cut-out splat is not alone structural but also quite comely. The center shell carving on the crest has a richness that is strategic for the chair. The shape of the splat resembles that of a vase, although some would say it resembles the back of a fiddle. These Queen Anne chairs are important because they show a restraint that is foreign to the European prototypes, which used walnut in the making. The line of the frame of the back is exceptionally pleasing and adds so much to the beauty of the chair. This model happens to be shown with a silk brocade used for the upholstery.

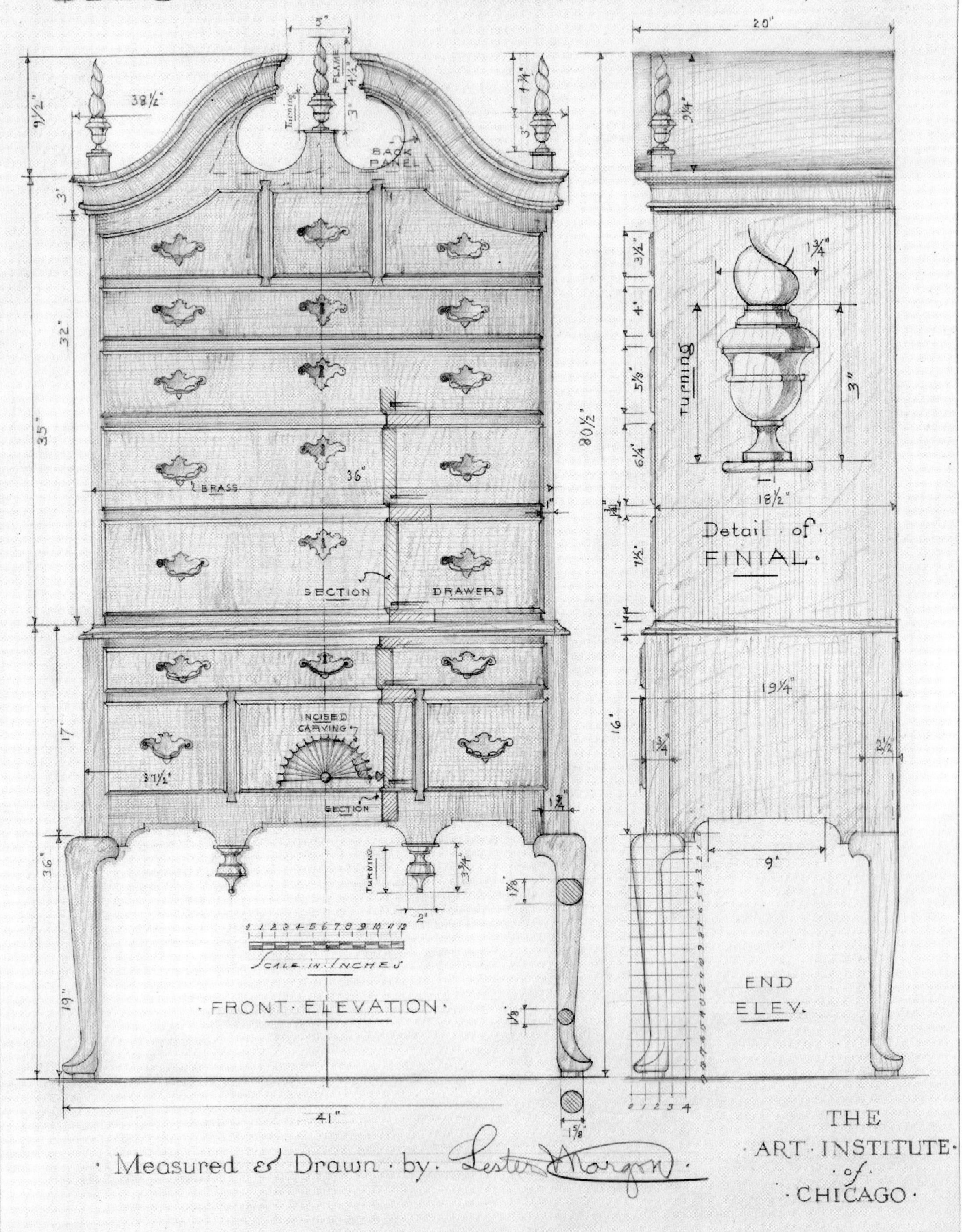

TIGER-STRIPED HIGHBOY

Art Institute of Chicago   Gift of Mrs. Emily Crane Chadbourne

What a splendid model! This tiger-striped maple highboy from Connecticut, *circa* 1740, is of Queen Anne inspiration. It is one of the best pieces fashioned of native curly maple, the grain of which is so pronounced and transcendental that the name "Tiger-Striped" appears warranted. It is of original design and shows the work of creative cabinetmakers. It shows what an inspired artist can develop from a prevailing form. The bonnet top is one of the most difficult forms to produce, and here it is broken and impregnated by curved lines holding a flamelike turning that is repeated above the cornice at the ends. The back of the bonnet is enclosed. The beauty of the selected maple is paramount and its effectiveness is obvious. The lower incised fan motif is well placed and the staunch simple cabriole legs appear to be most appropriate. The broken line of the bottom is fitted with dropped turnings. Although quite a tall piece, it has a certain airy lightness that is compelling. Seldom do we find such a decorative highboy that is so satisfying.

PHILADELPHIA HIGHBOY
Metropolitan Museum of Art

This imposing Philadelphia highboy in mahogany, dated 1760-1775, is by William Savory, who was active from 1742 to 1787, prominent in the Philadelphia School. Especially interesting is the scroll bonnet top, pierced by the flamboyant central ornament. Here the feature is the profuse use of carving — to our way of thinking, it is a bit too profuse. The Philadelphia School included, besides William Savory, Thomas Affleck, Benjamin Randolph, Thomas Tufft and Jonathan Gostelow.

HIGH CHEST OF DRAWERS
Museum of Art, Rhode Island School of Design

This is another type of Philadelphia high chest of drawers, fashioned after the Chippendale style. These highboys are among the most original and celebrated pieces of furniture made in America, *circa* 1760-1775. They are all different and varying in design and detail but they all represent a high standard of cabinetwork. The center and side finials seem to be missing but the effect is evident and the artistry compelling. These highboys can match anything that was produced in Europe.

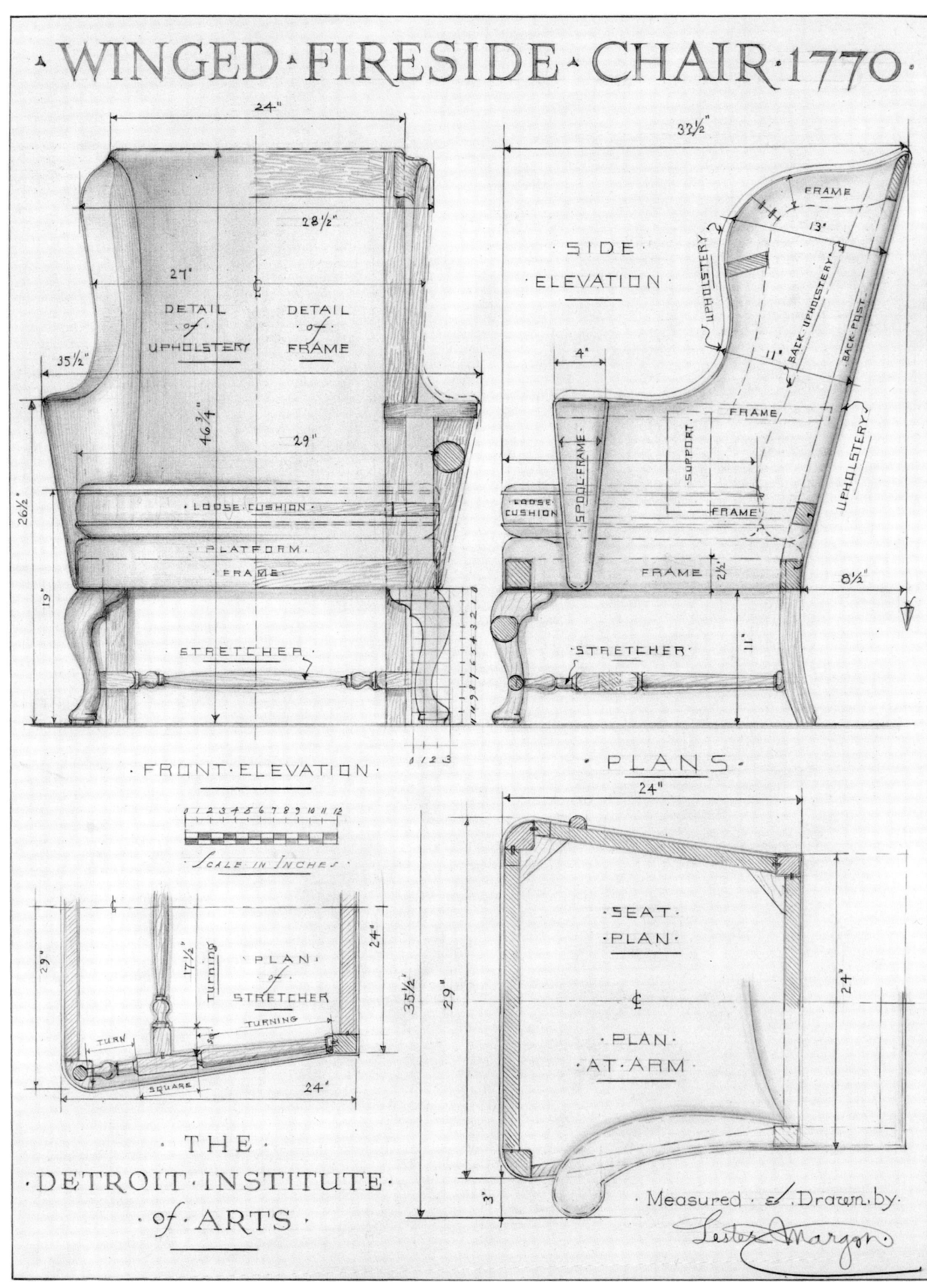

WING CHAIR
Detroit Institute of Arts

This elegant American wing chair, *circa* 1770, has a Queen Anne-type cabriole leg of walnut with turned stretchers. Sumptuous and inviting and fitting well into the drawing room of pre-Revolutionary Days, such a chair generally stood beside the hearth. It is completely covered in upholstery, broad of seat, with appropriate depth for lounging. The high back and the flaring wings are a protection from drafts. In chairs like this the line of the upholstery is more important than the wood showing, although the turned stretcher is a stand-by. Whereas these wing chairs continue to be popular, to find a measured drawing of the inner construction is a rarity. To most people the construction of these chairs is a mystery; just not knowing, they have to take the dealer's word for it that all is well in the interior. It is not a simple matter. Chairs of this character were used and made all over the country and were not indigenous to any special locality. Of course the three distinctive features of these chairs are the high backs, the line and spread of the wings and the breadth of the arms. Sometimes even the wood legs were partially hidden by a fringe or a valance.

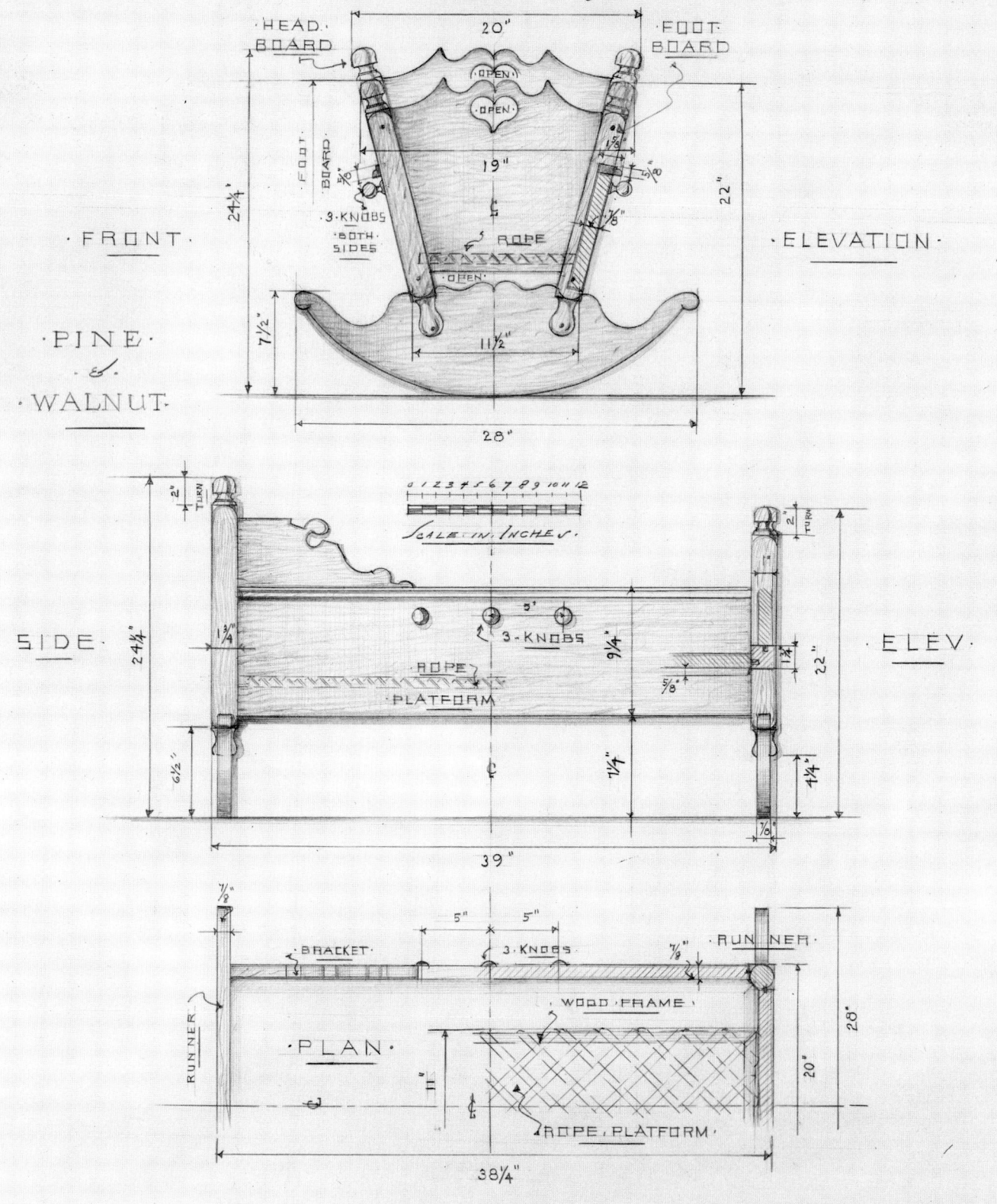

CRADLE

Philadelphia Museum of Art

This pine and walnut cradle is Pennsylvania German, *circa* 1750. Its design is consummate delight. What joy it must give to sit beside this cradle and rock the baby to sleep, sending the little one off to dreams. We found this cradle in the fabulous collection of Pennsylvania furniture and were most happy to include it in this compendium. The design is unique and attractive and the size of the cradle is ample so as to hold a youngster of several years if necessary. The cut-out heart motif in headboard and footboard seems to be especially appropriate for a child. Most cradles are more or less cut-and-dried affairs but this one has charm. Note the three knobs placed on the front and back of the bed to break up the long plain expanse. They serve as decoration. The cut-out brackets and the sweeping lines of the headboard and the footboard are delightful. Especially useful is the large radius of the runners that permits the cradle to rock endlessly. One unusual feature is the inside platform of the cradle, made of woven rope on a wooden frame. This permits of a certain give when the child is placed in it, much to the comfort of the little sleeper.

CRADLE

Wadsworth Atheneum

This Wetherfield cradle is also from the Wallace Nutting collection. It is made of oak, *circa* 1735. Here the maker did not spare the wood. It appears heavy and a bit cumbersome just to hold a little child. It is of the stile-and-rail construction. Note how the runners are boldly clamped onto the sides, are set back and well routed and given the effect of raised paneling. Sturdy is certainly the description of this cradle.

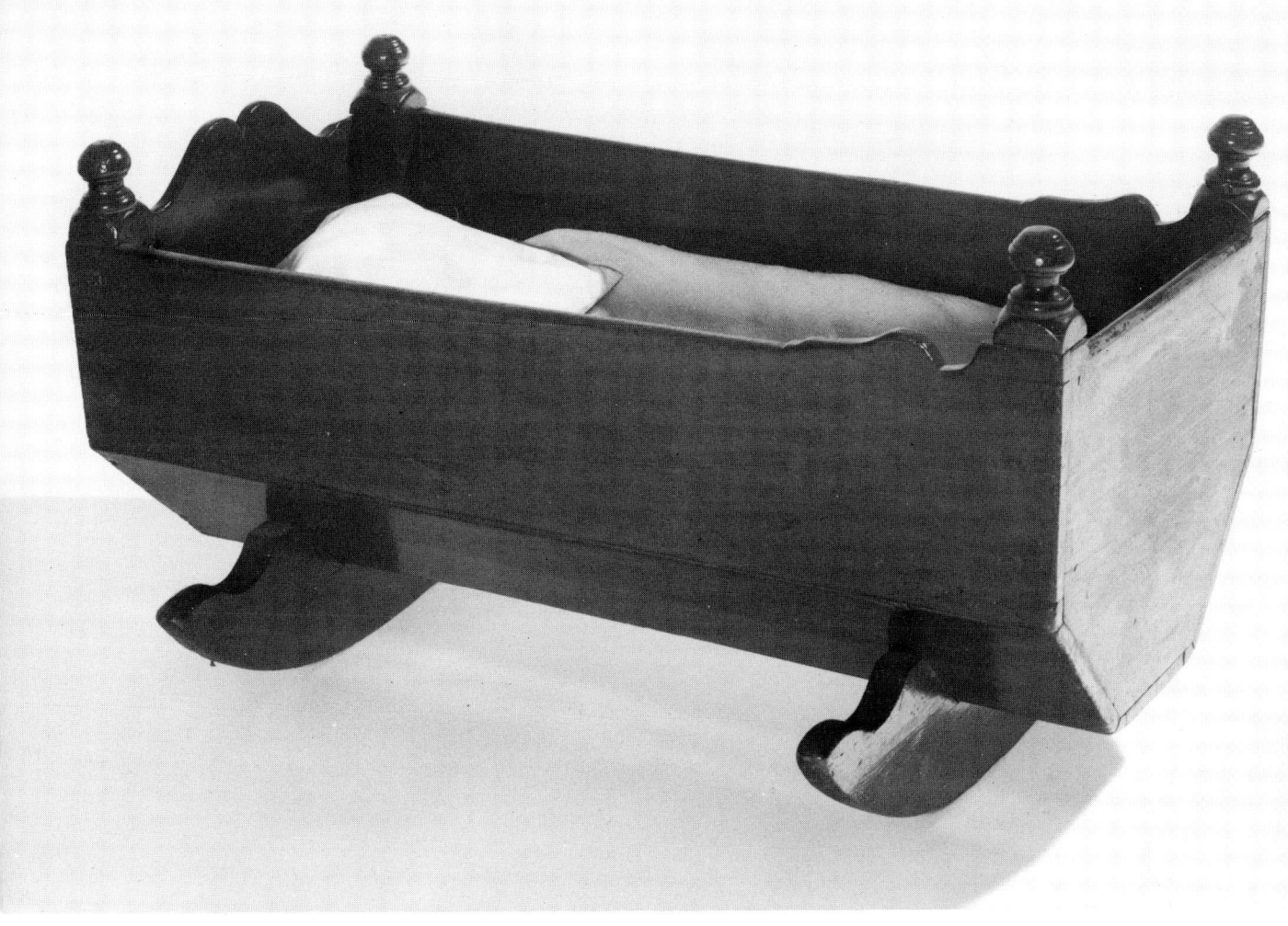

CRADLE
Brooklyn Museum

This cradle, from Long Island of the early eighteenth century, is of the Dutch type, made of a combination of pine and maple wood. Charming is the only fitting description. It is quaint, delicate and with a magic rhythm. The design is simple, the four turned posts are handles from which the cradle may be rocked. Note how the front and side panels are placed outside of the posts. What can be said of a cradle except that it is appropriate and fitting to hold a wee one?

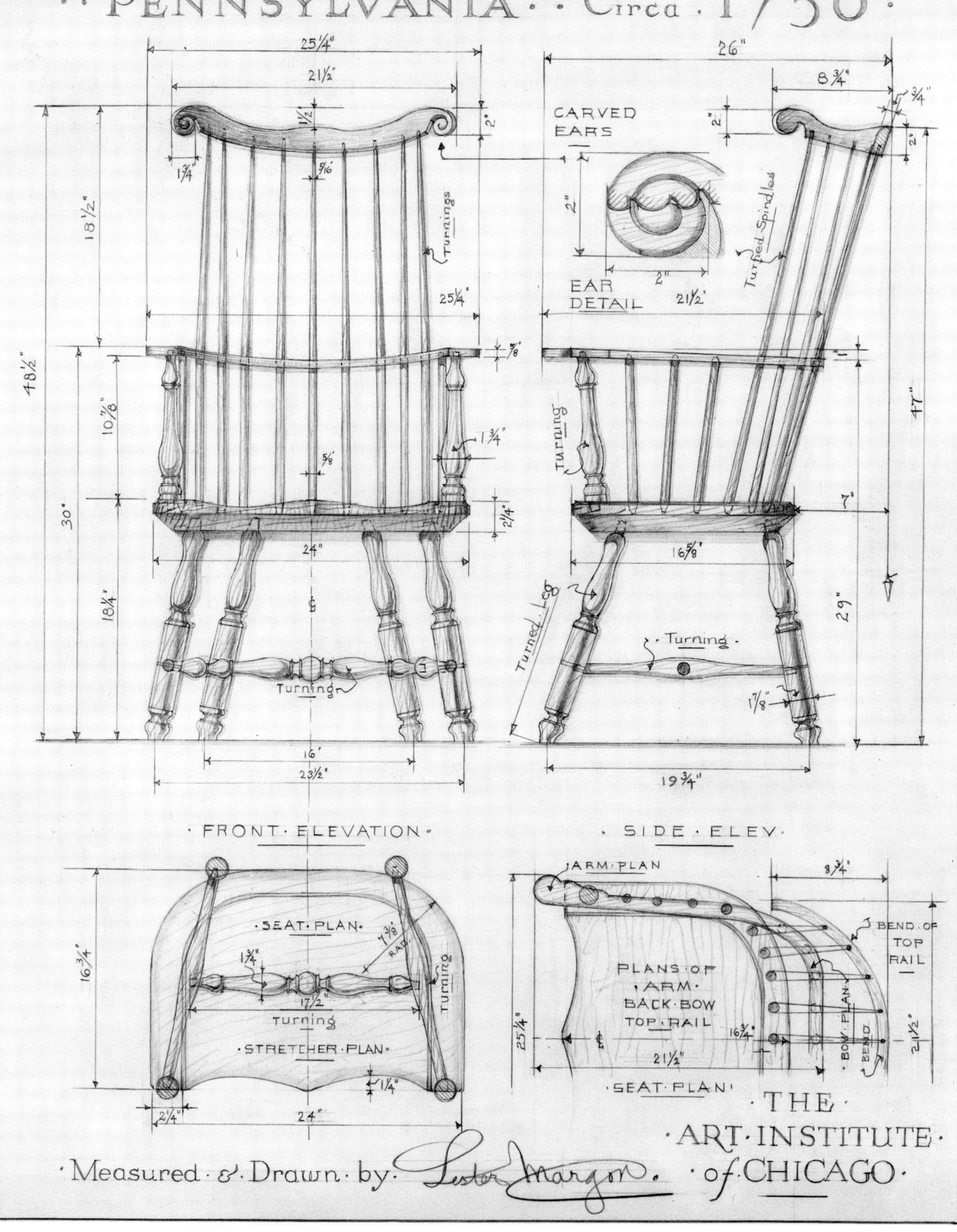

WINDSOR CHAIR
Art Institute of Chicago   *Gift of Mrs. Emily Crane Chadbourne*

This superb model of a comb-back Windsor chair with carved scroll "ears" is from Pennsylvania, *circa* 1750. The proportions are excellent and the saddle seat well balanced. The continuous center rail of the back forms the platform of the shaped arm rest. The turnings are unusual, especially in the legs. The long plain stretch is seldom found in these chairs. The fine rake to the legs affords a wide base, which is essential. In Colonial days practically every household had one or more of these Windsor chairs, including Mt. Vernon. Philadelphia was the principal center of manufacturing, but factories were soon set up in New York and Wilmington to meet the popular demand. Although originally derived from English models, these chairs were made so much better over here that it truly may be called an American invention. It later became the inspiration for Shaker chairs but those were simplified in the extreme.

WINDSOR CHAIR
Art Institute of Chicago

Coming from Fishkill, New York, of the third quarter of the eighteenth century, this typically American Windsor chair is an excellent model in which the arms break at the bend and turn upward to form the back. Of special interest are the superb matching turnings of the arm supports and the legs. The saddle seat is conservative in its shaping but the rake of the legs is sufficiently acute to afford a broad base for the chair, giving it a sense of unity and design equilibrium. There are fancier Windsor chairs but none better than this model. It is the gift of Mrs. Emily Crane Chadbourne.

FAN-BACK WINDSOR CHAIR
Art Institute of Chicago

This happens to be our favorite model of a Windsor chair. It is of the fan-back type from Pennsylvania, 1750-1780. Of special interest is the shaped top rail which extends beyond the back posts, these extensions being called "ears." The volute carving at each end creates the needed grace and balance to the chair. The legs are well raked, affording a broad base. The leg turnings are unusual, for seldom do we find such a large plain portion, but that gives the chair a certain individuality and distinction. Note that there is an extension on the back of the seat to receive two additional spindles for support. The chair is the gift of Elizabeth R. Vaughan.

WRITING-ARM WINDSOR CHAIR
Metropolitan Museum of Art

This New England Windsor chair is made from maple and pine. The right arm is expanded into a palette-shaped writing surface with an underslung drawer. There is another deeper drawer under the saddle seat. This is a curious chair but rather eloquent in appearance. The horseshoe shape of the arm extends around the back and intercepts the shaped spindles. The turnings are conventional and the stretchers seem to hold the monster together. It is probably from the vicinity of Philadelphia, *circa* 1740-1750. The chair is the gift of Mrs. Screven Lorillard, 1952.

SOUTHERN CELLARETTE
WALNUT · 1750-1775 ·

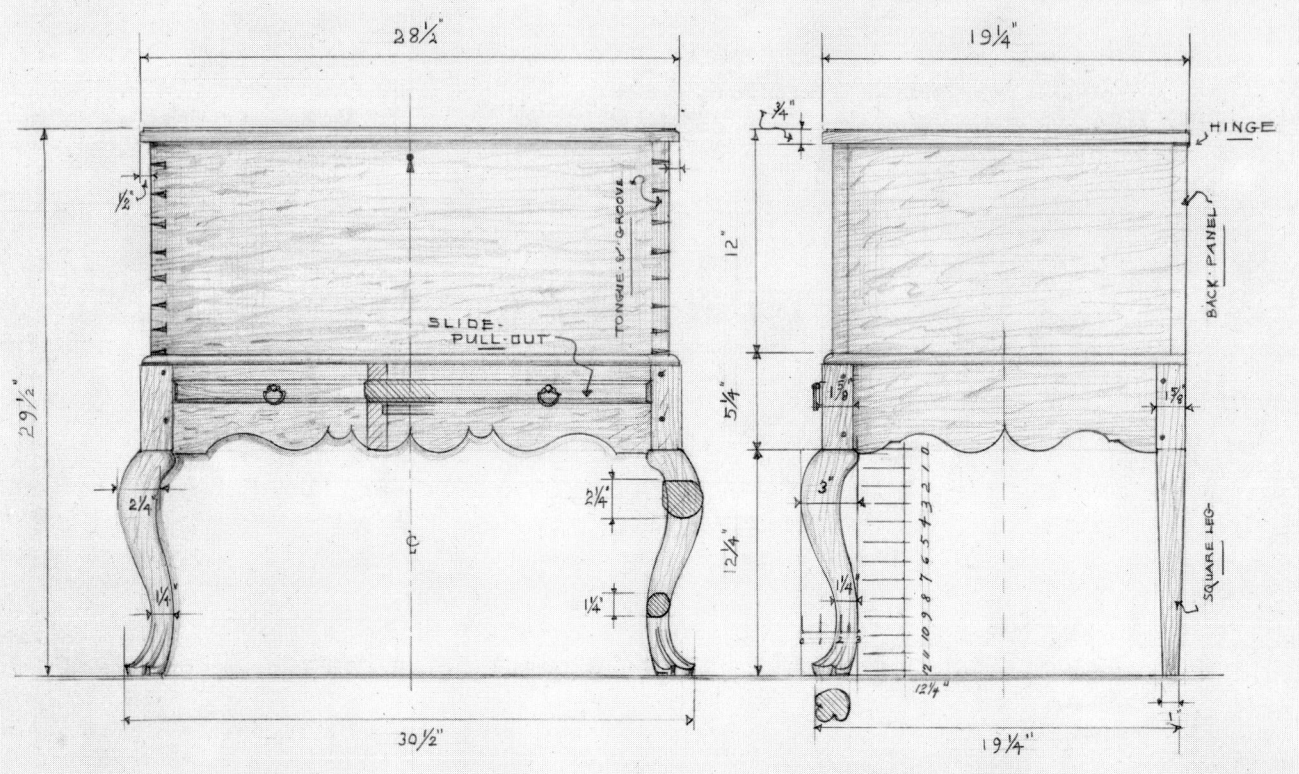

FRONT ELEVATION · END ELEV ·

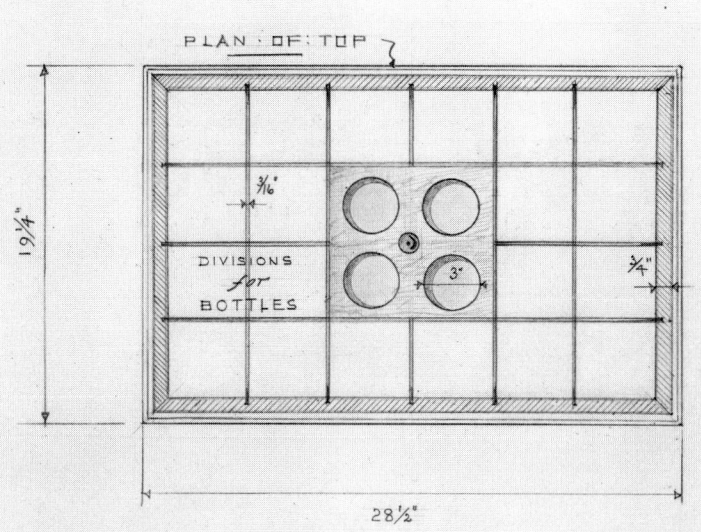

PLAN of INTERIOR

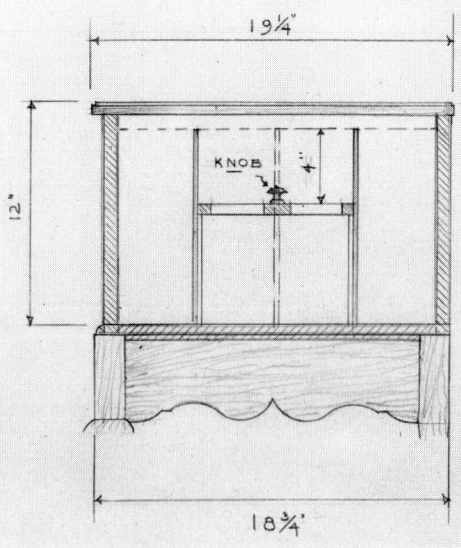

· SECTION of INTERIOR ·

Measured & Drawn by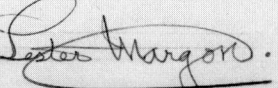

· BROOKLYN · MUSEUM ·
NEW YORK

CELLARETTE
Brooklyn Museum

The term "Southern" when applied to furniture has a far greater significance than merely the denoting of a section of the country. Southern furniture in Colonial days bespoke a certain graciousness and cordiality of the people. This furniture has a beguiling sensitiveness that must be encountered to be appreciated. This particular walnut cellarette, *circa* 1750-1775, is a good example. The cellarette or wine cooler was generally of boxlike proportions, of a height that permitted it to be placed under a side table in the dining room. The top was hinged and the interior was divided into appropriate spaces to receive the bottles. In the center, note the section provided for the sundries. In this instance there is a long lower slide that can be pulled out so the glasses can be placed thereon for service. The cellarette was indispensable in the formal dining room. Our model features the graceful cabriole legs with the Spanish toe, and the apron is handsomely treated. Note the dovetailing of the corners. This was a time when dining was a ceremony not to be hurried or underestimated, an important part of the social order.

CONSOLE TABLE
Philadelphia Museum of Art

This mahogany double-topped and shaped console table is of "The School of Duncan Phyfe" of the early nineteenth century. The double lyre supports and the four supporting legs just do not seem to go together. The table is interesting but it does not quite make the grade. It is heavy, lacking in grace and intuition. So many similar pieces were set up at this time that it is well to be a bit skeptical before attributing many of them to the master cabinetmaker.

SERVING TABLE
Brooklyn Museum

This slate-top serving table with the border of marqueterie is dated 1700. The rich walnut crotch on the front and the drawer panels are augmented by divisions of beads and double borders of herringbone inlay. The shaped lower apron is varied and the acorn drops add a punctilious note. The trumpet turnings are exemplary and the cross-stretcher is punctuated at the center by a supported ball. This is indeed a museum piece because it is so excellent in every particular.

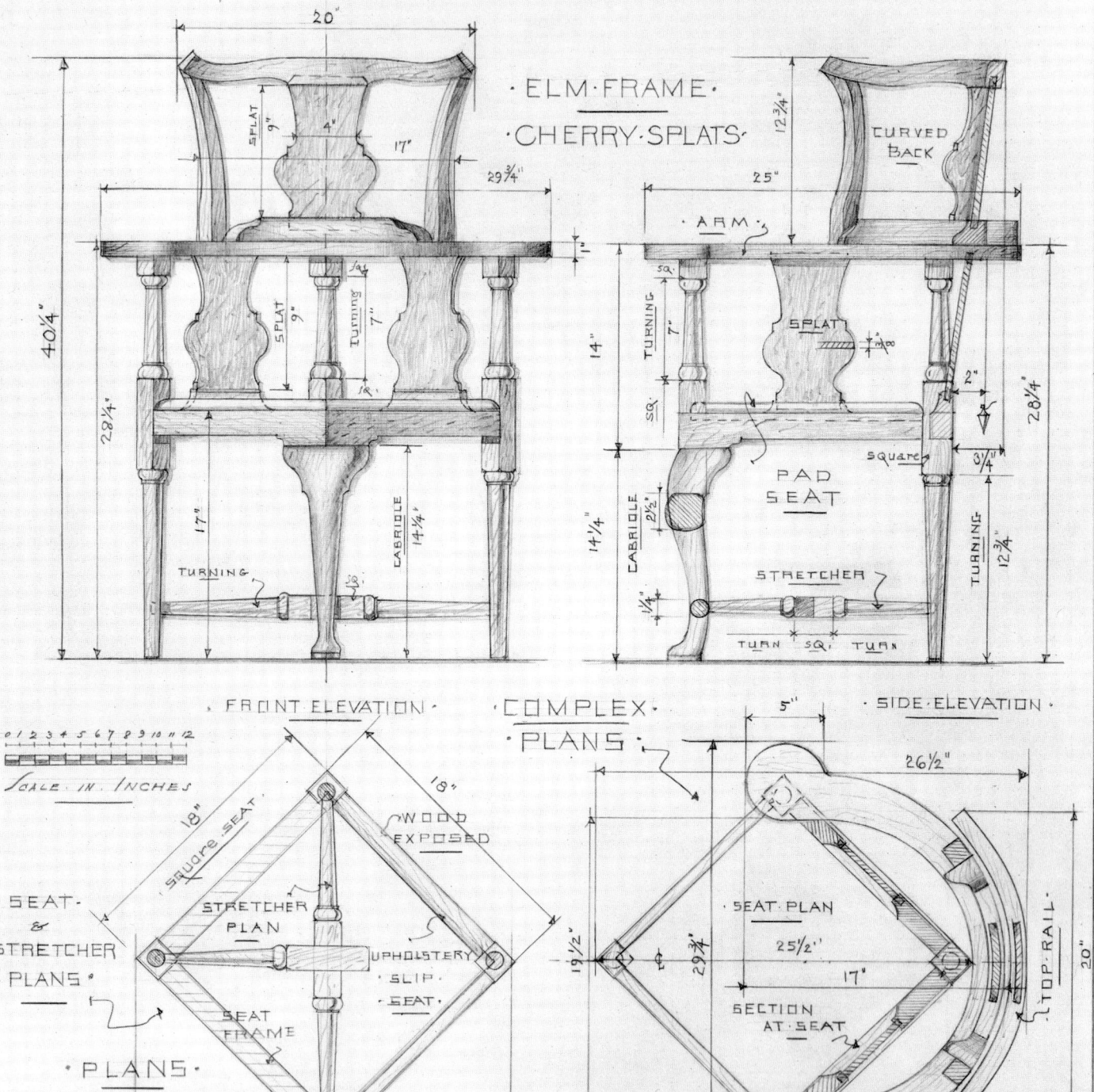

ROUNDABOUT CHAIR
Brooklyn Museum   Lent by George Drew Egbert

You may see single-back roundabout corner chairs often, but a double-back roundabout corner chair is indeed a rarity. This one has an elm-wood frame with cherry splats. The date is *circa* 1750. The effect of the front corner cabriole leg with the other three turned legs is rather unusual. The solid cut-out splats are a source of strength while the two-tier arrangement was probably contrived to offer greater seating comfort. The semi-circular arm and rail is generally made of three pieces of wood. These corner chairs were often made with rush seats and fancy cut-out splats, either with or without stretchers. Our model shows a turned cross-stretcher which is needed for support. At best, these round corner chairs are novel; one in any room should be quite sufficient. Whoever conceived of making this double-back roundabout chair took unto himself quite a problem; we get the impression that it is somewhat of a stunt, perching the back of one chair on top of another. However, it is unique and worthy of our attention.

BRIC-A-BRAC CABINET
Victoria and Albert Museum

This fantastic mixture of Oriental, Gothic and naturalistic motifs is certainly original. It is by Thomas Chippendale. One does not know where to look first; certainly it is the utmost in derangement and frolicsome chicanery. This is one instance where the famous English designer's imagination ran wildfire. Now we can well understand why the American designers did not want to perpetuate this type of thing. It was altogether foreign to their tastes and sense of discipline.

CHIPPENDALE SCONCE

Victoria and Albert Museum

Another flamboyant extravagance of Thomas Chippendale is this carved sconce. It is gilded and represents a conglomeration of Louis XV curvatures hung with naturalistic floral arrangements of roses, oak leaves and acorns punctuated by acanthus vagaries. The candleholders are almost obscured by the encumbrances. One cannot imagine this type of thing being used in an American ensemble: it is so utterly foreign to our taste and decorum that it is amusing. Note the frustrated columns at the side.

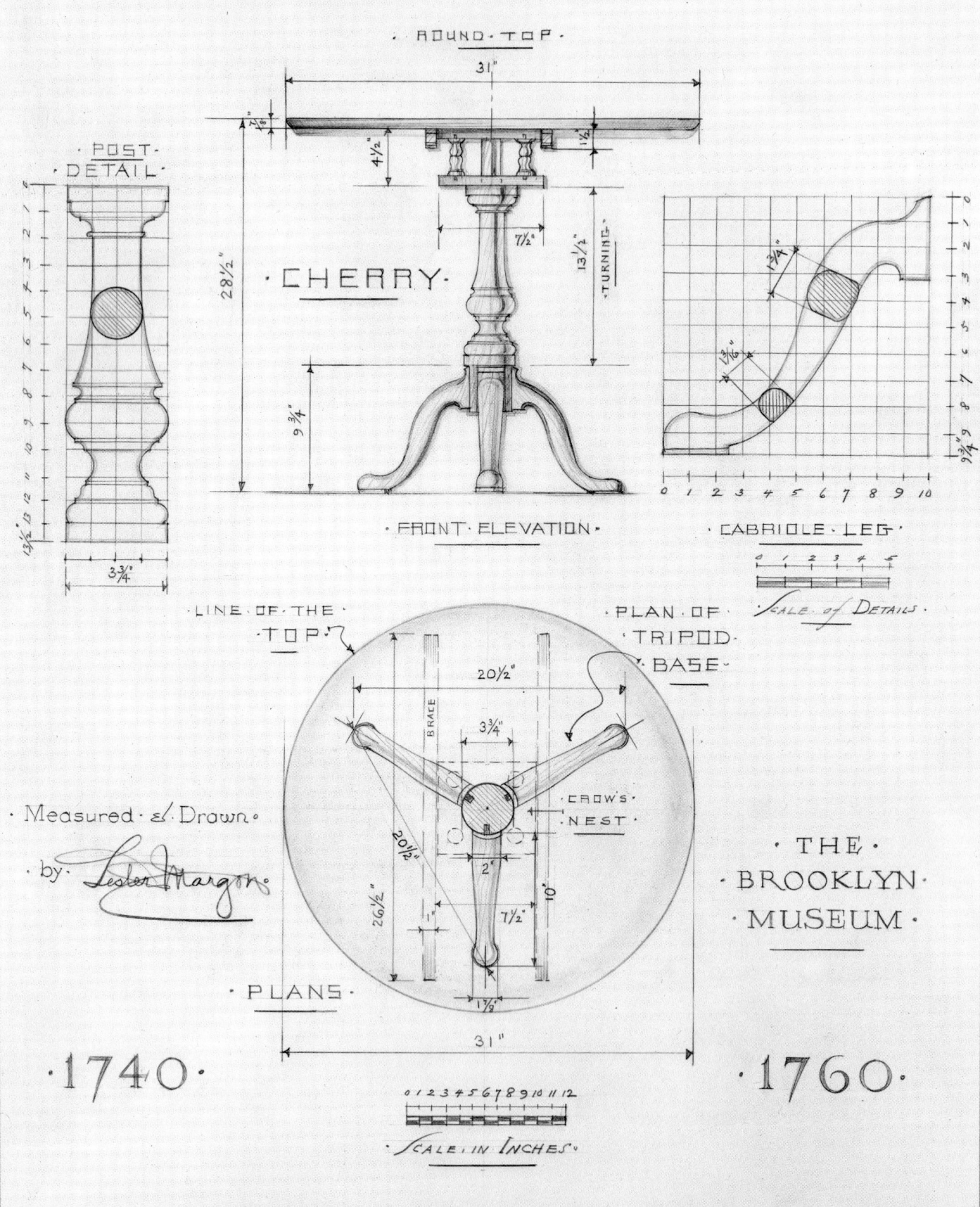

TIP-TOP TABLE
Brooklyn Museum

These tripod tip-top tables were very popular in Colonial America. They served many purposes and could be set aside when not in use. This example is in cherry in the Queen Anne style and is of Southern origin; its date is *circa* 1740-1760. This table is unique because it has a flush top, whereas most of these tabletops had a rim or some sort of molding around it. The birdcage beneath the top is typical and the turning support of the table has a certain Dutch character. The top may be tilted or revolved. Notice the two long pieces of wood called "cleats" which are screwed to the under side of the top and prevent warping. The base of the birdcage consists of a square piece of wood resting on the turned pedestal which extends loosely through a round opening in the base, thus permitting it to revolve. Chippendale tip-top tables are often much more elaborate, with carving on the cabriole legs and ball-and-claw feet. The tops, often shaped with piecrust moldings around the top circumference, are most often made of mahogany. The sizes of these tables vary from stands of twelve inches diameter to large tables sometimes forty-two inches across, depending on the use and purpose.

TRIPOD TABLE

Los Angeles County Museum of Art

This mahogany tripod table with the ball-and-claw feet and dish top is from Philadelphia, *circa* 1740. It follows all the rules and regulations of these tripod tables, with a top that drops, revolves or both. Beneath the top is the birdcage that regulates this manipulation. The turned pedestal is restrained and all in all a certain harmonious entity is created. This table is a museum purchase, the Denis Bequest.

DeLUXE TRIPOD TABLE
Museum of Art, Rhode Island School of Design

There are tripod tables and tripod tables galore, but this model is certainly superlative. It is in the Chippendale tradition, in mahogany, with a top having a piecrust edge, fluted column pedestal, ball-and-claw feet. The superb cabriole legs are carved at the knee by an acanthus leaf that is in itself a paragon of loveliness. The date is 1775-1800. The birdcage is conventional. What a joy it is to behold a table of such ultimate design and masterly execution!

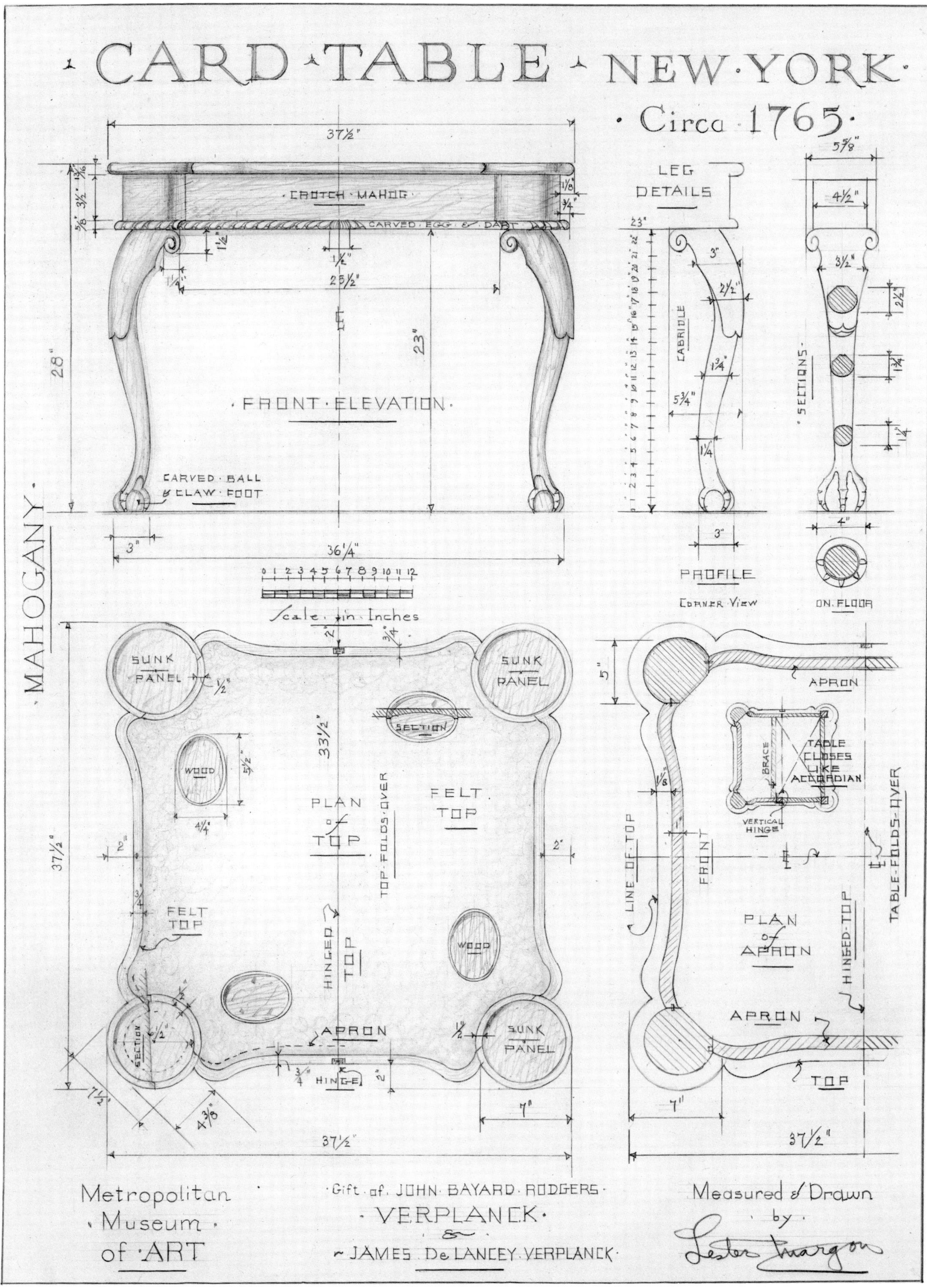

CARD TABLE · NEW YORK
Circa 1765

MAHOGANY

FRONT ELEVATION

CROTCH MAHOG
CARVED EGG & DART
CARVED BALL & CLAW FOOT

LEG DETAILS
CABRIOLE
PROFILE — Corner View
SECTIONS
ON FLOOR

Scale in Inches

PLAN of TOP
SUNK PANEL
WOOD
FELT TOP
HINGED TOP
APRON
SECTION
HINGE

PLAN of APRON
LINE OF TOP
FRONT
BRACE
TABLE CLOSES LIKE ACCORDIAN
VERTICAL HINGE
HINGED TOP
TABLE FOLDS OVER
APRON
TOP

Metropolitan Museum of Art

Gift of JOHN BAYARD RODGERS VERPLANCK & JAMES DeLANCEY VERPLANCK

Measured & Drawn by Lester Margon

CARD TABLE
Metropolitan Museum of Art
Gift of James De Lancey Verplanck and John Bayard Rogers Verplanck 1939

As the Colonies developed into lively communities, the card table became one criterion of gracious living. This mahogany specimen from New York, *circa* 1765, can be folded by means of a complicated accordion arrangement and set aside when not in use. Designs of these popular card tables varied but this one is of the finest, with its large rounded corners affording space for a platform for the chips. The four ashtrays are ingeniously set into the top. The unadorned cabriole legs with the ball-and-claw feet are impressive and the comparative austerity of the table is relieved by the carved egg-and-dart molding below the apron. This table is shown in the magnificent drawing room along with other Chippendale pieces of furniture. Even in those days the card table had a special attraction for the prosperous Colonists, who enjoyed games of chance just as we do today. There is the usual green felt top held in place by a wooden frame.

VERPLANCK ROOM
Metropolitan Museum of Art

This room was set up by the Metropolitan Museum of Art for the display of some pieces of the Verplanck Collection of furniture and photographed, January 1946. Here is shown that grandiose rococo gilded mirror, the card table illustrated in the measured drawing, several Chippendale-type chairs and a gracious sofa, along with the console with a white marble top. The room affords a fitting background for this fine furniture.

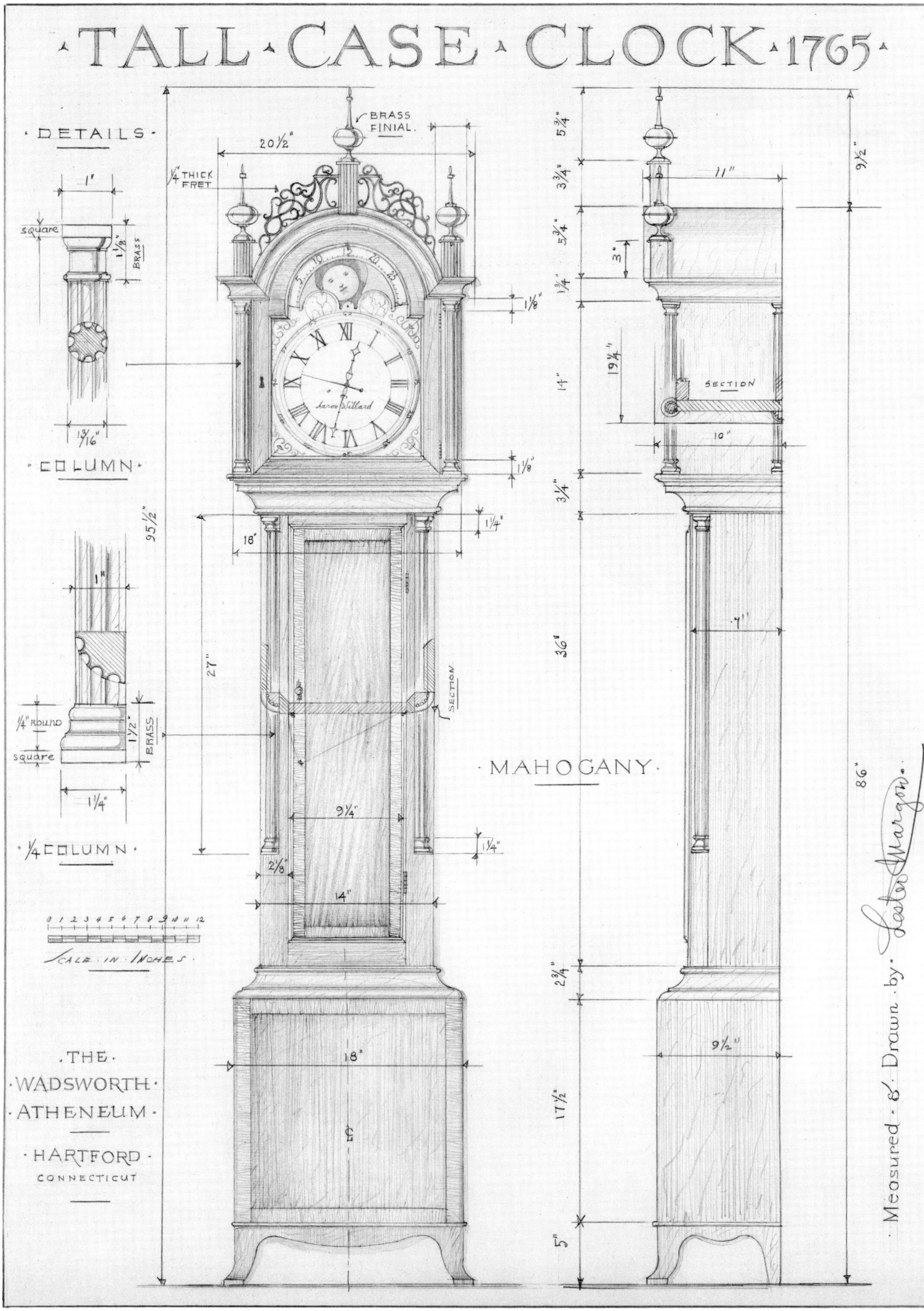

TALL·CASE·CLOCK·1765

·DETAILS·

·COLUMN·

¼ COLUMN

Scale in Inches

·THE·
·WADSWORTH·
·ATHENEUM·

·HARTFORD·
CONNECTICUT

·MAHOGANY·

Measured·&·Drawn·by·Lester Margon

TALL CASE CLOCK
Wadsworth Atheneum

Attributed to Aaron Willard, this Grandfather clock is in mahogany, *circa* 1765. The famous Massachusetts clockmaker family included Simon, Benjamin, Aaron and Ephraim; they worked simultaneously and produced similar creations. This one, a stately and impressive example of these tall clocks, is certainly an ambitious product. The stately proportions and the perfection of details are erudite. Its definite Hepplewhite inspiration in design can be determined by the flowing line of the base. The fretwork at the top is lacelike in perfection and the turned brass finials are eloquent in silhouette. The ormolu caps and bases on the inserted quarter-round columns add a sense of luxury. The works were probably made by Edward Massey. Up to the beginning of the eighteenth century, most clocks were imported from Europe. These tall clocks came into fashion early in the turn of the century, with Boston as headquarters. In many halls and living rooms at this time these Grandfather clocks kept vigil over the comings and the goings of the family, merely standing there and keeping a record of the passage of time.

BURNAP TALL CLOCK
Wadsworth Atheneum

This tall clock was made by Daniel Burnap of Andover, Massachusetts, *circa* 1780-1800. It is of mahogany and shows a rather severe and classical treatment in the design. It is a relief to see a tall clock that is not overburdened with detail. This one has an etched metal face with moon-face and calendar attachments. The works were of brass. If it resembles a coffin set on end, that should not be considered a deterrence to its really fine lines and proportions.

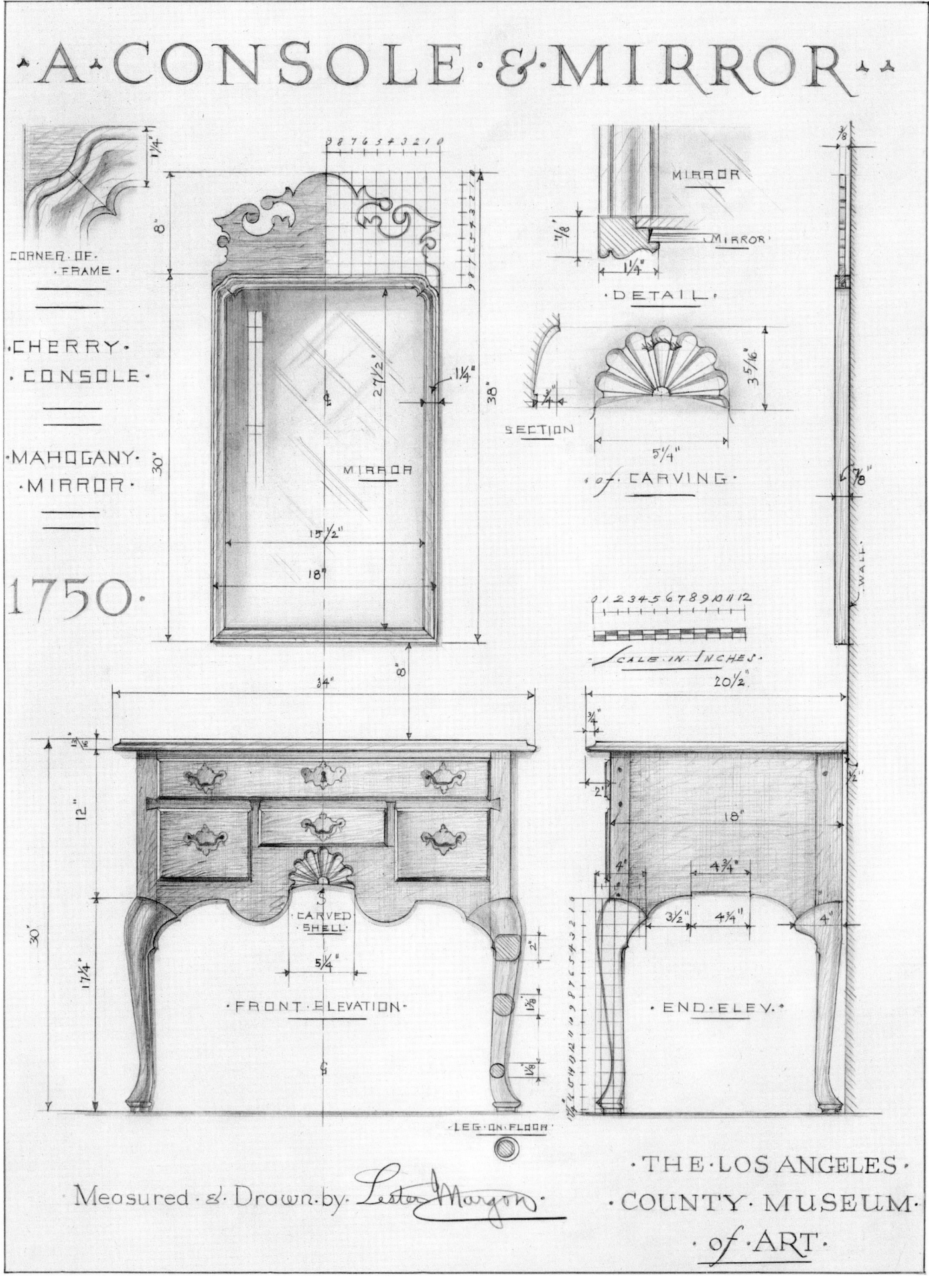

CHERRY LOWBOY
Los Angeles County Museum of Art   Museum Associates — The Balch Fund

This cherry console or lowboy is from Connecticut, *circa* 1740. The unadorned cabriole legs are distinctive and the rather unusual flow of the apron is enhanced by a bit of fan incised carving which is finer than on more florid examples. These pieces were also often used as small chests of drawers or as dressing tables with mirror, as indicated here. The drawer arrangement is unusual; however, this is an outstanding example of superb quality.

The accompanying mahogany mirror is a museum purchase, the Denis Bequest. It is in the Queen Anne tradition from Philadelphia, *circa* 1750. The elongated frame of the mirror is capped by a fretwork cresting cut in a floral pattern. There is a fine, sensitive rhythm in the line, with a not too complicated collection of curves and ramifications. Today the average foyer is often difficult to furnish. What shall we put in there? Here is a good suggestion — a console and a mirror. The upper corner of the frame is well handled.

ANOTHER LOWBOY
Museum of Art, Rhode Island School of Design

Although somewhat similar to the Sylmaris lowboy from the American Wing of the Metropolitan Museum of Art, this model is from the Pendleton Collection. It no doubt is from Philadelphia of approximately the same date. This lowboy has a little more grace and finesse in the treatment of the lower line of the shaped apron with the inclusion of the shell carving and the suggested scrolls. The carving of the legs does not seem to be quite as heedful. The Museum of Art labels it a chamber dressing table of the third quarter of the eighteenth century.

PHILADELPHIA LOWBOY
Metropolitan Museum of Art

This mahogany lowboy is of the Chippendale tradition from Philadelphia, *circa* 1770. From the famous Sylmaris Collection, it is a gift of George Coe Graves. The pierced hardware is effective, the center carved panel quite masterly and the treatment of the cabriole legs with the ball-and-claw feet excellent. What appears to us to be most ingratiating is the fine, low-relief acanthus carving on the knee of the legs. This is truly superlative in its refinement and appropriateness.

Religion Influences Design

LIST OF ILLUSTRATIONS

(Asterisks indicate photographs accompanied by measured drawings.)

KITCHEN DRESSER*
  Metropolitan Museum of Art
TABLE AND BENCHES
  Philadelphia Museum of Art
HANGING CABINET
  Philadelphia Museum of Art
SAWBUCK TABLE*
  Philadelphia Museum of Art
PINE TABLE
  Philadelphia Museum of Art
PEASANT TABLE
  Philadelphia Museum of Art
PAINTED CHESTS*
  Detroit Institute of Arts
WEDDING CHEST
  Metropolitan Museum of Art
PAINTED CHEST
  Art Institute of Chicago

BREADBOX*
  Philadelphia Museum of Art
STAIRWAY AND DOOR
  Philadelphia Museum of Art
KITCHEN FIREPLACE
  Philadelphia Museum of Art
SETTEE*
  Shaker Museum
STORAGE BENCH*
  Shaker Museum
CHEST WITH CUPBOARD*
  Shaker Museum
DINING TABLE*
  Shaker Museum
SHAKER TABLE
  New York State Historical Association
SHAKER TAILORESS'S TABLE
  New York State Historical Association

4

RELIGION INFLUENCES DESIGN

It will be interesting to note the different furniture developments of the Colonists in the various parts of the country where they settled. Take, for instance, the Pennsylvania German settlements during the latter part of the eighteenth century.

William Penn first influenced these German and Swiss peasants of the Palatinate to migrate to the Promised Land with the prospect of freedom of worship and the possibility of grants of fertile lands which they might work and cultivate. Many of them came from the Rhine Valley: Lutherans, Amish, Dunkers and Mennonites. They brought with them and adhered to their language and religious persuasions, their folklore and their customs. They were a self-centered people, averse to worldly pleasures, discouraged the use of mechanical implements on the farms and did not favor higher education for the younger generation. Later, motorized transportation was frowned upon and somber-clad bearded Amish farmers may be seen to this day driving hooded horse-drawn buggies. An industrious people, they were soon rewarded with fertile farmlands and barns full to overflowing. They promptly built modest houses of wood and depended solely upon traditional ceremonials for their community life. Settling originally in Pennsylvania around Germantown, Easton and Lancaster, their domain rapidly spread to New York, Baltimore and as far west as Pittsburgh.

Their furniture was simple in design, often crudely constructed, using pine, cherry and maple, or any wood that was available. Much of the early furniture was painted with decorations of peasant character.

Näive and fanciful representations of flowers, especially the tulip, animals and foliage were interspersed with conventional motifs such as scallops, crisscross patterns, linear arrangements, borders, rosettes and latticework. Representations of the heart became a popular device, with rays that rivaled the radiance of the sun. Angels made another favored subject for decoration, with imaginative representations of the heavenly hosts. Fabulous garlands and stylized drapery, dolphins of a nonexistent era and fantastically shaped vases overflowing with flowers and fruit were features of this peasant decoration.

Among the favored pieces of furniture built by the farmers, handymen and a few carpenters were tables, chairs, benches, beds, dower chests and tall cabinets with open shelves for display and storage purposes. Dough boxes, sawbuck tables, spinning wheels, chairs and desks were favored, while spice cabinets with innumerable drawers, candlestands, spoon racks and knife boxes were in demand. Framed heraldic representations of hand-lettered biblical stanzas with the glorification of the homely virtues appeared in every room. Many of these were beautifully drawn and illuminated. These farmers and field hands put their spare moments to useful endeavors and built worthwhile furniture. They were not influenced by outside tendencies or developments, with the result that their designs continue to be one of the freshest and richest sources of inspiration to this day. Being uninhibited, they expressed themselves freely and without restraint. They had a song in their hearts and were anxious to be heard.

Placed toward the pediments of these tall cabinets may be seen cherubs with outstretched arms and exalted expressions. Being deeply religious, these people put their faith in the Almighty and were joyous in His benefactions. Quaint verses found their way, often in Gothic lettering, on pillar and on post. One of these appearing, on the footboard of a bed, read as follows:

*"Ann Buchwalter is my name
and Heaven is my Destination,
Pennsylvania is my Dwelling Place
and Christ is my Salvation."*

Heretofore we have been inclined to relegate peasant decoration to European mountain locales, with a certain condescending attitude given similarly to the doodling of children. However, upon closer examination we stand transfixed at the profusion of details, the innate sense

Religion Influences Design

of color and the amazing placement of the design elements to be found in these Pennsylvania German creations. Some of the dower chests, especially those from Berks County, are truly fascinating. One in the American Wing of the Metropolitan Museum of Art is so impressive it might well rank with the finest examples of decorated furniture in the Colonial American category. There are three panels in the front, the center one depicting two unicorns which are invariably used as the guardians of fair maidenhood. The turtledoves, portrayed in thrushlike postures, sing their love songs in the prospect of a thrilling courtship. The two end panels portray the suitors on horseback making their speedy ways to claim the lady's fair hand. The excitement is intense. All this is held in place by borders of honeysuckle with whirling tendrils.

Mention should be made here of the variety of small painted boxes made by these people. Gay with naturalistic treatment of flowers, sparkling with choice selections of sentiment, these boxes were made to meet many an emergency. They were fashioned to hold candles for birthday cakes, pieces of jewelry and personal adornments; they were bride boxes and miniature hope chests. Some were no larger than seven inches and others as large as twenty. They were made in a myriad of shapes — square, rectangular, round, oval, hexagonal and in the shape of a diamond. Other boxes were for candies and bittersweets and pomegranate. Many bore delectable inscriptions such as "Ich liebe Dich." The name of the lady for which it was intended always appeared on the cover, which was fitted or hinged miraculously.

In the neighborhood of Ephrata, where the cloisters were located, a local schoolhouse became the gathering place of the young folks on Saturday night to dance and make merry. The older folks gathered in the neighboring houses and enjoyed salty gossip and conviviality. When the hour for departure arrived the family assembled and made their way home. It may not have been very exciting but it filled the social needs of those credulous people. Sunday was the day for worship, prayer and soul-searching. No work was done. Whoever disobeyed the ritual became an outcast in the social order. In this they were relentless. "Let us bow our heads and pray, let us thank the good Lord for his bounteous mercy." That was the chorus that could be heard everywhere.

The communities were noted for their fertile farmlands, neat stone houses and barns full to overflowing, the reward for industrious labor and dedication. Many of the one room houses had whitewashed walls, relieved only by a wooden mantel, baseboard, sometimes a dado and a wood cornice molding. Between these divisions was rough plaster, a fitting background for the colorful painted furniture and accessories. Most important were the neighboring barns, which often advanced to goodly proportions, always allowing large openings with flap-screens that could be lifted to permit air to enter. Across the façades of these barns were painted weird and threatening symbols to scare away the demons who might destroy the precious larder. These farmers were superstitious, and rightfully so. They took no chances with their produce.

As the Pennsylvania German settlements prospered, better types of furniture were made such as "slope desks," refectory tables, corner cupboards, chests, grandfather clocks, cherry beds with panel head and footboards supported by heavy turned posts. Very popular were those "storekeeper desks" with the right pedestal fitted with drawers and the left corner supported by a turned leg. Much of the later furniture was left in the natural wood, with not too much finish applied to hide its beauty. It could be that with progress came sophistication and that some of the early fervor for the homeland and the enthusiasm for the colorful painted furniture subsided. Probably the people became too busy and preoccupied with progress to trouble much about such variant matters. This is the penalty for becoming acclimated to the new surroundings and becoming acquainted with financial prosperity. Under these propitious circumstances it became difficult to remain naïve, natural and unsophisticated. One thing must be said in their favor — they have almost stubbornly stuck to their preconceived idea of the simple life with continued restrictions and limitation of action. Just what effect this will have on the younger generation is a problem.

Perhaps the finest ensemble of the Pennsylvania German furniture may be seen at the Philadelphia Museum of Art, in the Geesey Collection and in the furniture presented by the Du Ponts and shown in the settings of the rooms reconstructed and brought from the countryside to house and display these products and to show their diversity. Certainly the best rooms are from the House of the Miller of Millbach, 1752, the kitchen of which has been recreated in all its minutest details and fitted with all the pots and pans and paraphernalia. A splendid setting, it affords an excellent picture of the life of the Pennsylvania German people. Besides the excellent architectural features of the rooms, there are two splendid kitchen cupboards with open shelving at the top to permit the display of those fantastic pieces of decorated pottery for which they prided themselves so highly. This house was originally situated in the Valley of Mill Run in Lebanon County, Pennsylvania. The American Wing of the Metropolitan Museum of Art also has a splendid room of this same epoch,

Religion Influences Design

from Lancaster County, 1761, showing a group of varied and unusual chairs of the locale, including a child's high chair. Across the top of the mantel is stretched a blatant shotgun to welcome any intruder. There is a throbbing eagle perched on the top of a hanging cabinet, ready to take off at the slightest provocation, and a wrought-iron lighting fixture fitted with tapered candles hanging from the center of the ceiling above the dining table. The room, with its random boards as flooring held in place by pegs, is also a splendid reconstruction of the period.

THE SHAKERS

"Hands to work and hearts to God"

Another most interesting contribution to Colonial furniture design, and one strangely enough closely associated with religious indoctrination, is the Shaker furniture. To rightfully understand and appreciate the craftsmanship, its design, the perfection of workmanship in spite of the limitation of materials and the meager finish employed, one must be cognizant of the underlying circumstances and beliefs which brought this unusual sect into being.

From its very inception and its organization in eastern New York, it spread rapidly through New England, Kentucky and Ohio. The Shakers first gathered into community life at New Lebanon, New York, in 1787 as the "United Society of Believers in Christ's Second Coming." They were certain of the second coming of Christ during the millenium, as foretold in the Book of Revelation. Ann Lee, a factory worker from Manchester, England, was recognized as their spiritual leader. At the peak of the Society's membership, about 1840 to 1860, there were eighteen communities, housing units with approximately 6000 believers, stretching from Maine to Kentucky and Ohio. These workers, joiners, mechanics and artisans created a distinct and different style in furniture design which duly reflected and expressed the spirit and the practices of their convictions. Foresaking all worldly things, contributing their everything to the common good, withdrawing into secluded community life, they rejected all personal adornments and artifice, ostentation, display, vainglory and indulgences. They neither smoked nor drank and regarded all sexual relationships as heinous sins. Dedicated to celibacy, they were entities unto themselves. The Shakers believed in communism, a social system in which all goods were held in common and shared in common — certainly not the kind of communism that we are fighting today. They were ardent pacifists and believed in the public confession of sins. Their work in furniture was particularly praiseworthy. Sober in design, monastic in simplicity, restrained in composition, perfect in workmanship and always manifestly utilitarian, it possessed an honesty that seemed to be its main goal. Pursuing this work unaffectedly, they achieved a standard of craftsmanship that has seldom been approached. This was only possible by reason of their strict practice of apprenticeship. Their living quarters were immaculate, never cluttered; there was a place for everything and everything was in its place. Programs and procedures were carefully planned, there was no allowance for trial and error. Every inch of space was utilized to its best advantage. There was never cause for procrastination or abuse, for the Shakers attempted, and successfully, to perpetuate the ultimate in communal living.

In the dining halls there stood long tables with straight-back chairs of the one-slat type which were pushed under the tables or hung on the walls after the meals were ended. In the morning when the men went off to work they left their beds open. Later when the women were sure that none of the men was about they entered their rooms and made up the beds. The separation of the sexes was absolute and complete. The hands of the men and the women never touched; that would have indeed been considered blasphemy.

What exactly was the nature of this Shaker furniture? It precluded the nonessentials; smooth surfaces prevailed, for then things could readily be kept clean. The grain of the wood was never obscured by heavy finishes or varnishes. The beauty of the wood was permitted to shine through, sealing it only with a rubbing of wax. The lines of the furniture were straight, the corners sharp and true. This furniture was free from all subterfuge and needless elaboration. Behind it all was the sincere effort to get right down to the basic realities and to arrive as closely as possible to the perfect form, with proportions free of all undo variations and adulations. Though simple in the extreme, this Shaker furniture had majesty and was tremendously satisfying. Would it be too bold to suggest and imply that many of the foremost so-called "Modern" furniture designers have taken good note of this Shaker furniture and have incorporated many of its factors as their original designs? One thing is certain: the Shakers succeeded in combining beauty with utility and functionalism, without impairing the design. They incorporated a knowingness into this furniture that was in itself manifest.

Religion Influences Design

Because of its celibate persuasions, the sect had difficulty in surviving as time went on. They had hoped that their lofty ideals and aspirations would continue to attract new believers. This was not the case. The reasons for their decline and gradual extinction may be accredited to the wars and depressions which limited their funds and to competition, which deprived them of their industries. Inducements and attractions of the modern world took many of the younger people. Men and women failed to appreciate the cloistered life of routine, discipline, self-sacrifice and self-control. (This is from *The Shakers' Viewpoint*, by Eldress Emma B. King.)

Possibly this is to be regretted, for where in this woebegotten world today can we find such magnanimity? Visiting the Shakers' Home at Lebanon, New York, some years ago, we were struck by its homeliness, a restful atmosphere bespeaking peace and contentment. We were met at the door by Sister H. Rosetta Stephens, a little old lady wearing a black bonnet over her straight white hair. She was expecting us. We were welcome. Being shown into her little sitting room, we chatted about our personal interest in the cult and then was taken about. As she spoke and explained about this and that her face beamed with the enthusiasm of a child. The faces of all the elderly men and women about shone with the radiance of contentment. On our departure, Sister Rosetta eloquently expressed her pleasure in being able to give this little service to friends. It was a day to remember.

Nevertheless, it was not all work and no play. On Sunday evenings, the Shakers would forgather in the Assembly Hall and partake of a ritual dance which made them appear as "Shakers" to the nonbelievers, hence the name. The dance proceeded at an increasing pace, for there was no central figure as the choreographer but each member, men and women separately, participated, expressing his or her predilection in rhythmic exaltation. It was indeed a spectacle to behold and that great student and dancer, the late Doris Humphrey, presented memorable performances in her repertoire some years ago. The memory of her performance still makes the blood tingle. It is doubly unfortunate that this Shaker sect has now almost passed into oblivion because there is nothing to take its place. Today we are plagued with commercialism; the mighty dollar is the only source of recompense. The work and the doctrines of the Shakers were so outstanding and many of their procedures so laudable. Their failure to reproduce their kind was a fault of all cenobite groups. One verse among their many chants might be quoted because it so well expresses their zeal and faith in Salvation:

> *"I shall march through Mount Zion
> with my angelic band,
> I shall pass through the City
> with my fan in my hand."*

Persons who are interested may visit The Shaker Museum at Old Chatham, New York. It is now a nonprofit institution chartered by the Board of Regents of the State of New York. The famous Shakers' Ghost Town is at New Lebanon, New York, only a short distance away. Here may be seen the five-story stone barn, the settlement's former dormitory and laundry. You will see some of the Shakers' inventions, including the original washing machine, the dryers for clothes, the sturdy baskets, a practical bread slicer and safety knife racks. Among other noteworthy inventions were the tongue-and-groove machine, the screw propeller and a mechanical pea sheller. It is worthy to note that much of this designing was done by the craftswomen. This not alone predated woman suffrage but foreshadowed the day when women have taken their place in industry and no more may be considered the weaker sex. Their most persistent motto was:

> *"Do all your work as though
> you had a thousand years to
> live, and as you would if you
> knew you must die tomorrow."*

Religion Influences Design

Because of the fact that one main reason of the settlers coming to these shores was to escape from religious persecution, it is therefore not surprising to find this passion for celestial expression reflected in the designs of their furniture and household commodities. They brought with them fond memories coupled with the ritualistic restrictions which they sought to establish and observe here. This was especially true of the Pennsylvania Germans whose divine law prohibited the use of the human form in decoration except in the most allegorical aspects. The Shakers, on the other hand, eliminated all decoration from their furniture designs. Because of these enforced limitations, their work was not only individualistic but registered the tempo of their endeavors.

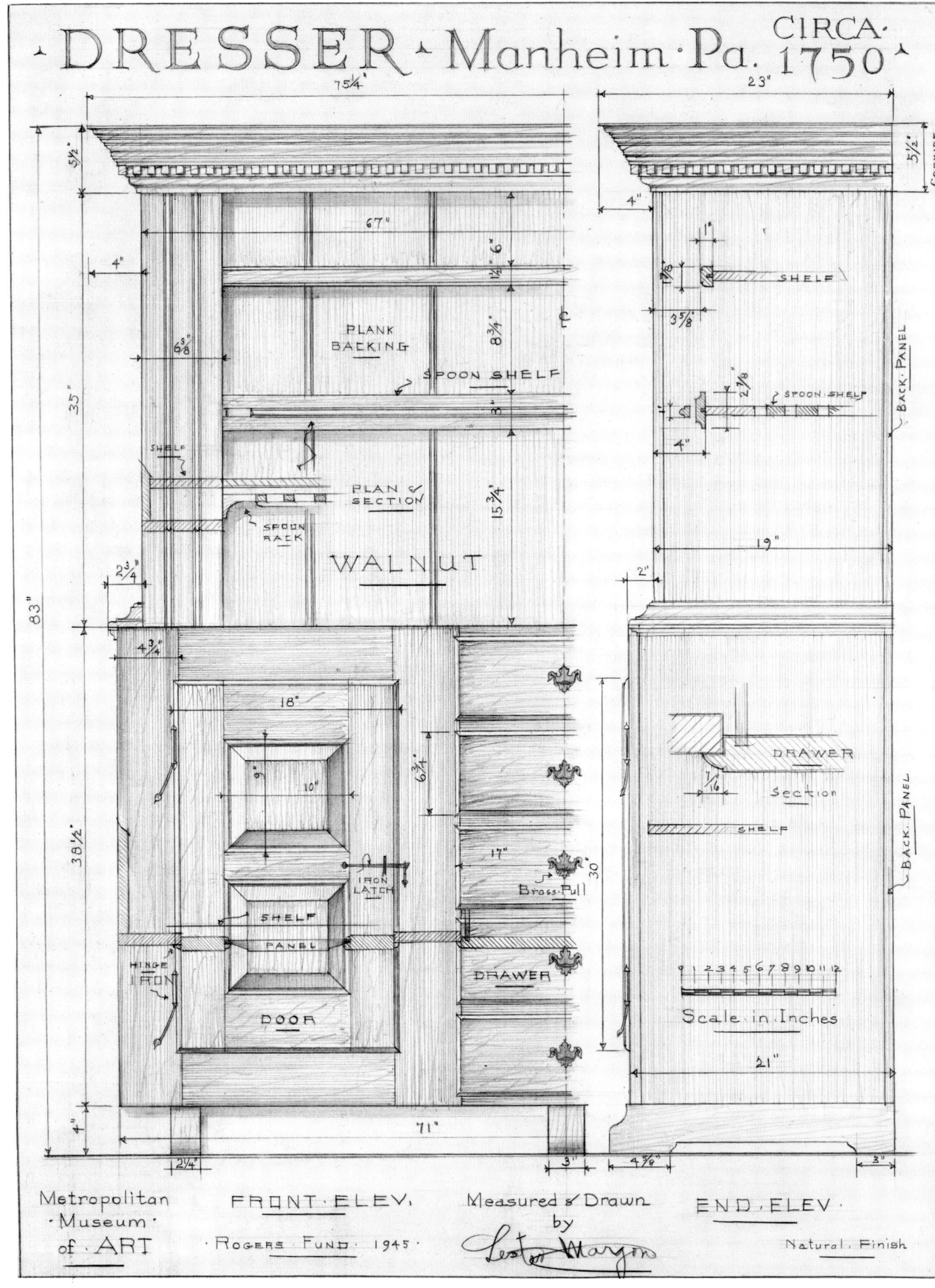

KITCHEN DRESSER
Metropolitan Museum of Art

This rather ponderous walnut kitchen dresser is Pennsylvania German from the town of Manheim, *circa* 1750, and is distinguished by its sturdy construction and honesty in design. It is the naïve expression of the local craftspeople who desired to produce a utilitarian cabinet that would take care of all the needs of a farmhouse kitchen. The piece has drawers, storage cabinets, open shelves and provision to hold cutlery. The upper part was used for the display of colorful ornamented pottery. While the general aspect of the piece is provincial, it nevertheless displays a very knowledgeable sense of design, for the detail of the cornice is quite Classical. In fact, there is a certain sculptural feeling about this piece that is inescapable. Worthy of note is the transparent finish on this dresser, resembling the color of running honey. It is surprising that walnut was used but no doubt it was close at hand; these pieces are most often made of pine. The wrought-iron hinges and pulls are interesting.

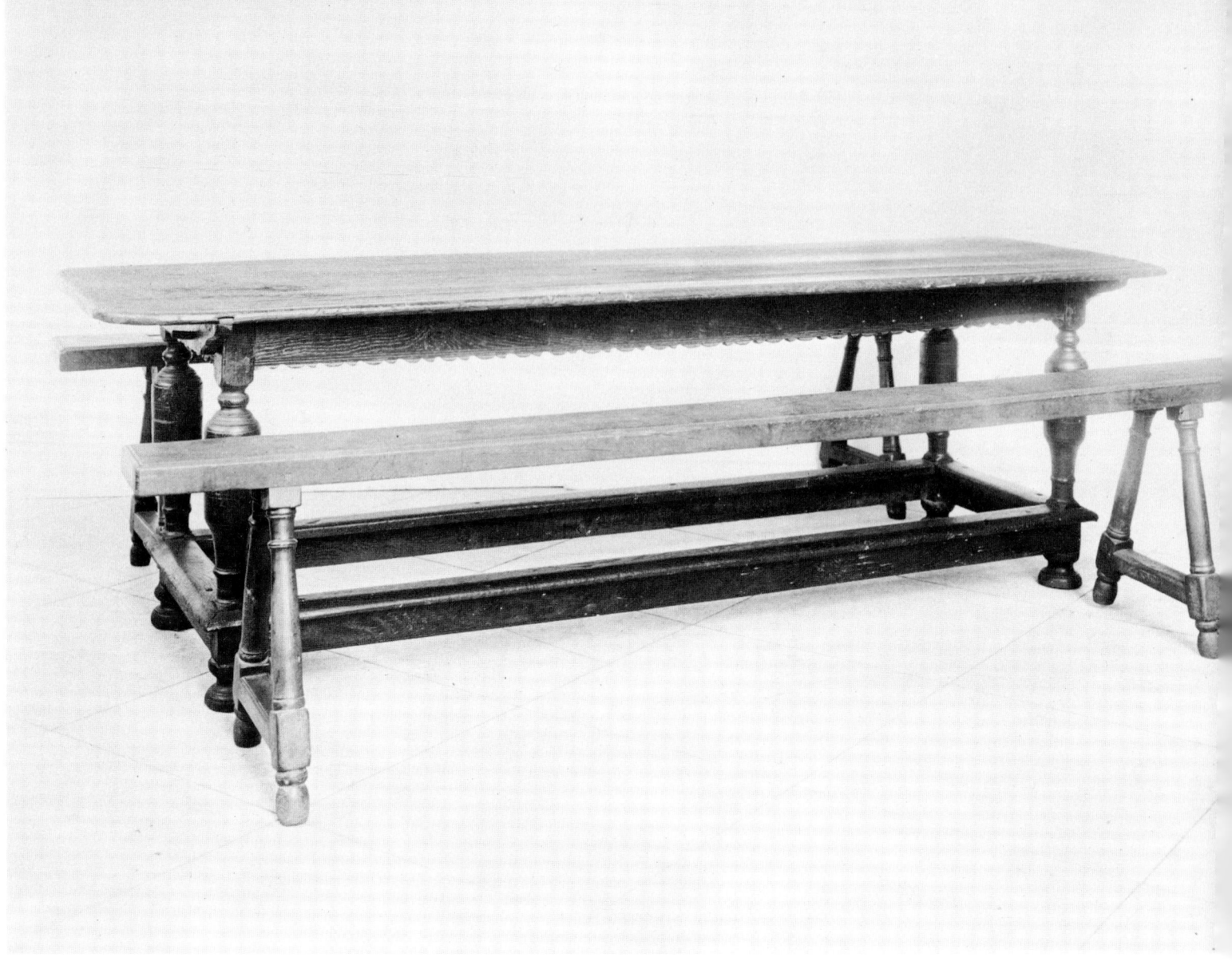

TABLE AND BENCHES
Philadelphia Museum of Art

This oak refectory table and two long benches, dated *circa* 1700, come from Pennsylvania. The benches are made from pear-wood and the Jacobean influence is apparent. The table top, made up of several planks, held in place by a wooden cleat, has large rounded corners. The broken line of the apron does much to defeat the rather monastic appearance. The table's bulbous legs are held in place by the heavy stretcher, which affords a welcome resting place for the tired wayfarer. The benches do not appear so sturdy, with stretchers only at the ends.

PENNSYLVANIA GERMAN ODDITIES
Metropolitan Museum of Art

Even in the small household accessories, these Pennsylvania Germans showed interest and consideration. This frolicsome hanging pipe rack is not alone carved but painted as well. The broad and heavy pounder used in pressing, elaborately ornamented with the ever faithful tulip motif, is likewise painted and decorated. Note the interesting texture evident in the background. They believed that nothing was too small or insignificant to be made beautiful. Going through the department stores and viewing the accessories counters today, don't we wish that a little more thought and attention were given to these articles?

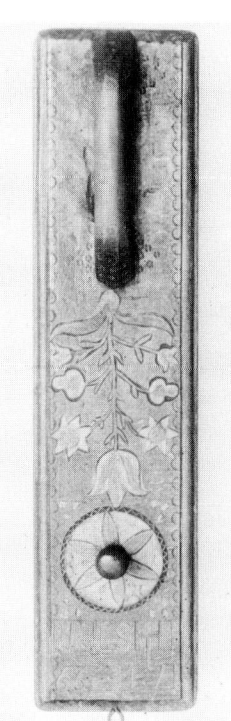

HANGING CABINET
Philadelphia Museum of Art

This hanging corner cabinet of pine, Pennsylvania German from the middle of the eighteenth century, is shown in the rooms from the House of the Miller of Millbach, the gift of the Du Ponts. It is a simple well-balanced piece, sturdy but having a certain flair, with the top proscenium effect for the display of a piece of precious pottery. Below are a cupboard and a small drawer. It is a delightful conception that would grace the corner of any room.

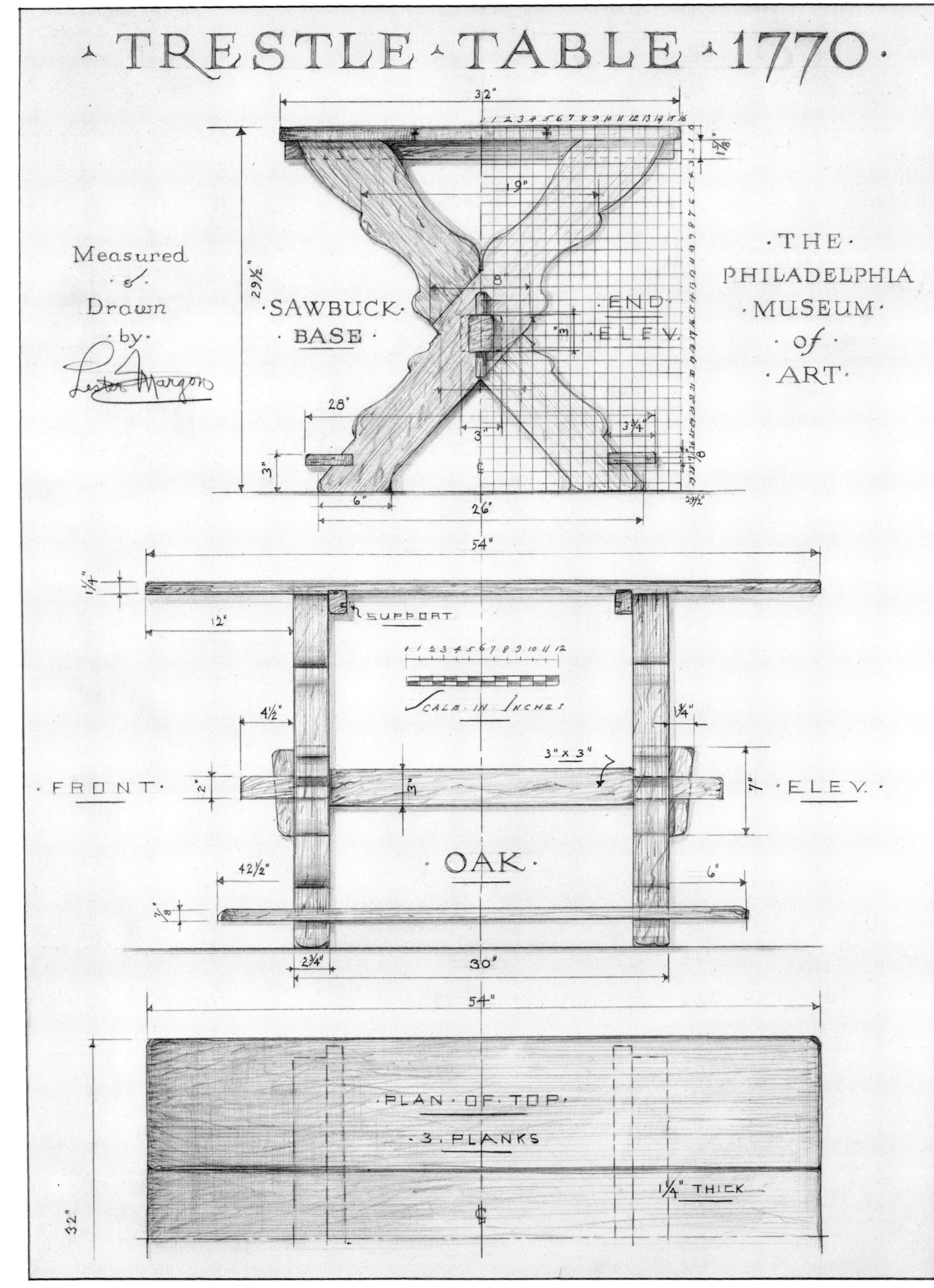

SAWBUCK TABLE
Philadelphia Museum of Art

Sawbuck tables are most often found in peasant dining areas all through the Tyrol and Central Europe. The Pennsylvania Germans probably saw fit to copy these tables for their use. The construction is basic but by no means simple. This model, made of oak, dates from the middle of the 18th century. The table's cross side supports, made of heavy stock, are spliced at the intersection and held in place by a center stretcher that is pierced and fastened by a shaped dart. At the bottom, on each side, are foot-rests which also serve as stretchers for the table. Note that the top is made of three planks joined together and braced by cleats inside the upright supports. Of course this type of table is perfect for a provincial setting and the more crude it appears, the better. Many have a long drawer beneath the top, as is evidenced by a similar table in the American Wing of the Metropolitan Museum of Art. Tables of this type no doubt were made in the early times, there being a certain primitive logic in crossing two pieces of wood and fastening them at the center.

PINE TABLE
Philadelphia Museum of Art

This oval-top pine table is from Pennsylvania, the date 1750. The edges of the top, which is made of planks, appear to be badly worn. The table has one drawer, the lower apron is shaped and the legs are turned and well splayed to afford a wide base. It is a good example of the work of these peasant settlers in its frankness and direct means of expression. It is on display in the Pennsylvania German rooms.

PEASANT TABLE
Philadelphia Museum of Art

Pennsylvania is the locale, the early part of the eighteenth century the date. This walnut table is certainly substantial-looking, with the shaped square legs supported by heavy stretchers. There is one drawer and the apron is rich in curvatures. The wide overhang of the top permits of better seating around the table. The top, made of planks, is held together by side strips and by cleats inserted below. A peasant-type table, it expresses the sturdy individuality of the Pennsylvania German people.

· PAINTED · CHEST · 1790 ·

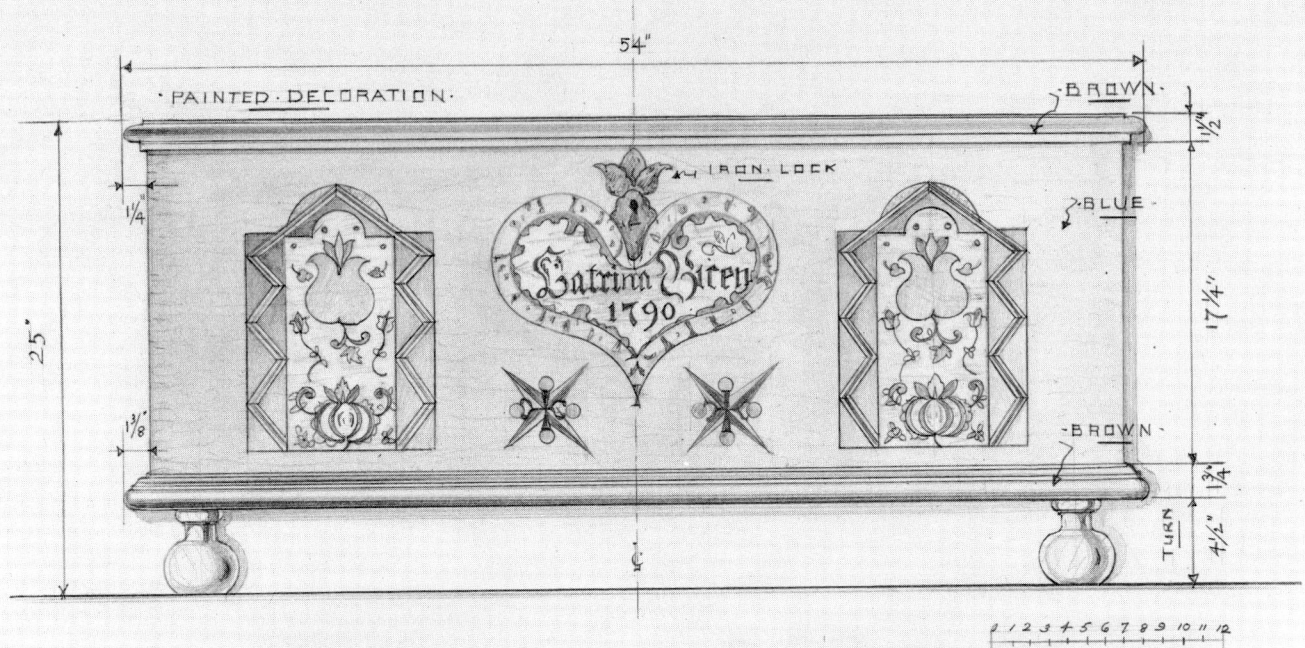

· FRONT · ELEVATION ·

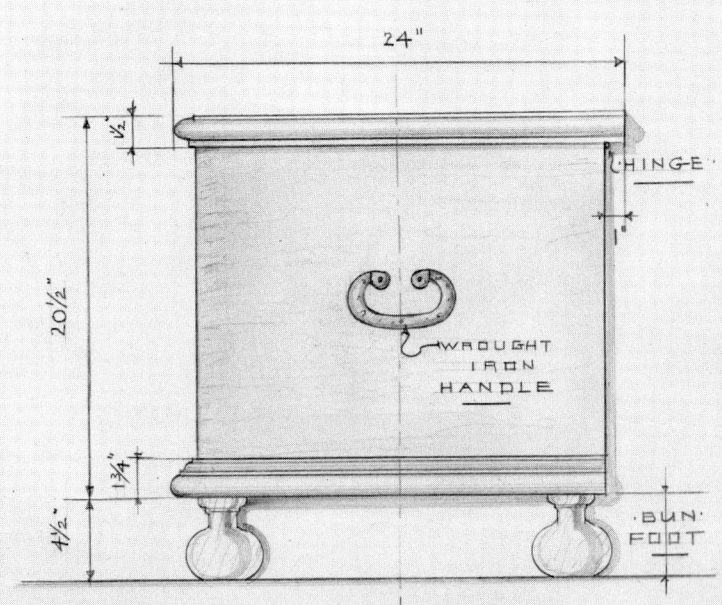

· END · ELEV ·

· Measured · & · Drawn · by · Lester Morgan

· THE ·
· DETROIT · INSTITUTE ·
· of · ARTS ·

PAINTED CHEST
Detroit Institute of Arts

These Pennsylvania German dowry chests, *circa* 1790, are among the most colorful and distinctive contributions to American Colonial furniture. The term "dowry" indicates the property which a woman owns and brings to her husband at the time of their marriage. This chest, belonging to Latrina Vicen and dated 1790, is an excellent example, glamorous in detail and propitious in conception. Again the tulip plays an important rôle in the painted decoration, with the heart as the central motif. As used here, it could be the symbol of promised happiness. The two glittering stars below shine brightly for the future. The two side panels are rich in detail and full of rapture. The wrought-iron handles at the ends are ready to help transport the chest to its destination. The background of the chest is painted blue, with top and bottom moldings brown; that of the side panels is white and the decoration brilliant in color. Many of these early chests were made without drawers.

These painted chests had no connection with any other section of the Colonies. They were exclusively the product of the Pennsylvania German people, with their original type of decoration.

WEDDING CHEST
Metropolitan Museum of Art

This painted Pennsylvania German chest is probably one of the finest. It is described in detail in the text. It has two lower drawers under the box of the upper part, which has a hinged top. This chest in particular is certainly a bit of glorious decoration. Space division, design and coloring are all superb. Gay, pulsating, beyond compare, it is doubly interesting because it is decorated also on the top and the side. This chest was purchased by the Rogers Fund, 1923.

PAINTED CHEST
Art Institute of Chicago

Our delight in viewing many of these Pennsylvania painted chests knows no bounds. This wedding chest, dating from 1785, was painted by Christian Selzer. It features the architectural pilasters, which divide the front into three arched panels, producing three splendid areas for decoration. The two end panels are for floral vase arrangements, with the Star of Bethlehem above. The central panel bears the date 1785. These chests are always a source of wonderment. No two are ever alike. This chest was purchased by the Museum from the Avery Fund.

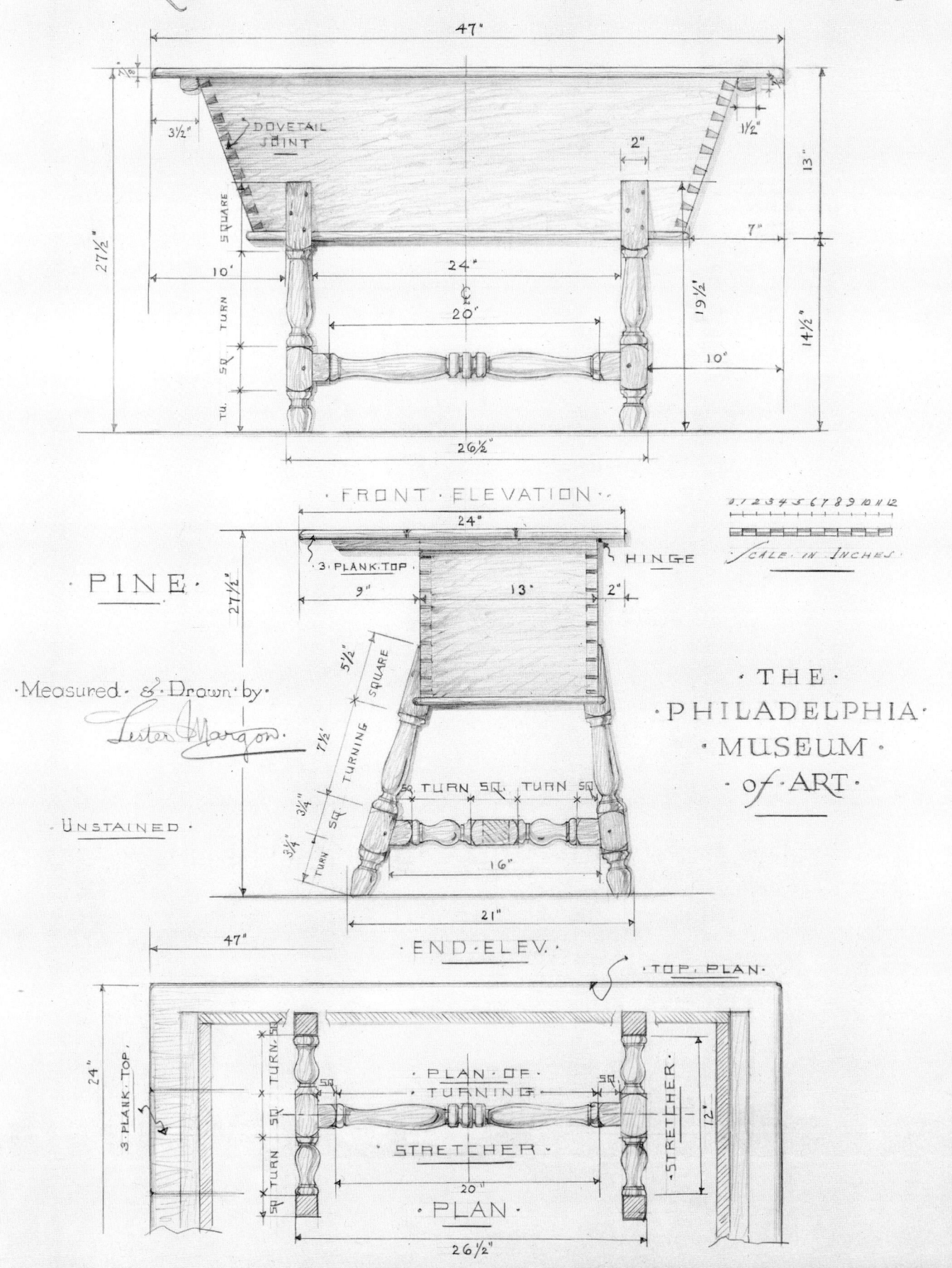

BREADBOX

Philadelphia Museum of Art

This kneading trough-table, dough or bread-preparation box, is a typical Pennsylvania German kitchen unit, *circa* 1750. Made of unstained pine, this is a provincial piece that has much charm despite its utilitarian aspect. The dough was mixed and kneaded on the broad top and then put into the box for raising and safekeeping. When wanted, it is taken out and made ready for the oven in whatever shape or purpose desired. The turnings are well lined and the sturdy stretchers give the necessary support. The top is made of three broad planks held in place by cleats at the ends. These peasant pieces are so interesting because the dovetailing is clearly indicated and becomes part of the design. This one is set against a wall in the kitchen of the House of the Miller of Millbach. This furniture is the expression of the people who made it, sturdy, individual and altogether honest. There is no attempt at subterfuge, no beating around the bush. They knew what they wanted and made it in the most simple and satisfactory manner. Their interiors were ascetic and simple, but the austerity of their whitewashed walls was relieved by wood moldings and colorful decorated furniture.

STAIRWAY AND DOOR
Philadelphia Museum of Art

This view of a stairway, entirely of wood, is from the House of the Miller of Millbach, Lebanon County, Pennsylvania, dated 1752. The design of the oblong-shaped pillar supports or balustrade follows in line the slope of the stairs. The front post is square and massive, meeting a heavy shaped rail. Note the elegant beamed ceiling and the fine wall paneling. Of special interest is the double door, excellently paneled, with the butterfly wrought-iron hinges.

KITCHEN FIREPLACE
Philadelphia Museum of Art

The kitchen fireplace and a far corner from the House of the Miller of Millbach from Lebanon County, Pennsylvania, 1752. It shows the heavy wooden shelf and the interior of the hearth with all its pots, pans and paraphernalia associated with cooking. The furniture shown includes two wainscot chairs, the sawbuck table, a corner hanging cabinet and the old faithful salt box. The jug and the pewter plates are typical. Note that the walls of the room are roughly plastered and the interior of the hearth is faced with stones from the fields.

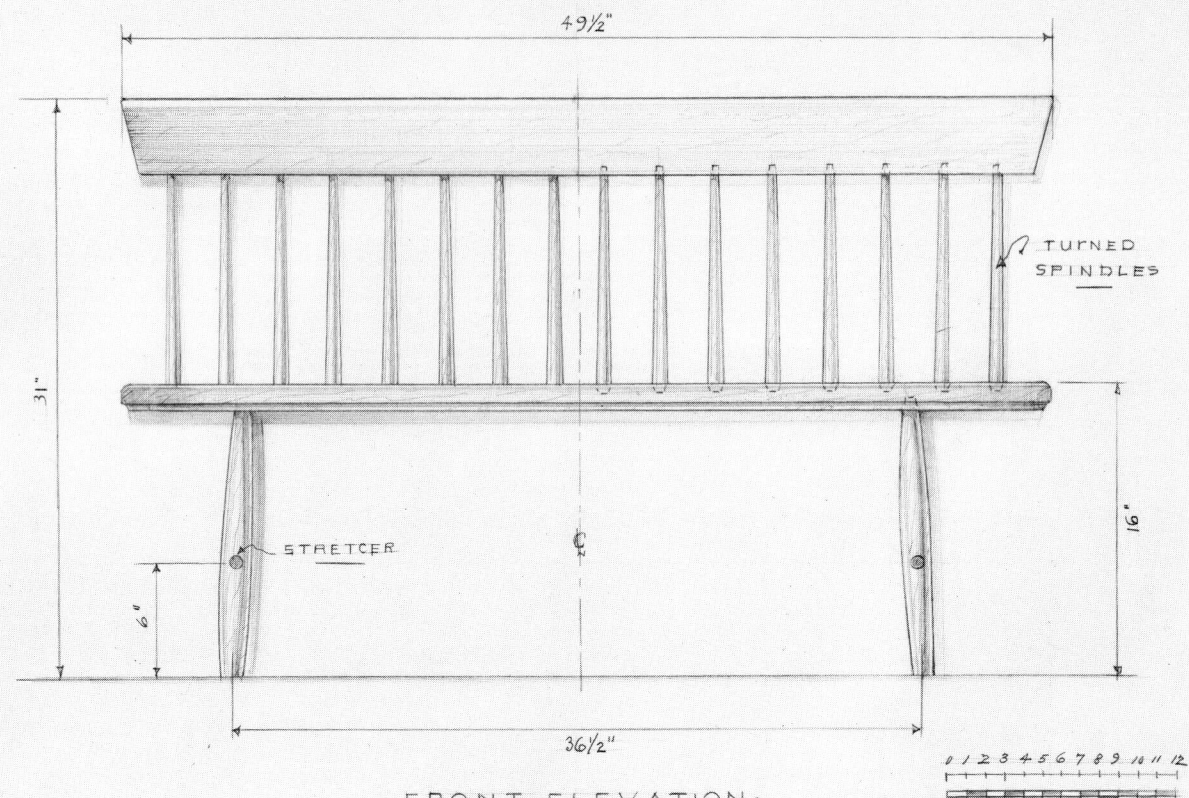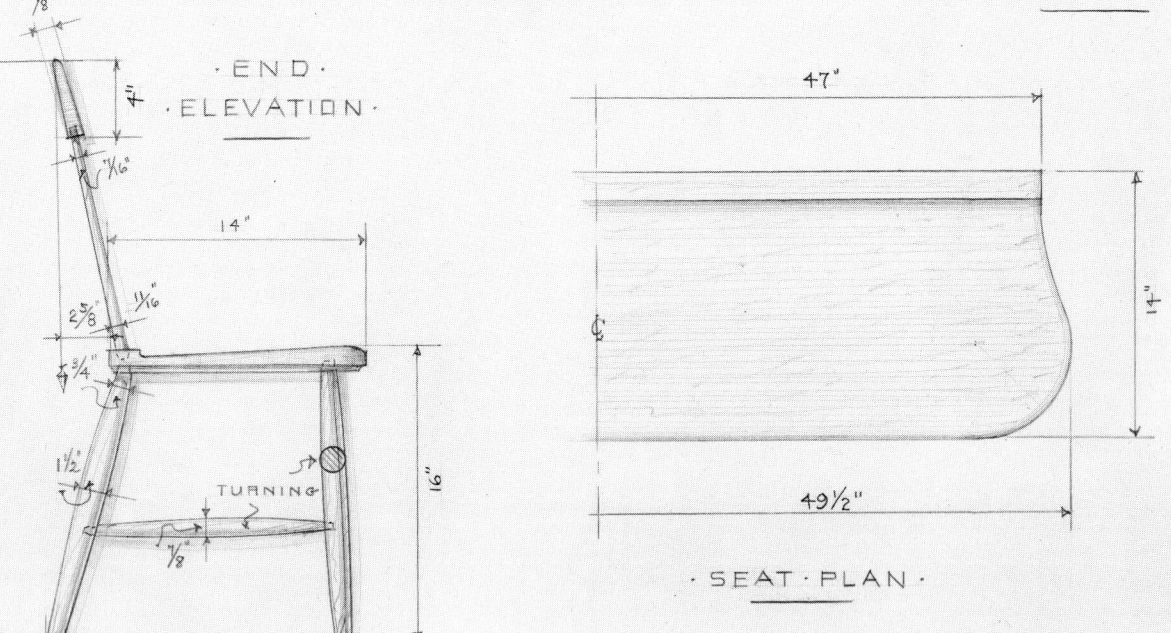

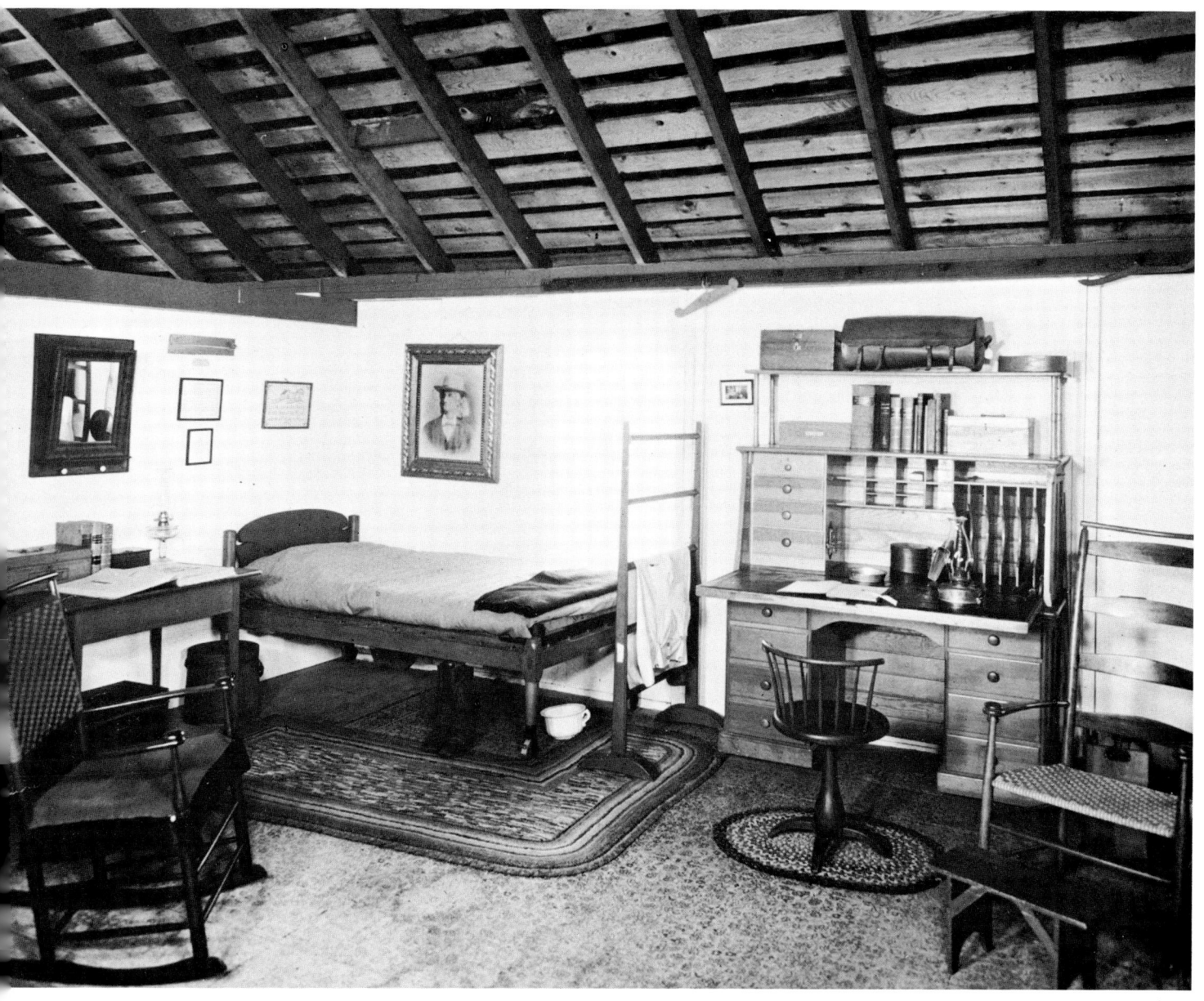

SETTEE
Shaker Museum

In this settee the Shaker craftsmen seem to have taken a leaf from the Windsor-type products although they have simplified it to the extreme. The form is beautiful and the shaped plain turnings are certainly effective. This bench is from Canterbury. Note the bend of the back and the slight rake of the legs, with the stretchers only on the ends for support. The shape of the saddle seat is well conceived and affords just the right seating comfort. If there is a certain institutional aspect to its severity — well, that is the sort of thing the Shakers wanted to create. The slant of the back leg produces just the right restraint.

This is a photograph of a Brother's room. Again it seems to be a combination bedroom and office with the pedestal desk and the drawers and files above and so many pigeonholes. Pay special attention to the ingenious swivel chair. It is as modern as tomorrow. The rocker and the armchair with the footrest are said to be of the finest. The rafter ceiling with the space between the boards for ventilation provides air conditioning. There is a spot rug under the bed and a braided oval rug beneath the swivel chair. It is quite a compact setting.

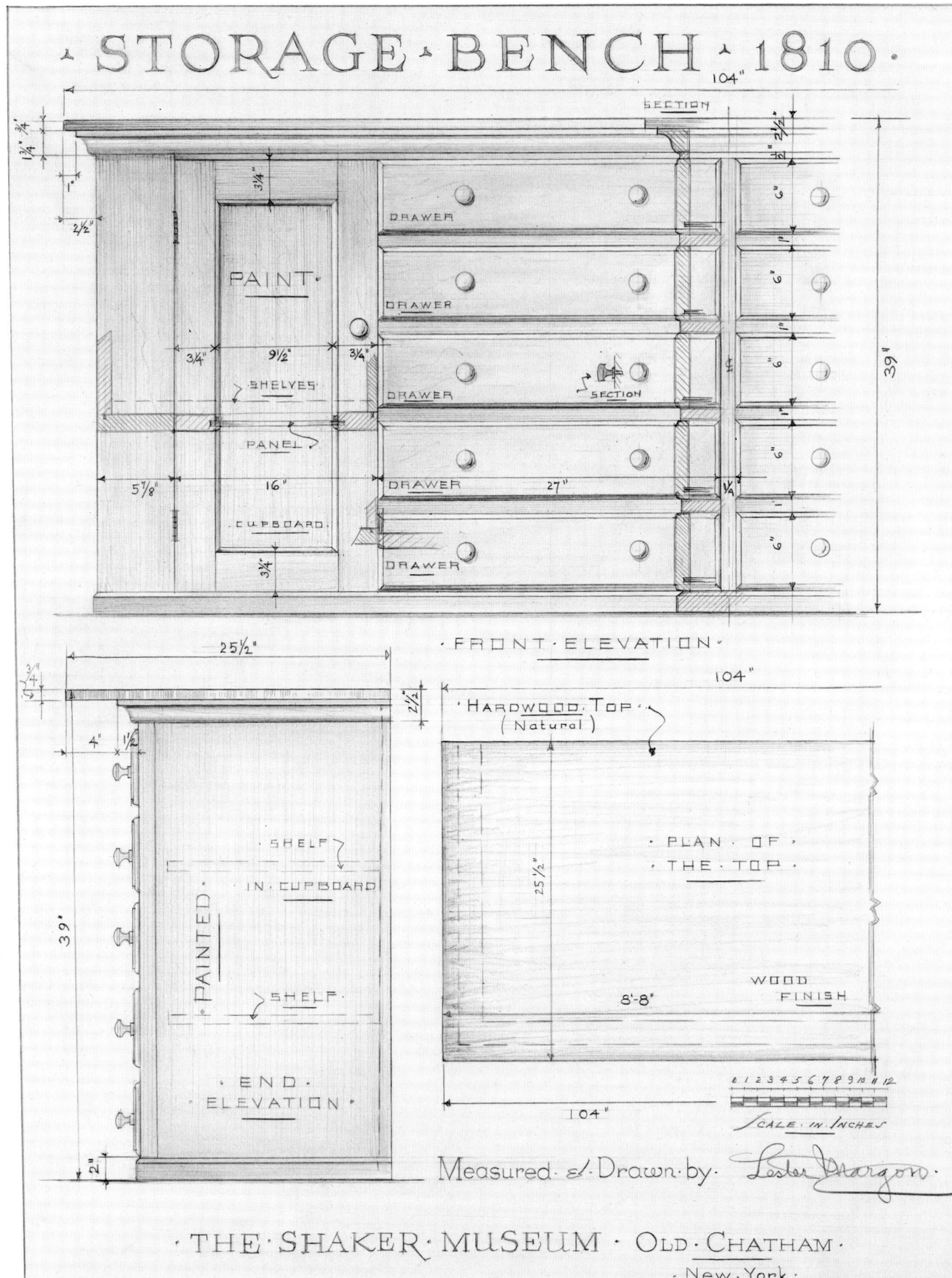

STORAGE BENCH
Shaker Museum

What would one give today to find a storage bench of this size and capacity? Study the piece, for it displays the magic of space allotment. Consisting of only two end cupboards and eight equal-sized center drawers, the effect is most pleasing and decorative. It was part of the Shaker establishment at Lebanon, New York. Besides the vast storage space, the top was used for working. Note the large extension of the top at the front to permit of better standing. This storage bench comes from the Canterbury Church, 1792. The accompanying photograph shows the Trustee's Office, now installed at the Shaker Museum at Old Chatham, New York. The walnut desk and the cherry cupboard are from Pleasant Hill, Kentucky. The extended wall clothes rack is interesting and the round high stool with the legs bent outward is something that should be noted by today's manufacturers. Note the large woven basket and the two rockers. These are claimed to be the finest in execution and seating comfort. This Shaker furniture had a way of producing a sense of adequacy and fulfillment. There never could be a question of its practicability.

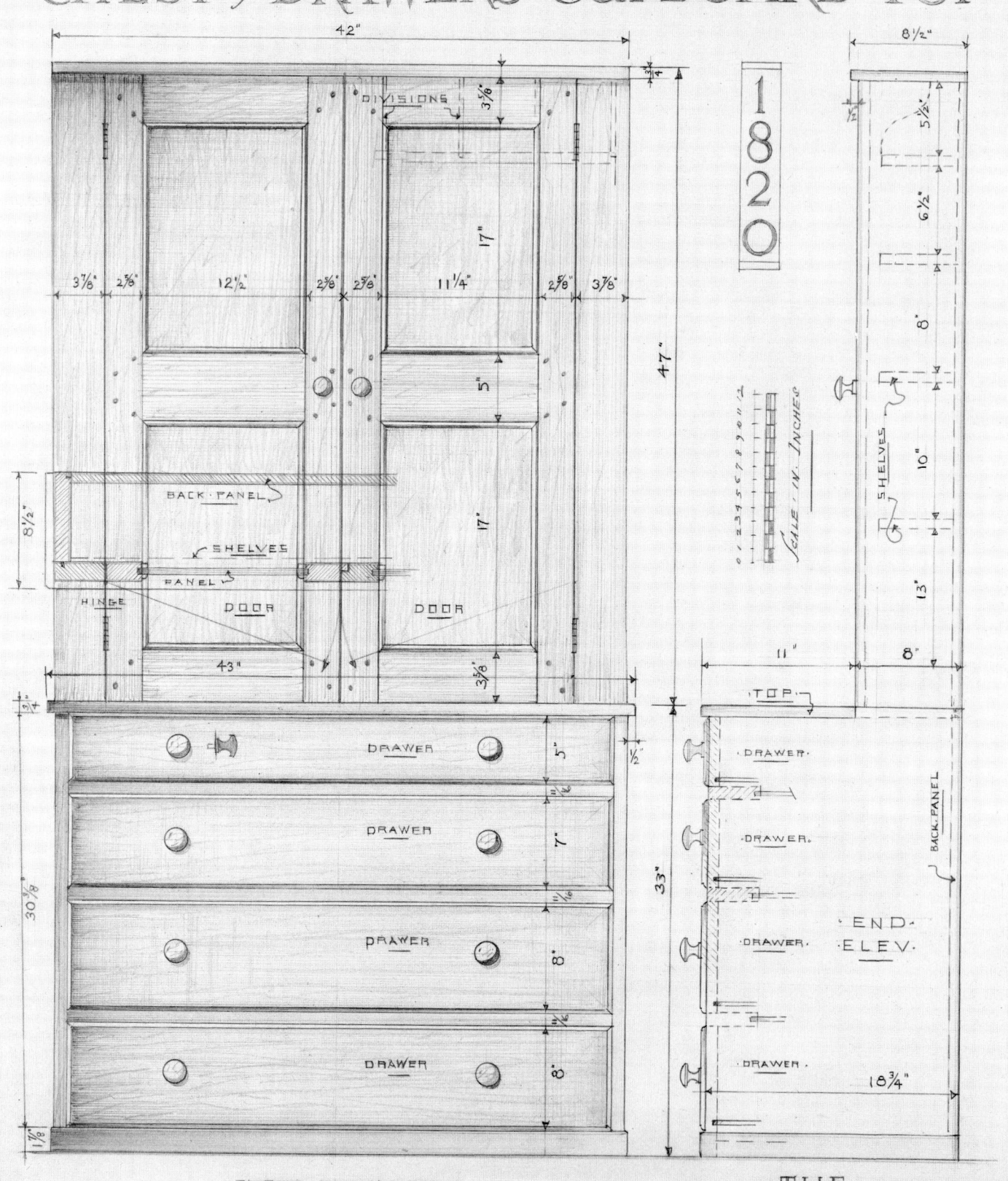

CHEST WITH CUPBOARD
Shaker Museum

This tall combination-piece of a chest of drawers surmounted by a cupboard exemplifies the chastity of Shaker furniture. It is one hundred-percent utilitarian, and every inch of space inside is utilized to advantage. The piece, *circa* 1775, is of maple with turned wooden knobs and belonged to the Church family of Mount Lebanon, New York. Inside the cupboard are shelves and the top space is divided for the storage of smaller miscellanea. The piece is tall but by clever space divisions and paneling of the cupboard doors, the effect is pleasing. In the room photograph we see stark beauty achieved through functional simplicity of design, expressing a deep tenet of these people's religious beliefs. This is a sitting room showing a round pedestal table and a collection of varied types and sizes of chairs and rockers, while crayon portraits in carved gilded frames look down in compassionate understanding. One can picture an assembly of the Sisters, each busily engaged with some handicraft, enjoying a bit of leisure and perhaps even a little gossip. Here one may see how well this chest with cupboard fits into a room setting of this type. Note the sewing-rocker with drawers under the seat. Beside the entrance stands Elder Benjamin Young's trunk on a trunk stand. He was famous for long missionary journeys made on foot.

DINING TABLE 1807

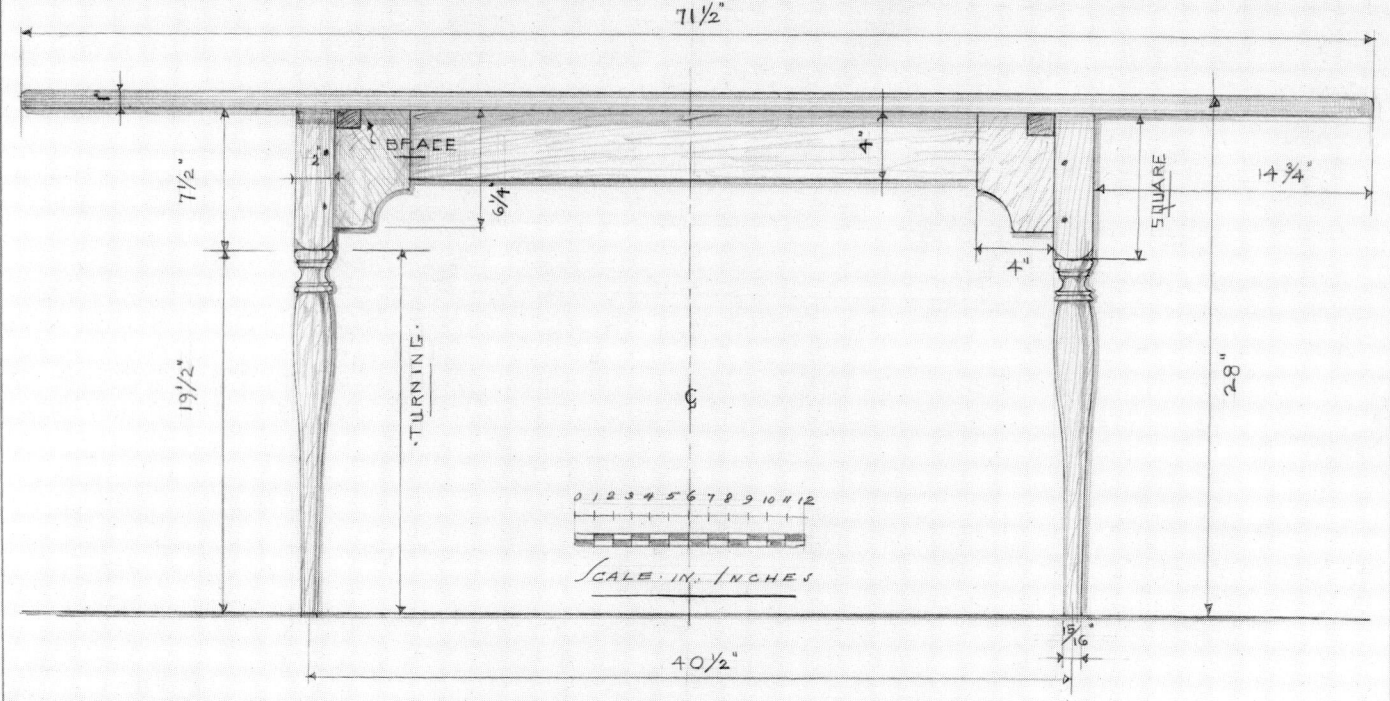

FRONT ELEVATION

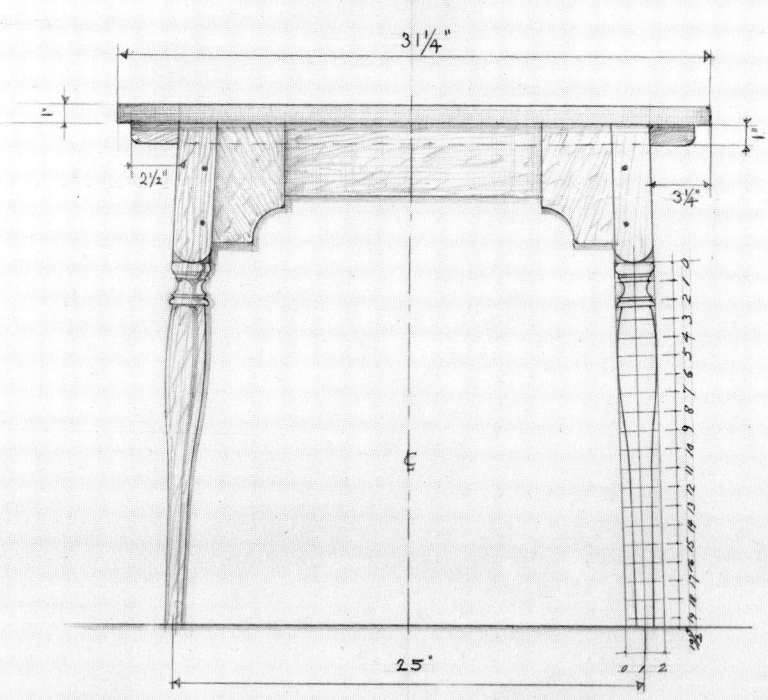

END ELEV.

Measured & Drawn by Lester Margon

THE SHAKER MUSEUM

OLD CHATHAM NEW YORK

DINING TABLE
Shaker Museum

This long and narrow table, probably used for dining, was part of the original furniture in a Shaker home — that of the Church family of New Lebanon, New York. The slight spread of the legs gives the table the required stability. The subtlety of the turned leg is astonishing — when has one ever seen anything like it? The nuances are infinite. The generous overhang of the top at each end makes seating more comfortable. The room is the Sister's bedroom, showing the dropleaf table, the iron foot warmer, the cupboard with drawers, the footstool and inviting arm- chairs and rockers. There are Shaker hand-woven bed covers and a good-size basket. Seen here as a typical room, it presents a picture of not only adequacy but even of creature comforts. One can almost picture the sisters scurrying about. This was not alone a bedroom but probably served as workroom, sitting room and office when necessary. The furniture is simple, adequate and certainly utilitarian; it is free from frills and inconsequentials. One immediately sees the purpose for which it was intended. That is one of the secrets of Shaker furniture.

SHAKER TABLE
New York State Historical Association

Exhibited in the Fenimore House in the Restoration of the New York State Historical Association at Cooperstown, N.Y., is this Shaker refectory table. Note the unusual turned legs, the inclusion of two drawers in the apron for cutlery and linens. This long dining table is interesting because of the large overhang at each end to permit of more comfortable sitting. The top is made of several planks with narrow strips of wood between them. Cooperstown, well known for the Baseball Hall of Fame, should be equally well known for its marvelous displays of houses and Americana.

SHAKER TAILORESS'S TABLE
New York State Historical Association

Again we are impressed by the utmost in utilitarianism in the Shaker Tailoress's table. Especially in furniture the Shakers achieved beauty through functional simplicity of design. Note the wide drop-flap at the back that can be raised to afford a greater working surface. The six long drawers of varied sizes can well take care of the supplies and materials to be sewed. The top is made of planks set together and held by side strips. The wood was maple with very little finish and that was rubbed in.

Style and Three Great Designers

LIST OF ILLUSTRATIONS

(Asterisks indicate photographs accompanied by measured drawings.)

DUNCAN PHYFE SOFA*
   Detroit Institute of Arts
EMPIRE SOFA
   Metropolitan Museum of Art
WINDOW BENCH
   Museum of the City of New York
DUNCAN PHYFE TABLE
   Detroit Institute of Arts
DUNCAN PHYFE SIDE CHAIR
   Detroit Institute of Arts
DUNCAN PHYFE SOFA
   Museum of the City of New York
GODDARD "BURO" TABLE*
   *Museum of Art, Rhode Island
School of Design*
BLOCK-FRONT CHEST
   Metropolitan Museum of Art

SHAPED CHEST OF DRAWERS*
   *Museum of Art, Rhode Island
School of Design*
McINTIRE SOFA*
   Metropolitan Museum of Art
SAMUEL McINTIRE DETAILS
   Los Angeles County Museum of Art
McINTIRE SHIELD-BACK CHAIR
   Los Angeles County Museum of Art
DETAILS OF CARVING
(DUNCAN PHYFE SOFA)
   Museum of the City of New York
DETAILS OF CARVING
(McINTIRE SOFA)
   Metropolitan Museum of Art

5

STYLE AND THREE GREAT DESIGNERS

STYLE is the quality that gives distinction, character and excellence to any artistic expression. Style in furniture design is the summary of the prevailing tastes, cultural development and technical advancement of a particular period as seen against the ethnic image. We are all more or less familiar with the styles in Colonial American furniture; many of its designations were borrowed from the English periods such as Queen Anne, William and Mary, the Georgian and the Victorian. More appropriately these styles should have been called Early American, Revolutionary, Federal, etc., etc. Style suggests a certain chronological order in the development of craftsmanship and design in a given time. It is the recognized label for a step forward in production and perception. Style mirrors the fashion trends of an epoch in technology. Most of all, in furniture design, it records the recognition of certain design developments as promulgated by the master designers and cabinetmakers. But style has a still greater significance in that it assembles the different current propensities and molds them into a definite category. Style is that all-embracing consideration that takes the different existing propensities and converts them into a definite embodiment. Style is that alluding phenomenon which crystallizes the gradual changes to something more tangible and more to our liking. Style is that transitory wonderment, any attempt to define it being somewhat like aiming your arrow at a shooting star. We all know perfectly well what style is, we are cognizant of it, but who can define its essentials? It is as varying and unstable as feminine whims and as difficult to penetrate. Therefore, let us suggest that style is a certain ephemeral matter that pleases us at the moment but is destined to change. Let us sum it all up by stating that style is the distinctive or intrinsic mode of presentation, construction and execution in any of the arts. It is that unique quality that gives accelerated impetus to artistic expression. Style then is the epitome of the summation of trends, developments and fulfillments of a certain progressive autonomy. The further one delves into this enigma of style the more involved it will become.

DUNCAN PHYFE

The very first cabinetmaker who seems to be pre-eminent in Colonial American furniture during the latter part of the eighteenth century and the first quarter of the nineteenth century is one Duncan Phyfe. We have selected three great designers of that era to investigate and determine, if possible, just what made them tick. In this analysis we are going to try to substantiate the conviction that they all were leaders in their craft. In this way we shall be able better to appreciate just what they promulgated in good design and their contributions in creating furniture that was more beautiful than had been made theretofore. These three men had vision and foresight and commanded the means and the facility to use them in good taste, judgment and imagination. All pioneers, no matter in what field, must be advance agents of possible future developments and be able to transform their imageries into realities. They must not alone be well acquainted with what has been done in the past but be cognizant of what is being accomplished in the present.

Duncan Phyfe is certainly the best known name in Colonial American furniture of the Federal period, 1780 to 1830. Coming to New York in 1784 from Scotland, he learned his trade in Albany but returned to New York City in 1790. Self-confident to a major degree, he immediately went into business at No. 2 Broad Street. His prompt and almost phenomenal success put him into the very first rank of the cabinetmakers of the day. At the early age of thirty he was well established and his fame placed him among the foremost designers and makers of fine furniture. Undoubtedly his best work was done approaching the turn of the century. Besides being an accomplished artisan he proved himself to be an astute businessman and cannily manipulated his production to suit the dictates of changing fashions. He knew when to stop, abandon and go ahead.

Style and Three Great Designers

At this time his furniture was refined, elegant, urbane, graceful and distinctive. Catering to a wealthy and a fastidious clientele, he combined restraint, good taste and felicity. With the tremendous increase in the erection of fine houses, his furniture was designed to fit graciously into these new settings. He possessed that sixth sense of knowing what his public wanted and was proficient in measuring up to their needs. Until the advent of the Empire onslaught, Duncan Phyfe did excellent work and prospered. Following the dictates of Sheraton, Hepplewhite and Chippendale, he had the exceptional ability of fusing all these foreign dictates into his own channels and tempering them into a style that was unquestionably his own. With the introduction of the Regency and the Empire styles his fine and delicate work lost favor. He did try to switch and worked for a time in Consulate developments but his output was heavy and lacked the French touch and understanding. His Empire work did not find favor. Criticism began to be adverse and like so many distinguished artists, his last years were not happy. Because of the turn of events, coupled with financial difficulties, he died a much embittered and disillusioned man at the age of eighty-six, in 1854.

Most of Duncan Phyfe's furniture was made of mahogany, of excellent proportions and in the grand manner. In the chair backs he used such artifices as the lyre, the Grecian urn and crisscross arrangements punctuated in the center by rosettes. The water leaf was one of his favored enrichments and assumed all shapes and proportions, often covering the fronts of legs and embellishing the bowl sections of supporting pedestal urns. On the feet he placed brass shoes and for heavy pieces, such as tables, settees and consoles, he used castors. He made almost every kind of furniture and did all surprisingly well, including chairs, settees, sofas, console and extension tables, pedestal consoles, sewing cabinets, window benches, washstands, parlor upholstered chairs, cradles and even dolls' furniture.

During his most productive period he was known to have in his employ over a hundred workmen. Of course it would be ridiculous to suggest that Duncan Phyfe did much of the work himself. If he succeeded in supervising and directing the tremendous output he was doing well. However, since so much of the furniture produced during these years was influenced by him, let us rightfully attribute it to him under the general classification of "The School of Duncan Phyfe."

A clever business executive, he had that unique ability of adapting foreign influences to his advantage. Whereas all designers seek inspiration from diverse sources, it has been said that all geniuses are a combination

MASTERPIECES OF AMERICAN FURNITURE

of charlatan and Michelangelo. Duncan Phyfe had the knack of selecting and using such elements as fitted into his work complacently. Records show that he was a calculating man. He imported the finest mahogany from the West Indies and Cuba. The fabricators, appreciating his cunning and perspicacity, reserved the broadest timber for his purpose, often making him pay fabulous sums for the selected logs. He appreciated the beauty and the sales potentialities of crotch-mahogany panels framed in linings and borders of rich cross-banding of tulip wood. He played upon this combination incessantly.

Because of the tremendous productivity, many museums throughout the country have groups of Duncan Phyfe furniture and much of it is still in private collections. The American Wing of the Metropolitan Museum of Art has a very fine settee, an extension dining table, chairs and drop-leaf consoles. The Detroit Institute of Arts, the Cleveland Museum and the Museum of Cooper Union all have splendid examples. The small but delightful Taft Museum in Cincinnati, Ohio, has some remarkable examples and the lady curator made a special effort to acquaint us with the fact. The Albany, New York, Institute of History and Art, has a Duncan Phyfe sewing table that for its elaborate carving is magnificent.

Great quantities of so-called Duncan Phyfe furniture have been reproduced by leading manufacturers, to their great credit. However, as is always the case, some of these would-be reproductions are quite miserable. Price being a factor, good reproductions must be expensive because much of the detail work cannot be done by machines. It requires considerable handwork and touching-up to get the desired effect. Then too, finishing mahogany is not a simple matter. Whereas the undercoating may be sprayed on, the final finishing, rubbing and sealing should be done by hand to get that satiny, translucent aspect. This requires skillful and experienced handling and can be a costly procedure.

The name "Duncan Phyfe" is magic! It conjures up all kinds of representations in the public's mind. In the hands of unscrupulous dealers it can be misrepresented with dire results. Therefore it would be well for persons considering the purchase of Duncan Phyfe-style furniture to become a little acquainted with the historical facts and know the outstanding features of this furniture beforehand. The store salesman will be of little help. He is out to sell what is on the floor and will have no inclination to warrant the authenticity of the design of the furniture.

JOHN GODDARD

The second Colonial American designer and cabinetmaker that comes to our attention is John Goddard, Rhode Island, and his son, John Townsend Goddard, who worked in Newport from 1750 to 1776. Their forte was the production of desks, dressing tables, bureaux, highboys and lowboys. These pieces were almost always made of mahogany. This was the pre-Revolutionary era, when the wealthy inhabitants of Newport, Salem, Charleston and Baltimore were not to be outdone by such rival cities as New York, Philadelphia and Boston in their demands or the appreciation of fine furniture.

The Goddards worked mostly in the tradition of Queen Anne, taking some arbitrary pointers from Sheraton, Hepplewhite and even Chippendale. They were not particularly innovators, although many of their pieces are individual, distinctive and above all prepossessing. Possibly their principal contribution to Colonial American furniture design was their adroit handling of the blockfront with the cockleshell ornament carved right into the panel. This originally was a Queen Anne feature but they used it most decoratively on the case pieces. The fronts were divided into three panels or sections, with the outer two convex and the central panel concave. In most cases the bracket foot was used in many variations, from simple to most elaborate. To produce these massive blockfronts required the use of substantial blocks of wood, as they were carved from a single piece, never built-up or glued together. While mahogany was the preferred wood, sometimes walnut or cherry had to be used.

Besides case goods, John Goddard produced desks, secrétaires, bookcases with scrolls, bonnet and broken pediment tops, with shell carvings and flamelike finials. In the case of kneehole desks, often used as dressing tables, the arched setback door at the center also had the shell carving. These were the utmost in refinement of these Goddard pieces. The Georgian-type pulls and escutcheon plates used were often heavily engraved. The top plan was generally rectangular, following the shape of the body proper. These pieces were prized because of the propitious manner in which they were carried out. One of these superb "buros" was presented to the Art Museum of the Rhode Island School of Design by Miss Mary Lemoine Potter.

Masterpieces of American Furniture

Not being content with making splendid furniture, John Goddard was bent on producing most attractive wood coffins. To be laid to rest in one of these ostentatious sarcophagi was indeed a great honor in his day. What St. Peter said when these entombments arrived is still a matter of conjecture. Goddard also made a number of game tables with serpentine blocking on the skirt. These tables were invariably supported by cabriole legs handsomely carved with ball-and-claw feet. They folded to console size by means of an accordion mechanism. He also made tall clocks, using blockfronts for the center panel. The works for these clocks were generally imported from England. While John Goddard and his son were not the sole cabinetmakers of the time who specialized in the blockfront with shell carvings, they were the foremost exponents of this particular type of furniture and they reached the heights in doing so. Their designs were sophisticated, the workmanship paramount and the general effect produced was brilliant by reason of the most carefully worked-out details. The shell carvings, because of the intricate delineation and radiating perplexities, were often a revelation of exquisite artistry. These carvings were different on every piece, to conform with the particular space and placement.

Although John Goddard was unquestionably a traditionalist, his contribution to Colonial American furniture design was manifest because he gave fresh impetus and finer interpretation and renewed emphasis to the adaptation of preceding styles. His work found wide acceptance and appreciation and a genuine Goddard piece today is considered a veritable treasure and its price can only be estimated in gold. Even though much of his work was not original it needs no apologies, invites no preamble. It is fine, it is elegant, it is worthy.

Every designer cannot be original but he can do a fine job of whatever he undertakes to accomplish. This furniture can stand on its own merits and is altogether important. You may never see a John Goddard chair but one of his case pieces cannot be mistaken for anything else.

SAMUEL McINTIRE

And now a third famous personality warrants our attention. Samuel McIntire was a designer, cabinetmaker, carver, architect and a man of many other accomplishments. He worked in the post-Revolutionary period, 1757 to 1811. Many authorities question his wide scope of accomplishments because they feel that one man could not actually do so many things well. Professor Fiske Kimball led the investigation but documents at the Essex Institute in Salem, Massachusetts, seem to give the necessary evidence that he was indeed a man of many phases and endeavors. He was not only a master carpenter, craftsman and furniture designer, but also an eminent architect. He designed some of the finest residences in Salem, always in the best Classical tradition. The Peabody House in Massachusetts clearly shows the knowledgeable way in which he interpreted the Adam style. The details of the trim are minute, the mantelpieces are masterpieces of delineation, while the handling of the arches and cornices cannot be described in words. Every now and then we come across a man of many faces and accomplishments. He seems to do everything with ease, knowledge and proficiency. Samuel McIntire was evidently such a man. Not content with doing his own work, he took in assignments in carving from other people. All this we know to be a fact. Of course he may not have done everything himself but it all was certainly done under his knowledge and direction. So let us not quibble over the abilities of this man, for he has left examples of his works.

His products can be readily identified by his penchant for the use of carved baskets of fruit and flowers, garlands, horns of plenty, eagles, festoons, swags entwined with flowers, sheaths of wheat, borders interpolated by linear arrangements and fantastic ribbon organizations. That he had a true affinity for texture may be seen in the carved panels on the tops of his sofas. The backgrounds of these panels are tooled, punctuated and travailed, but all is held in place by a narrow, flat border. His appreciation of graceful curves and flowing lines is evident in the McIntire sofa from Salem, 1800, now in the American Wing of the Metropolitan Museum of Art. It is an outstanding piece of furniture design, with the back center panel depicting a basket overflowing with fruit and flowers and with a branch of laurel extending from each side. The details are eloquent and punctilious, carved and fluted, turned or reeded, the utmost in refinement and decorum. There is no seat frame showing. The upholstery is inviting. Certainly there can be no question of his stylistic *savoir faire*.

While he was a great architect, here we are more concerned with Samuel McIntire as a furniture designer. He was at home in all forms of decoration and used them deliberately. In his work there never could be detected the slightest sign of hesitancy. He knew what he set out to accomplish and achieved it brilliantly. This is the essential objective of a master designer. He knows and does. In the run-of-the-mill collection of artisans, many of us fear to attempt. His attributes seemed to know no bounds and his capacity for work was unlimited. If because of these facts his works have been discredited it is unfortunate. For a time he was assisted by his son but the younger man's work was inferior and perfunctory. The association with his father had little influence on the work produced during his tenure.

Just as the treatment of the interiors was affected by the Greek Revival and the excavations being undertaken at Pompeii and Herculaneum and studied personally by the Brothers Adam on location, this influence was evident in America in the furniture design at this time. Pilasters were introduced, architectural motifs interpolated and bas-relief and painted panels incorporated. It was a period when Classicism was taking the helm and Samuel McIntire was one of the perpetrators who worked with glowing enthusiasm.

Style and Three Great Designers

In all fields of endeavor there appear leaders who seem to possess that seventh sense of anticipating what is to come and possess that talent and tenacity to put their predilections into action. This was true most particularly in furniture design during the latter part of the eighteenth century. However, there were definite influences that made their efforts not alone feasible but culminated in the effluorescence and final acceptance of their efforts. Without sound preparation and knowledge, combined with influential backing, their efforts might have fallen amiss. Therefore in the three designers selected for consideration, we can follow the propitious circumstances which augmented their development and their successful careers.

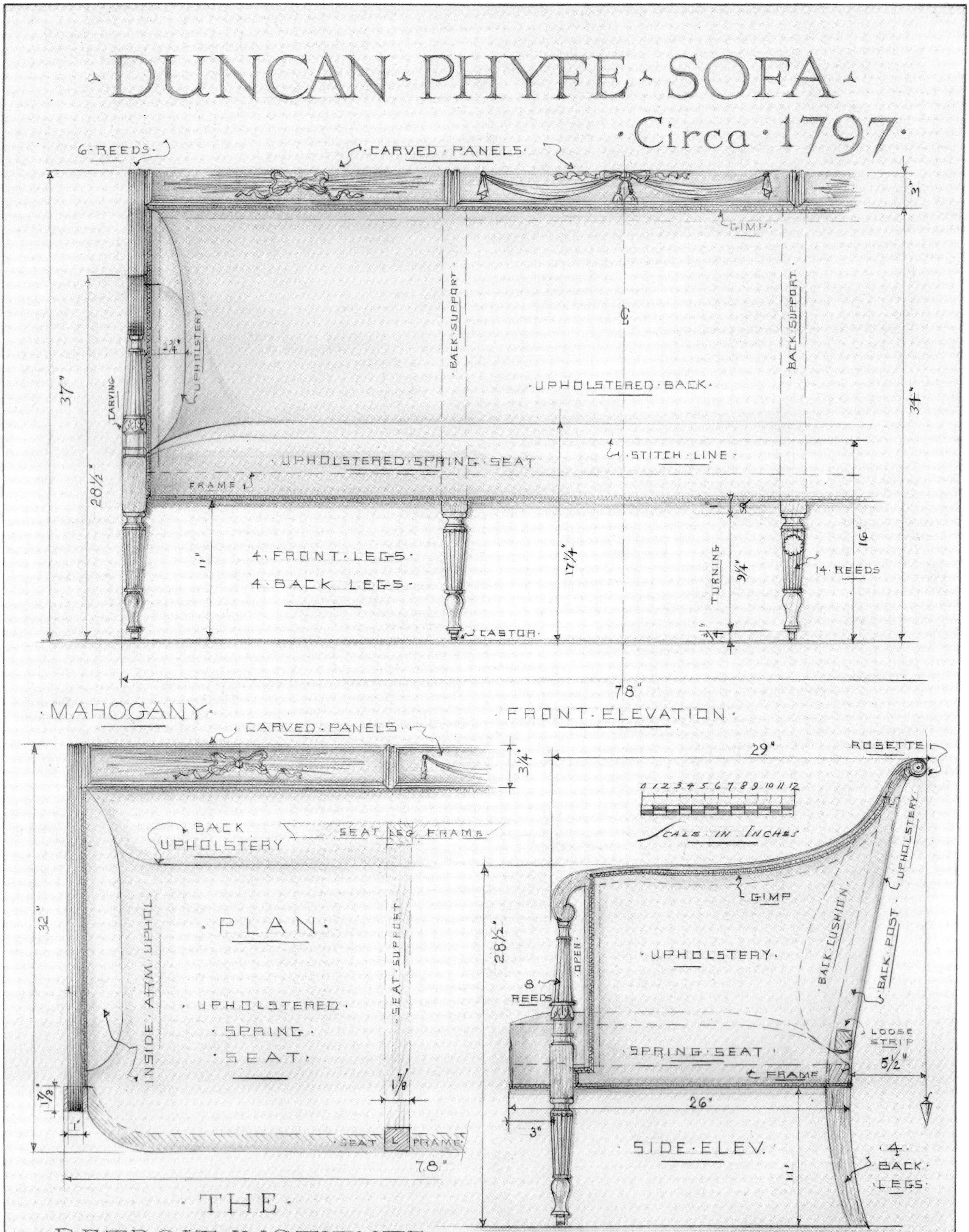

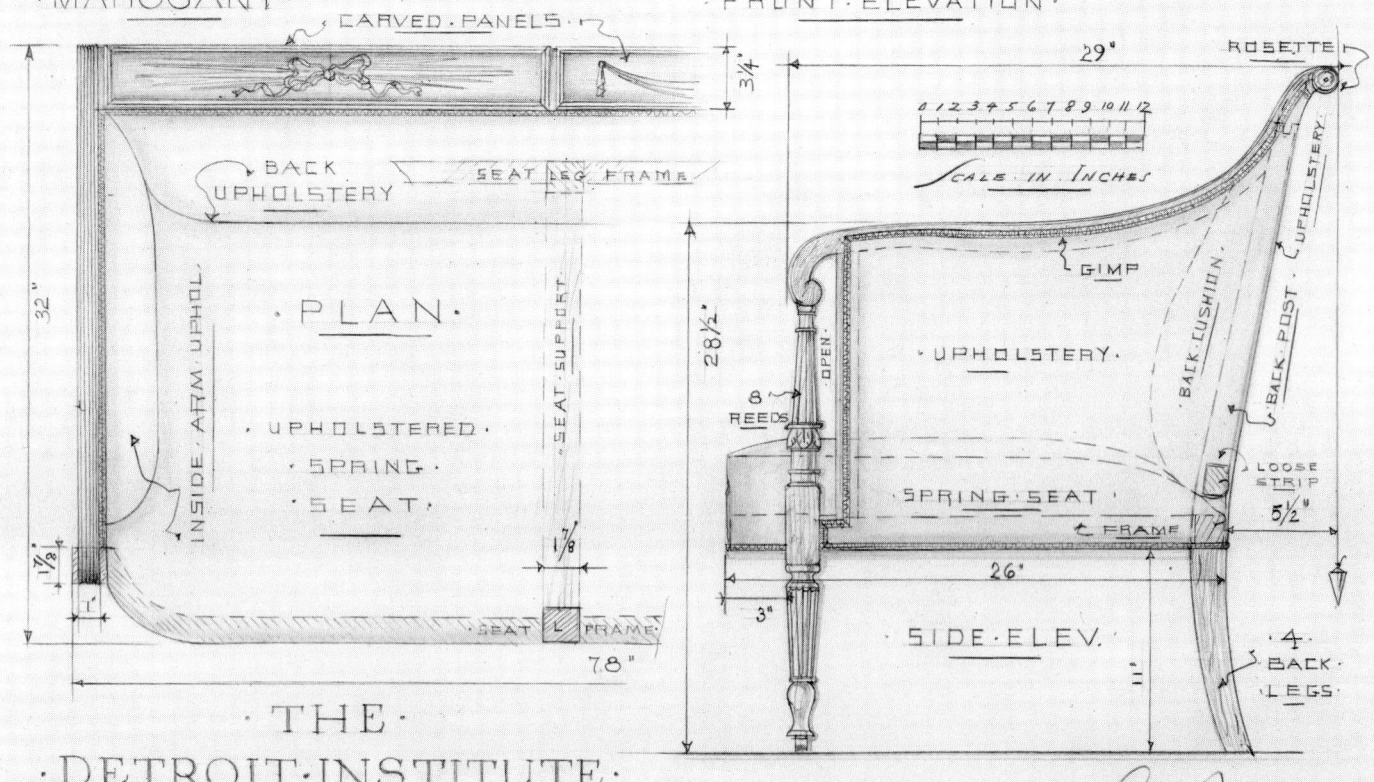

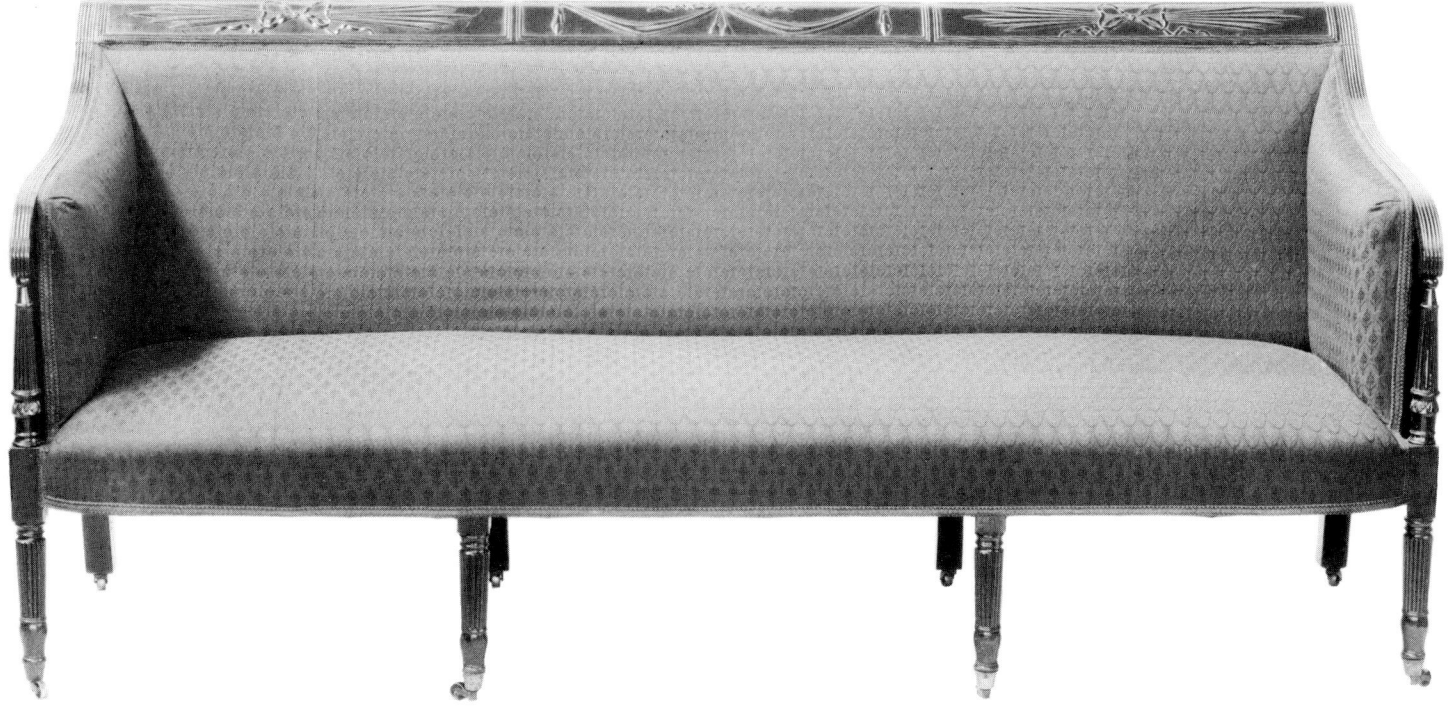

DUNCAN PHYFE SOFA
Detroit Institute of Arts

This Sheraton-style sofa, made by Duncan Phyfe, New York, *circa* 1800, was probably the most expensive sofa that he produced. The finely carved panels in the back and the finely reeded turned legs are certainly of the highest craftsmanship. Of special interest is the graceful slope of the arm, terminating in the scroll at the arm post. The central panel of the back shows a double swag and the two side panels depict sheafs of wheat tied by a fabulous ribbon bowknot with flowing ends. The carving is low in relief and crisp but the background has been left untouched. What makes these Duncan Phyfe sofas so extraordinary is the fine restraint shown, the excellence of the proportions and the rightness of the conception. A similar model may be seen in the collection of the Museum of the City of New York. The designer's best work was done in the Sheraton and Hepplewhite periods although he always added a touch that was distinctly his own in the exquisite carving and fine detail. One of his earliest admirers and backers was John Jacob Astor. He furnished the houses of the aristocracy, including Stuyvesant, the Van Rensselaers and the Van Cortlandt Mansion.

EMPIRE SOFA
Metropolitan Museum of Art

This sofa by Duncan Phyfe is a little too curvy for his best type of work. It somehow does not possess the repose which we have become accustomed to expect. There is a profusion of busy currents which do not seem to synchronize into a pleasing harmony. It looks as if he has taken two chairs and made them the base for the sofa. No, it is not altogether pleasing. It shows the work of the cabinetmaker after he had reached the heights and was coming down the incline to desperation. However, the enlarged detail of the back carving is excellent.

WINDOW BENCH
Museum of the City of New York

This mahogany window seat, one of a pair, is by Duncan Phyfe, New York, *circa* 1800. It is graceful and restrained in design, a fitting seat for a lady behind the lace curtains at the window, watching the horses and carriages roll by. Sheraton in inspiration, it nevertheless appears to be original in conception. The benches belonged to the Hawley family and were the gift of Miss Adelaide de Groot.

DUNCAN PHYFE TABLE
Detroit Institute of Arts

This genuine drop-leaf mahogany table, *circa* 1780, is a superlative example of this master's work. The shaped drop leaves are supported by swing brackets. There is a drawer supported by four turned and carved posts from which develop four shaped legs topped with water-leaf carving. It is the fine detail and the crispness of the carving that command our attention. The brass claw-feet are supported by castors. The turned drops at the corners create just the proper balance for the table.

DUNCAN PHYFE SIDE CHAIR
Detroit Institute of Arts

This late-Sheraton-style side chair by Duncan Phyfe, New York, *circa* 1810-1812, is a masterpiece in its right. The feature is the carved lyre in the back, for which he was justly renowned. The chair has grace, majesty and all the attributes that we have come to expect of the works of the master cabinetmaker. The chair is of mahogany. There are so many fine features that it is difficult to pick out any one that is outstanding. The double-top console table, we believe, should be said to belong to "The School of Duncan Phyfe." It just does not measure up to the standard.

DUNCAN PHYFE SOFA
Museum of the City of New York

In a New York drawing room of the period from an old house in Greenwich, Connecticut, *circa* 1810, this finest of the Duncan Phyfe sofas holds the center of the stage. Its detail is finite and expressive and represents possibly one of the most expensive of his products. No doubt the most intriguing feature is the way the sweep of the side, starting at the back, swings down and around to meet the turned and reeded arm support. This is a most difficult procedure and caps anything that he had attempted heretofore. The three carved panels of the back are paragons of the carver's craft.

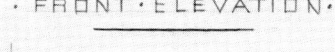
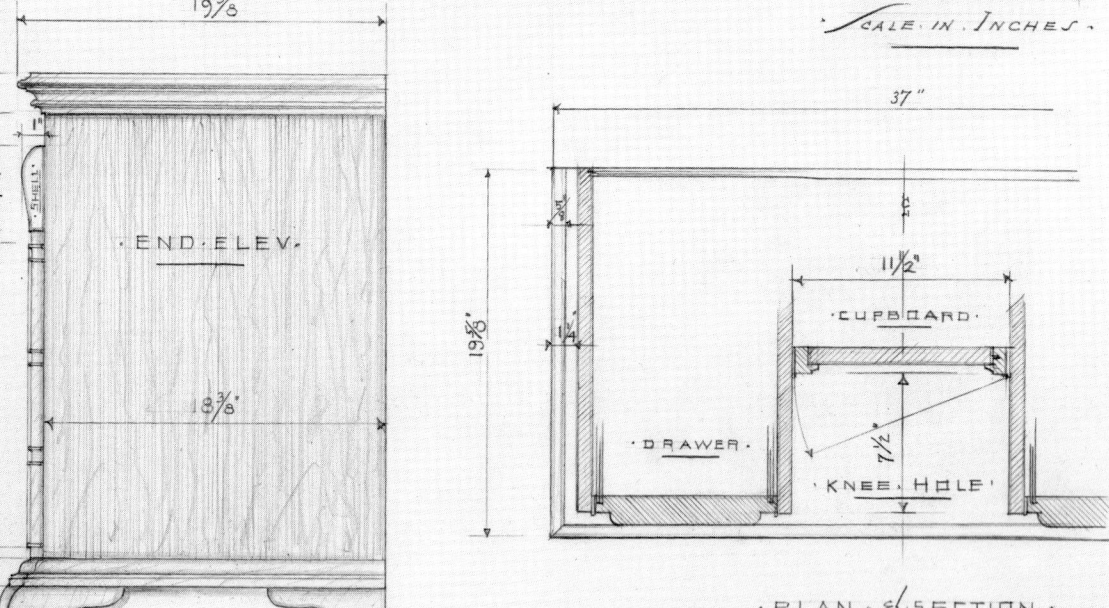

"BURO" TABLE
Museum of Art, Rhode Island School of Design
The Gift of Mary Lemoine Potter

This mahogany kneehole desk or dressing table is by one John Goddard (1723-1785). It was made in Newport, Rhode Island, *circa* 1750-1775. The "buro," as Goddard preferred to call it, is a combination of the Queen Anne and the Chippendale styles. The feature, of course, is the block front with the shell carving. These fronts were fashioned out of solid blocks of mahogany, never of pieces joined together. The intricacy of the shell carving is considered the most important motif in American design. Note how well all the details go together; the blocked front drawers, the shell carving, the carved scroll of the bracket feet and the illustrious pierced brass pulls and escutcheon plates. It is believed that this buro was made to order for Stephen Hopkins, one of the signers of the Declaration of Independence. The arched recessed door in the kneehole is the ultimate in refinement.

This is indeed a masterpiece of Newport craftsmanship. Note that the shell motif is used both in relief and also as an incised bit of decoration. The choice of a mottled mahogany adds to the effectiveness of the piece. We hold this to be one of the most grandiose expressions of developed design and cabinetwork in America.

BLOCK FRONT CHEST
Metropolitan Museum of Art

This block-front bureau was made by John Townsend of Newport, Rhode Island, and bears his label. The three block-front panels surmounted by the cockleshell carvings are similar to the work turned out by John Goddard. The curved bracket foot is used on these pieces. The date is *circa* 1775. This represents the finest in American cabinetwork. Townsend also made tall clocks using the block panel as the main decoration on the front. This chest was purchased through the Rogers Fund, 1927.

CHEST of DRAWERS · 1760

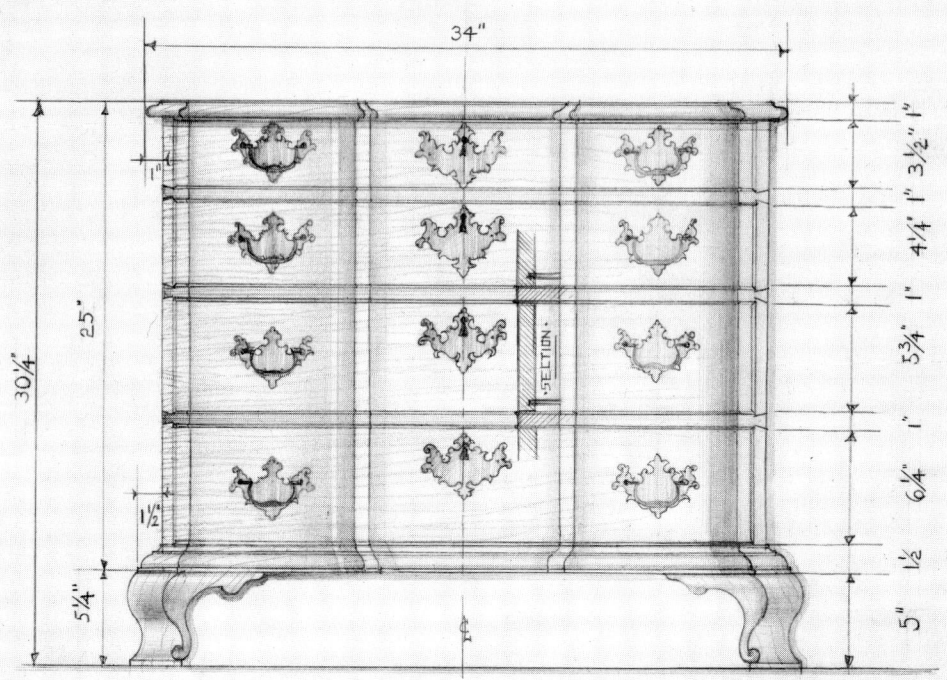

· FRONT · ELEVATION ·

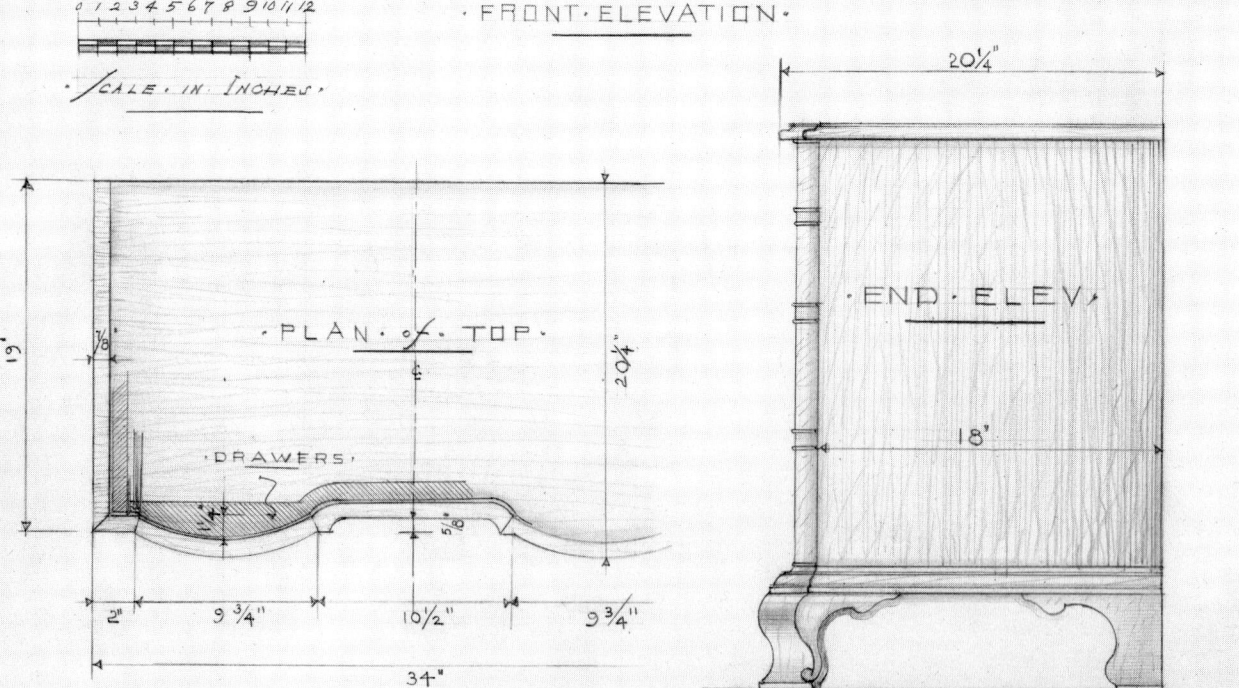

· Measured & Drawn by · Lester Margon

· THE ·
MUSEUM · of · ART ·
Rhode · Island · School ·
· of · Design ·

SHAPED CHEST OF DRAWERS
Museum of Art, Rhode Island School of Design

This Pendleton Collection's magnificent shaped chest of drawers in mahogany is probably from Newport, Rhode Island, *circa* 1760. The secondary woods are pine and spruce. While it does not contain the brilliant effects of the works of Townsend and Goddard, in quality and design it nevertheless is equal to anything they produced. The large shaped brass pulls and escutcheon plates give the chest a rare appearance of elegance. The shaped blocked front produces a play of light and shade that is transcendental. The shaped and carved bracket feet are most effective. The straight-grained mahogany veneers used, not too flamboyant, are just right to produce the essential dignity for this chest. Note the simple treatment of the back leg to permit the chest to rest easily against the wall. This is certainly one of the finest pieces that have come to our attention.

EIGHTEENTH CENTURY GALLERY
Museum of Fine Arts, Boston

In the American Eighteenth Century Gallery we see the bow-front mahogany chest of drawers in the Sheraton style and the attractive shaped mirror above. The treatment of the top panel is unique. Looking through the opening, note the cases of American glass, while at the end of the corridor stands a double paneled door from *circa* 1740. The Department of Decorative Arts of America is one of the finest in its collection of Colonial American material, including the fabulous M. & M. Karolik Collection.

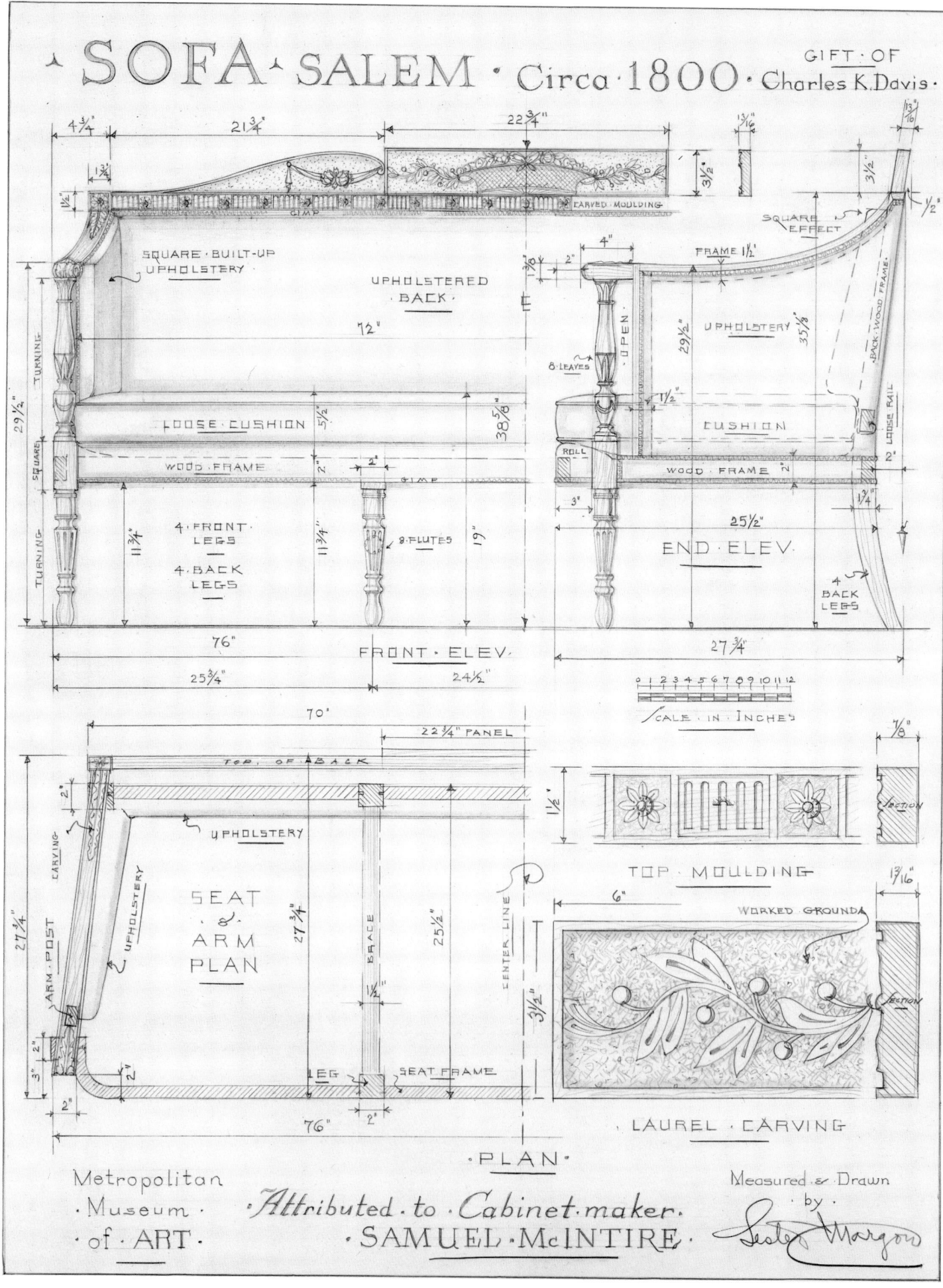

McINTIRE SOFA

Metropolitan Museum of Art   Gift of Charles K. Davis 1946

This magnificent Sheraton-style sofa is attributed to Samuel McIntire of Salem, Massachusetts, *circa* 1800. It is made of mahogany. Probably built by Salem craftsmen and carved to order by McIntire, this is indeed an American classic. Whether or not McIntire actually did the carving personally is a matter of conjecture. However, the design, character and decoration are so typical that it is sufficient to believe that at least it was done under his direction. The basket of fruit and flowers was a favorite subject and appears in variations on many of his pieces. The urn carving of the arm supports and the restrained turning of the fluted legs are meticulous. As to the central carved panel, pay particular attention to the background. It is actually hammered, tooled and travailed to secure the desired rich texture, all held in place by a narrow, flat border. McIntire did several of these sofas, very similar in style and detail. One of them may be seen at the Boston Museum of Fine Arts, a part of the famous M. & M. Karolik Collection. This measured drawing shows the sofa with a modern version of the seat upholstery for more comfort.

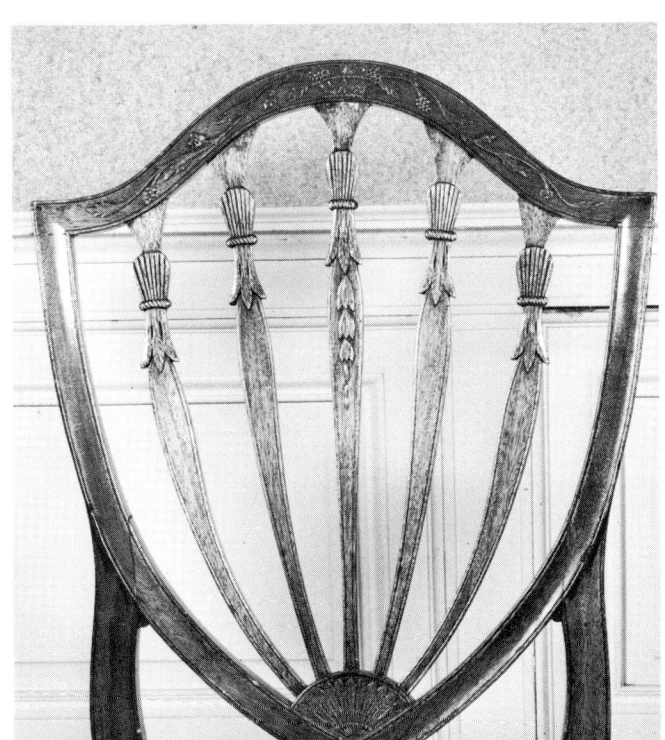

SAMUEL McINTIRE DETAILS

Los Angeles County Museum of Art

It is seldom that we are privileged to see an enlarged detail of an example of carving by Samuel McIntire. In this shield-back chair, its excellence is apparent. This chair of distinction, included in the catalogue of the M. & M. Karolik collection, was acquired by the Museum through the Balch Fund. Especially interesting are the varied slats and their decorative treatment. The treatment of the rail carving on the cresting is almost medallic in fineness. See the accompanying photograph of the complete chair.

McINTIRE SHIELD-BACK CHAIR
Los Angeles County Museum of Art

Here we see the full view of the Hepplewhite shield-back chair of mahogany with the plain square tapered legs. The chair is from Salem, Massachusetts, *circa* 1800. The scalloped treatment of the nail-heads adds to the effectiveness of the upholstery. Here we can see the excellence of the design and the brilliance of the proportions. The carving on the cresting appears to be secondary but the eloquence of the varied splats is evident. These McIntire Hepplewhite chairs are considered the finest by reason of their originality, proportions and workmanship.

SHIELD-BACK CHAIR
Los Angeles County Museum of Art

Here is a simplified version of the shield-back chair attributed to Samuel McIntire. In this instance there is no carving of the cresting of the shield and only a bit of water-leaf carving enhances the termination of the splats. It has only four splats instead of the customary five. The square tapered legs are inlaid with V-shaped shaded satinwood panels with linings and a band of inlay towards the bottom. It is an unique model that appears to be not altogether satisfactory. By comparison of different chairs we are able to arrive at an understanding.

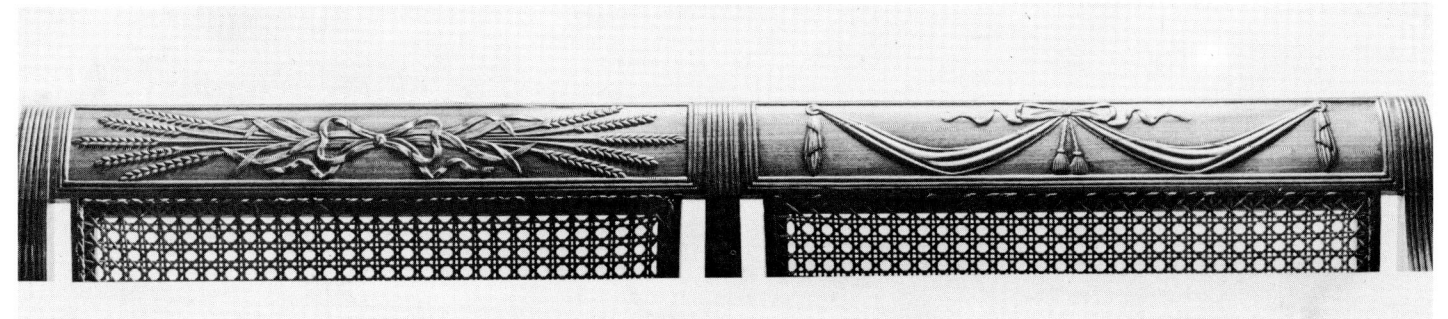

DETAILS OF CARVING

(Above) Enlarged detail of a Duncan Phyfe sofa, identical with the carving on the back of the sofa shown from the Museum of the City of New York. Here we can see clearly the excellence of this carving which may not be seen clearly in the complete sofa photographs. The two end panels portray sheaths of wheat tied by a ribbon bow and flowing ends. The center panel shows double swag tied at the center by a ribbon with tassels.

(Below) Enlarged detail of the back carving on the Samuel McIntire sofa from the Metropolitan Museum of Art clearly shows the high proficiency and the artistry of this master. The excellence of the composition, the definiteness of the detail and the handling of the background all accentuate his greatness. It is indeed a pleasure to be able to study these details at close range.

After the Revolution

LIST OF ILLUSTRATIONS

(Asterisks indicate photographs accompanied by measured drawings.)

CORNER CUPBOARD*
  Metropolitan Museum of Art
CORNER CABINET
  Art Institute of Chicago
TALL CABINET
  Philadelphia Museum of Art
SIDEBOARD*
  Art Institute of Chicago
PEMBROKE TABLE*
  Los Angeles County Museum of Art
PEMBROKE TABLE
  Detroit Institute of Arts
SIDE CHAIR*
  Metropolitan Museum of Art
SHERATON ARMCHAIR
  Los Angeles County Museum of Art
MAIN GALLERY
  Metropolitan Museum of Art
MANTEL CLOCK*
  Old Sturbridge Village
BRACKET CLOCK
  Metropolitan Museum of Art
SPICE CABINET
  Old Sturbridge Village
EAGLE CHAIR*
  Art Institute of Chicago
1812 CHAIR
  Brooklyn Museum
WASHSTAND*
  Metropolitan Museum of Art

DECORATED WASHSTAND
  Art Institute of Chicago
MINIATURE CLOCK*
  Metropolitan Museum of Art
SIDE CHAIR*
  Metropolitan Museum of Art
FANCY CHAIR
  Los Angeles County Museum of Art
HITCHCOCK ROCKER
  Brooklyn Museum
HITCHCOCK CHAIR
  Art Institute of Chicago
HITCHCOCK CHAIR
  Brooklyn Museum
GONDOLA CHAIR
  Metropolitan Museum of Art
LOUIS XV BERGÈRE
  Metropolitan Museum of Art
EMPIRE SETTING
  Metropolitan Museum of Art
SIDE VIEW OF EMPIRE CHAIR
  Gothenburg Museum
ADAM PAINTED CHAIR
  Metropolitan Museum of Art
EMPIRE ARMCHAIR
  Gothenburg Museum
EARLY VICTORIAN ROOM
  Metropolitan Museum of Art
VICTORIAN PARLOR
  Brooklyn Museum

6

AFTER THE REVOLUTION: Victorian

AFTER the winning of the American Revolution and the establishment of the new republic, a wave of patriotism swept over the country like wildfire. With the adoption of the eagle as the central figure in the United States emblem in 1782, its extensive use in decoration and on furniture was imminent. The eagle proved to be the favored motif for interior design in all its phases and appeared on many articles of everyday usage, such as silverware, china, hardware, on tops of clocks, mirrors, lighting fixtures, on the top of tall cabinets, for inlay, painted and sculptured panels. In fact, representations of the eagle could be found in every home and in every shape and form. Coupled with the Liberty Bell, the eagle appeared on the coins and paper currency of the nation.

The third element of design, not so much in evidence as the eagle, was the American flag, with its thirteen stars arranged in a circle. Red, white and blue were the national colors, white standing for peace, red to commemorate the soldiers who gave their lifeblood for the new freedom and the blue for the preservation of liberty and justice. The eagle persisted and spread its wings in protective custody over the nation. To this day it holds forth as the insignia of the United States Army Quartermaster Corps, the Air Force, the Medical and Dental Divisions and the Wings. Its presence is manifold in more or less ferocious postures, fullfront, profile, always ready to take off in defense of the country. Business firms incorporated the eagle in their trademarks as a sign of patriotism and as good business.

The excitement of the Revolution and the successful establishment of the new government brought forth a wave of jubilant prosperity across the nation. Fine houses continued to be built and furnished elegantly. Duncan Phyfe was at his most exalted height and all seemed well with the world. Gradually the atmosphere changed. Following the excitement of the forming of the new government came the inevitable reaction. There was a letdown in trade and in creativity. The inevitable lull had set in and the people had to settle down and prepare themselves for the difficult days that were to follow. The period was disconcerting. It also marked a decisive halt in the development of furniture design in America.

In England at this time the Brothers Adam were influential in fostering the Greek Revival which had its repercussions over here. The graceful Colonial style suffered a setback. Fortunately the designs based on Classical derivatives were fundamentally sound. This led to the introduction of such decorative features as the use of pilasters and free-standing columns, sunken paneling, applied moldings, medallions enriched with portrait bas-reliefs and ornaments featuring the honeysuckle, frets and urns, the laurel leaf, fluted friezes, rosettes and husks arranged as drop-ornaments and tied with ribbons and bows.

Josiah Wedgwood, inspired by the findings in Pompeii and Herculaneum, produced the splendid Wedgwood ware and such individual showpieces as the Jasper Vase. The distinguished painter and medallist, Angelica Kauffmann, lent her skills in England to the trend in furniture design and created colorful allegorical medallions often appearing on satinwood cabinets and credenzas. All this had influence on furniture production over here and Adam blue became the dominant color for interior decoration. All this was very fine but it certainly was not American. Its popularity faltered and we were at a loss as to what to do or where to go.

The close association of France and the United States after the Revolution introduced many symbolic elements into furniture design, such as the lion's foot, conventionalized eagles' wings as settee supports and full in the round representations of eagles as pedestals for tables. The French Revolution and the following Reign of Terror caused many craftspeople in France to find themselves in dire circumstances. Much of the art and skills of the eighteenth century was jeopardized. Many of the aristocrats, out of favor with the new regime, fled for their lives to America, taking with them many of their prized possessions, including furniture. This had considerable effect on the work that was being done

After the Revolution

here. The cabinetmakers of the United States found it almost impossible to reproduce the French models or to even approach them in finesse, opulence and artistry. It was all too involved, delicate and elaborate. The use of intricate marqueterie, the placement of those incredible bits of ormolu and the multiplication of the seemingly endless succession of ridiculous curves, was just too much for their credence. Our cabinetmakers did not have the necessary background or the training, the knowledge or the skills, required for the making of this French furniture. Most of all, they did not have the "touch," that indefinable quality that makes many French products so superior and unapproachable to this day.

Of course Napoleon, with his mania for military rapport, nurtured the development of the Empire Style. Under his direction and patronage, the young architects Perçier and Fontaine gratified his cravings for regal splendor. Walls were draped and supported by speared posts, heraldic columns representing Victory were interpolated. It was all majestic, military and triumphant. The trumpets blared, horns bleated and drums rolled in silent visionary interludes. Wine reds, rich purples, forest greens, brilliant yellows and vibrant blues, always interspersed with gold, were the favored colors. All this was enhanced by latticework, rosettes and Victory wreaths, always featuring the initial "N," the chosen symbol of Napoleon. This martial madness had its repercussions in the United States, as was to be expected. The American craftsmen did their best to approximate the French furniture but in all fairness it must be noted that they did not succumb to the use of sphinxes and other military embellishments but substituted the American eagle, the horn of plenty and the baskets of fruit and flowers.

After Napoleon met his Waterloo, the fanfare and adulation for the Empire manifestations subsided. Over here there was an increasing desire and tendency to return to design normalcy and the sane approbation of former days. An effort was made to discard the pomp and circumstance of the military fever and to return to beauty of line, good proportions and the basic principles of palatable design. Some progress was made but the necessary leadership and inspiration were lacking. It was one of those latent periods when there was no direct approach to creativity.

Then came the War of 1812, with the accompanying wave of renewed patriotism which spread over the nation. Patriotic insignia appeared everywhere and the Stars and Stripes fluttered in the breeze. Since all wars require renewed artificial stimulation of the emotions of the populace, this time was no exception. The eagle supported brackets, the arms of chairs, became pedestal supports for tables and was cast into brass finials on cabinets, clocks, mirror frames and was used wherever possible. Patriotism was further ignited by the use of painted decoration and decalcomanias depicting naval engagements and placed in the upper panels of Sheraton mirrors and on the lower portions of shelf-clocks. These scenes were painted on the backs of the glass. Depiction of the Stars and Stripes was never neglected. So it is in the periods of stress and strain — clear thinking is at a premium and we become misled by false reports. We become confused with ulterior matters and tend to forego the essentials. When emotions get the upper hand reason flies out the window.

Soon something new appeared on the furniture horizon. In Riverton, Connecticut, Lambert Hitchcock was its promulgator. He produced a new type of chair that won vast and immediate acceptance throughout the countryside. Successful farmers and small landowners, particularly in New England, fell for his designs. These chairs were a clever combination of Sheraton and Empire forms with what might be called the American Provincial. The legs were turned with reeds running horizontally and splayed. The seats were slightly shaped, made of rush and framed in wood. The cushion backs had a top rail which was slightly bent and a center slat which was saw-cut of adequate dimensions to permit of decoration of a unique powder-gold stencil design of fruit and flowers. Much gold was used in the trim and striping. An excellent example was on exhibition at the De Young Memorial Museum in San Francisco, California, a loan from the Elizabeth B. Norton Collection. Here the center back panel was decorated with the stencil of a double horn of plenty. The effect was most interesting. The chair was painted black.

The firm of Hitchcock & Alford in Connecticut later produced a line of rockers to match, of goodly proportions and probably the best and most comfortable of their kind. In fact, these chairs are some of the few pieces of furniture that may be called typically and originally American. They seem to have found a ready welcome on almost every porch throughout the country. In the case of these Hitchcock rockers, the thin back slats were shaped to conform with the body. The heavy shaped and bent toprails were often cut-out in fanciful outlines. The seats were made from a heavy chunk of wood and cut in the shape of an inverted scroll affording the utmost in seating comfort. Back, front and side stretchers braced the legs and runners, which were set right into the bottom of the turned legs. Many of these rockers were left in the wood finish and unadorned but some were painted with stencil decoration. We recall one excellent model which was exhibited at the Brooklyn Museum through the courtesy of Mr. Arthur W. Clement.

After the Revolution

Following every war there is a period of dearth, depletion and insolvency. The nation is exhausted, fortunes have changed hands and creative activities are at a standstill. People are trying to get a second breath, put their houses in order and begin planning for the future. Under such circumstances furniture design reached a low ebb. There did not seem to be any leaders who were willing to carry the torch. European influences persisted but American designers were not enthusiastic about them for they did not express what the populace was seeking. It was only after the new nation experienced a definite sense of security that activities were undertaken in building, interior design and furniture.

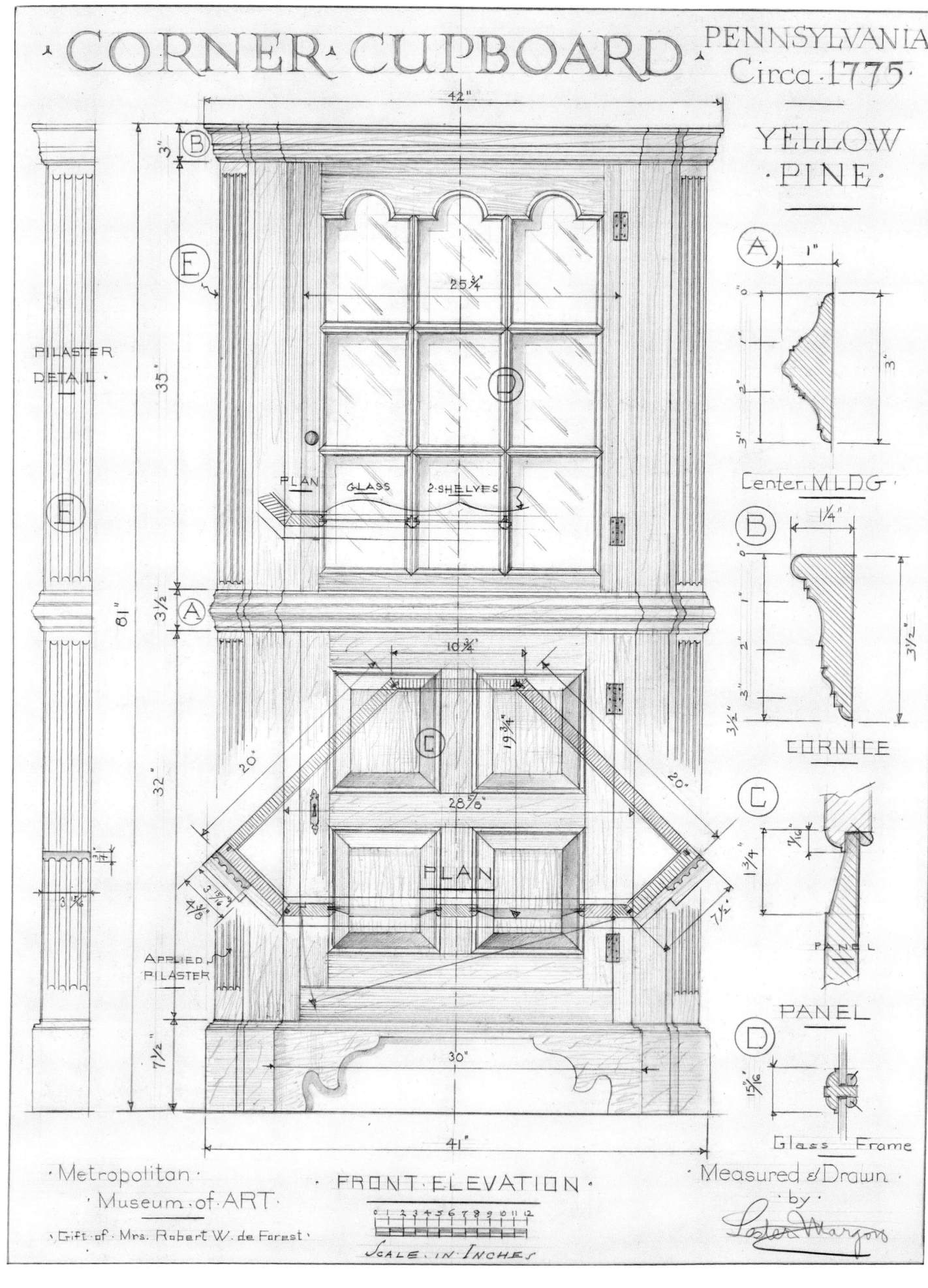

CORNER CUPBOARD
Metropolitan Museum of Art   Gift of Mrs. Robert W. de Forest 1933

Most corner cabinets are movable but so planned that they become part of the interior design of a room. This model is from Pennsylvania, *circa* 1775, and is made of yellow pine. The design is simple, a sort of combination of the Provincial and the Classical. The fluted pilasters, the paneled door of the lower storage compartment and the frolicsome line of the base are all rather happy features. The thing that gives this piece a special character is the arched treatment of the divided glass door. Glass at this time was still at a premium and the use of small pieces was mandatory.

Many of these corner cabinets had painted interiors, with variegated shaping of the interior shelving, all adding to their delightful appearance. The glass door top was used for the display of precious china. One unusual feature in this model is its division almost definitely in half. This is against all rules and yet the over-all effect is definitely pleasing. Many of these corner cabinets are so architectural in form that they cannot be classified as furniture, and in that case they were generally "built in."

CORNER CABINET
Art Institute of Chicago

Corner cabinets were very popular during the early nineteenth century. This walnut model from eastern Ohio is simple and dignified and fulfills the utilitarian requirements for storage and display. The restraint shown in the design is excellent, its simplicity beguiling. This cabinet was a purchase, made through the Elizabeth R. Vaughan Fund.

A TALL CABINET
Philadelphia Museum of Art

Here we find a Hepplewhite tall cabinet of cherry from the late eighteenth century. It is Pennsylvania German, as is evidenced by the introduction of the carved tulip motif at the center of the top and the side finials. The scrolls at the top are accentuated by carved rosettes. This piece is a combination of chest of drawers and a glass-door cupboard for display. It is from the noted Geesey Collection, a gift of Mr. Titus C. Geesey of Wilmington, Delaware, to the Museum. It is not a large collection, but some of the pieces of furniture included are of rare quality.

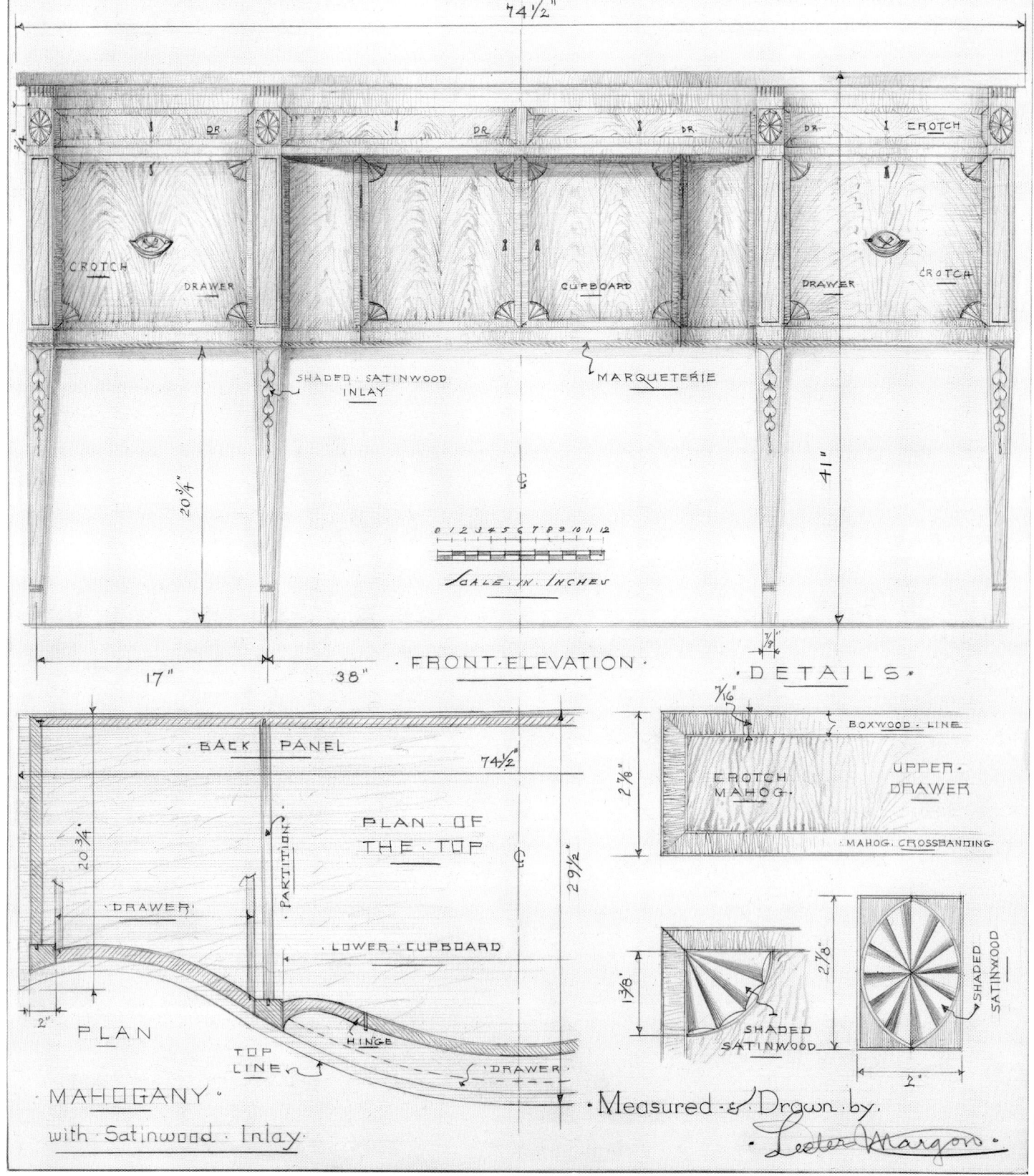

SIDEBOARD

Art Institute of Chicago *Gift of the Antiquarian Society through the Mrs. Clive Runnells Fund*

This prepossessing mahogany sideboard, attributed to Mathew Egerton, is from New Jersey, *circa* 1790. The serpentine front is divided into three main sections, the two ends being cupboards and the lower setback section one long cupboard with rounded ends to fill out the line. Above these cupboards is a line of four drawers, all of approximately equal size. The setback central cupboard produces an interesting shadow effect. Its delicacy and refinement of detail indicate the highest standard of work produced by the American cabinetmakers at this time. The splendid proportion of the tapering square legs gives the sideboard a sense of lightness and a most graceful appearance. One gets the sense that this heavy bulk is actually floating in the air. The fine shaded satinwood inlay and the boxwood linings, along with the wealth of the cross-banding, are outstanding. The rich selected and matched mahogany crotch veneers are superlative. This is indeed a masterpiece, possibly the most elaborate of its type. For the record, it might be well to classify this sideboard as of Hepplewhite inspiration.

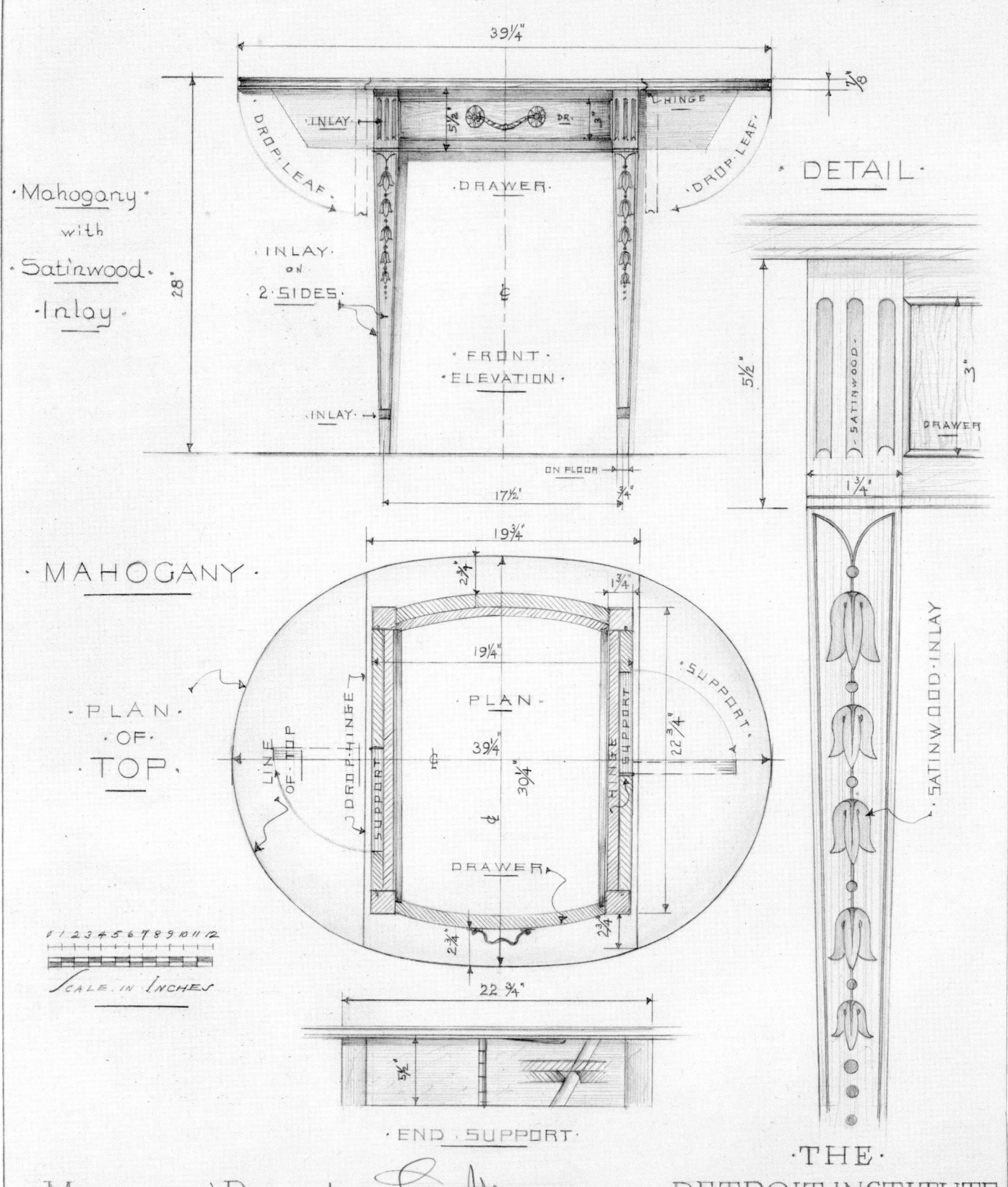

PEMBROKE TABLE
Los Angeles County Museum of Art

This Pembroke table of cherry with drop leaves, probably by Lemuel Adams of Hartford, has an oval top, square tapered legs and one drawer. The shape of the drawer follows the line of the top. The legs have long, pointed, shaded inlaid drops of satinwood. The leaves are supported by pull-out lopers. The date is *circa* 1790, the place Connecticut. This is another piece from the Kenneth B. Pattison Collection.

PEMBROKE TABLE
Detroit Institute of Arts

Pembroke tables of Hepplewhite inspiration were made in Baltimore, *circa* 1790. Of mahogany with bellflower inlay of shaded satinwood and fine inlaid lining, they represented the acme of perfection in urbane design. The oval top with the drop leaves was used by the ladies and gentlemen to breakfast on, very often in the bedroom. This model has one drawer, the front of which is curved to follow the line of the top. The drop leaves are supported by brackets which swing out under them. There are no stretchers. The tapered legs had a band of inlay toward the bottom. The two accompanying chairs are magnificent. The shield-back or heart-shaped side chair of mahogany has the delicate and graceful pierced center panel in the Hepplewhite style. The armchair, also of mahogany, is of Sheraton inspiration; this is a New York model, *circa* 1800. It too is a chair perfect in design and execution, the center carved splat contained within the arched area so well balanced and handsomely carved. The tapered legs with the spade foot are correct features. There are no stretchers.

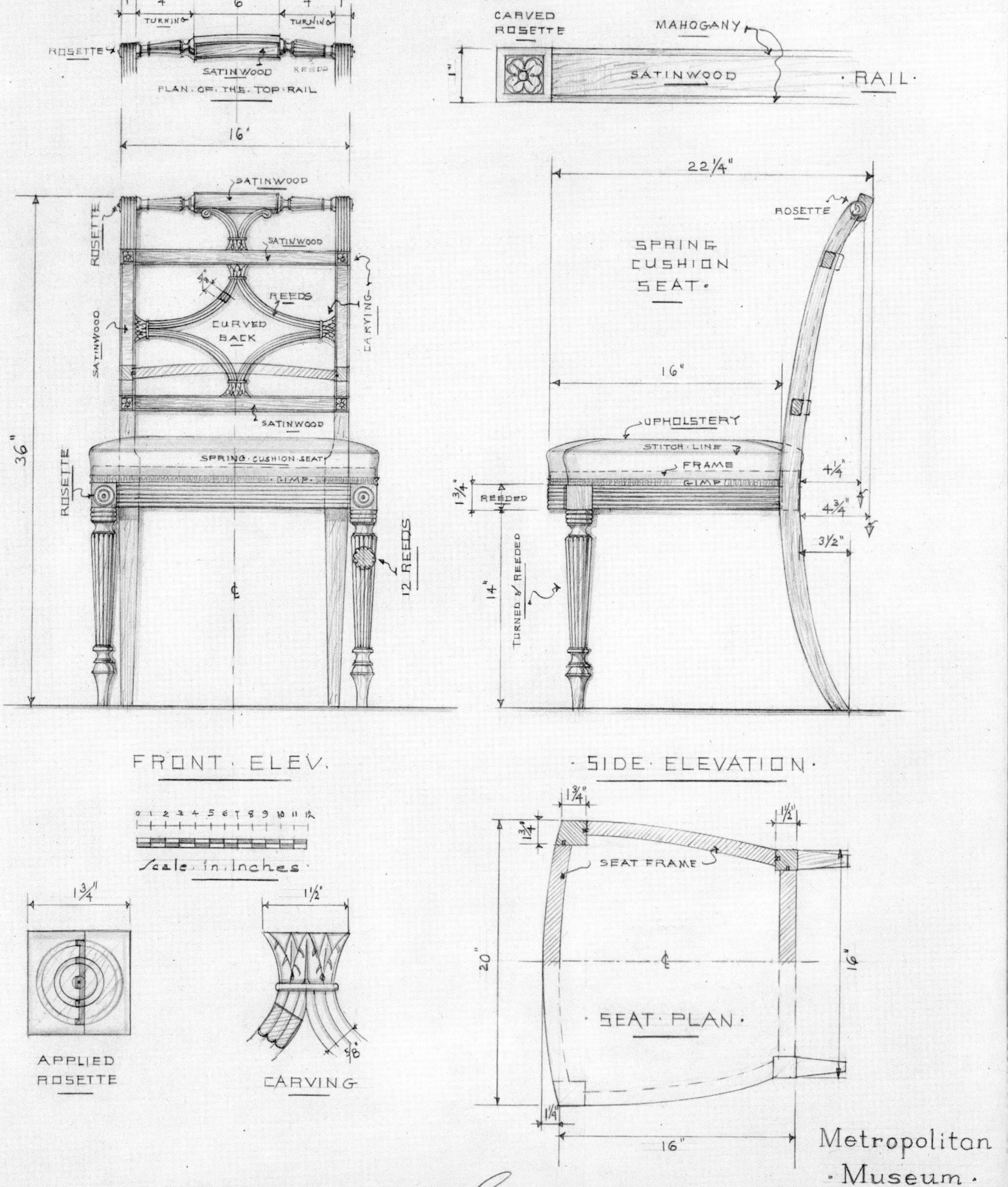

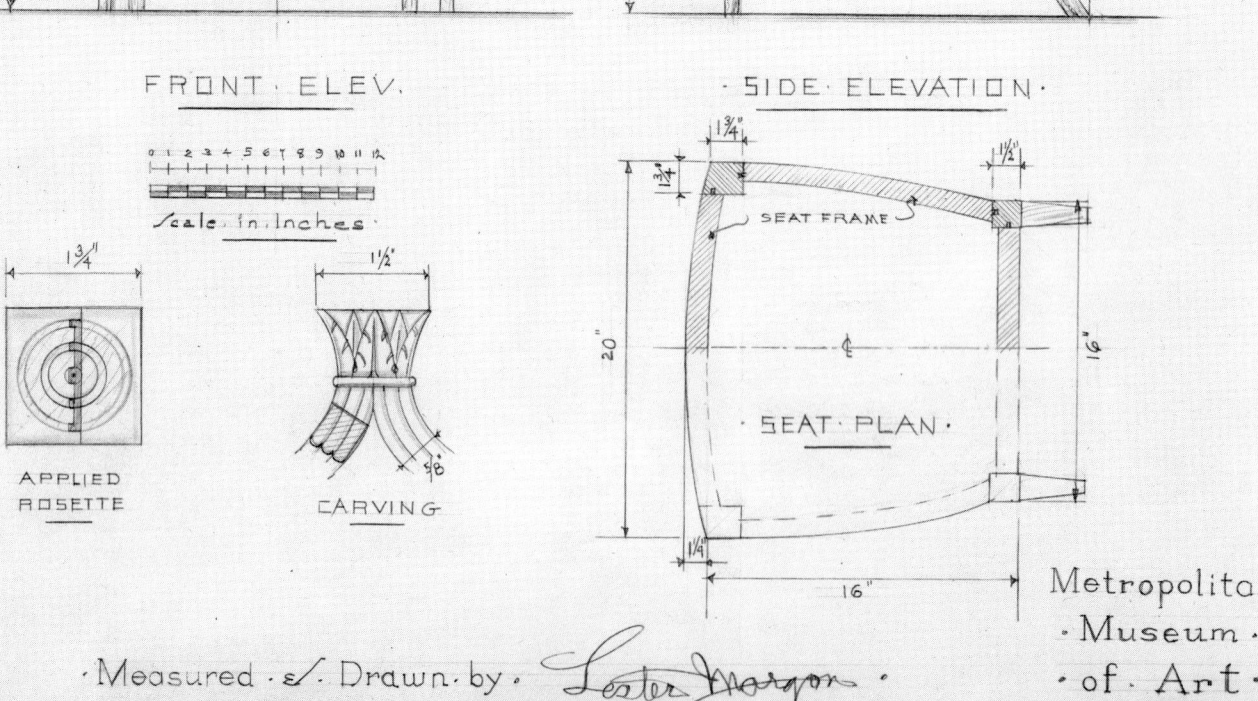

SIDE CHAIR
Metropolitan Museum of Art   Gift of Mrs. Russell Sage 1909

This elegant Sheraton-style chair, *circa* 1800, was formerly in the Bolles Collection and is made of mahogany. It is attributed to John Seymour of Boston. This chair is distinguished by refinements of form and the beauty and contrast of the satinwood inlay on the pillow-back top rail and on the back posts. Note the fine reeding and the straightforward turning of the front legs. The reeding on the seat frame and the corner rosettes are also typical of the work of Duncan Phyfe. The complex composition of the back panel and the noticeable curve of the back are departures from the early Federal period. The neoclassic approach in this chair is typical of Sheraton's later designs. This was one of the chairs featured in the exhibit, "The Anatomy of the Chair," in 1962 at the Museum. The work of the Seymour family of Boston is distinguished by just such intricacy of form and of the contrasting inlay. It marks a time when the designs were becoming more severe and selective; this chair heralded the nineteenth century.

SHERATON ARMCHAIR
Los Angeles County Museum of Art

This armchair from Massachusetts is made of mahogany with satinwood inlay, high upholstered back, stop-fluted arm supports and turned and reeded front legs. The date is *circa* 1800. In Wallace Nutting's *Treasury* there is illustrated a very similar chair, from Groton, Massachusetts. This present one is a Museum purchase, the Denis Bequest. This is one of the most popular models of upholstered high-back chairs, the reason being self-evident. It appears important, with infinite grace, and abounds in seating comfort.

MAIN GALLERY
Metropolitan Museum of Art

This elegant American alcove from a main gallery shows woodwork from Boston and Salem, *circa* 1800, a selection of furniture mostly after the Sheraton style. The mantelpiece is from a house by Charles Bulfinch, one of the first native trained architects in America and a fervent follower of the Adam style. The cornice happens to be an original from the Cook-Oliver House in Salem, Massachusetts, built shortly after 1804 from plans by Samuel McIntire. This is a typical residential New England interior where light colors and delicate moldings are combined with a fineness of scale. The scenic wallpaper is most colorful.

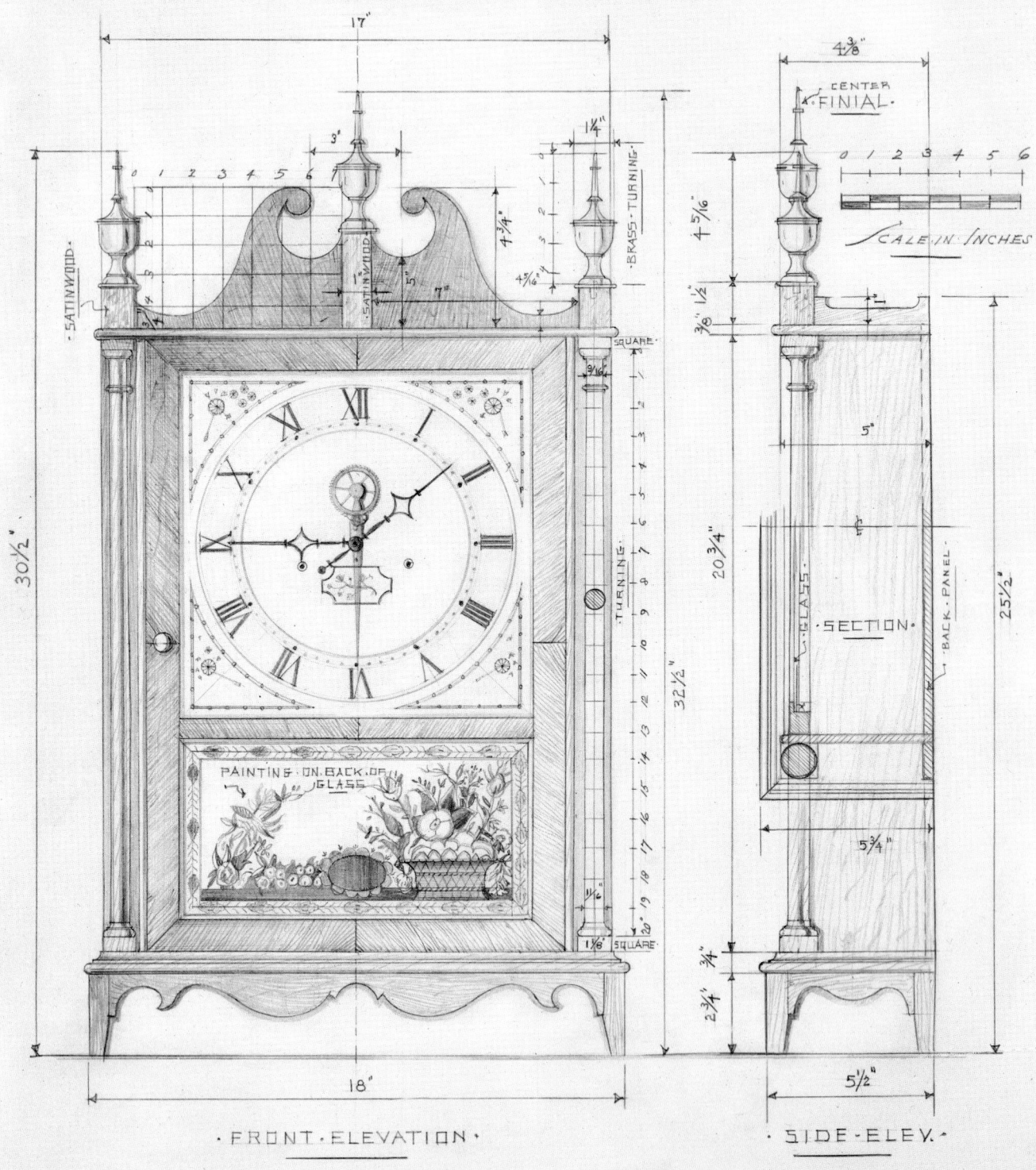

MANTEL CLOCK
Old Sturbridge Village

This Sheraton-style mahogany and satinwood mantel clock has been purposely drawn to a larger scale to permit of the showing of the details and to illustrate the painting in the lower panel. This design, universally accepted as Colonial, has elegance, simplicity and charm. The clock, dated 1816, is attributed to Eli Terry and is believed to have been patented by him. He was the mechanical genius of the clock world at that time and worked on his creations constantly, striving for perfection. This pillar-and-scroll model found immediate favor and the sales were tremendous throughout the land. The finely chased brass finials are exquisite and the scroll forms excellent. The face of the clock is well delineated and the hands delicately fashioned. Of interest is the lower painted panel, which was done on the inside of the glass for preservation and effect. These clocks had wooden works and struck the hour on a cast-iron bell. With iron weights for power, the clocks ran for thirty days on a winding. Similar clocks were made at this time by Seth Thomas, who seemed to be his business rival and antagonist.

BRACKET CLOCK
Metropolitan Museum of Art

This mahogany bracket clock by Seth Thomas (1774-1859) shows how very similar his products were to the clocks made by Eli Terry and his family. The detail is not quite so fine, nor is the face of the clock as finely delineated. The decorated scenic panel below looks as though it might be decalcomania. However, the general design is practically identical. In our opinion they lacked the refinements and the delicacy of the Terry clocks. Later, Terry sold out to Seth Thomas.

SPICE CABINET
Old Sturbridge Village

This hanging spice cabinet, with many 4" x 5" drawers, is most useful and decorative. The frame is painted a combination of gray with black moldings around the drawers; the drawer panels are of bird's-eye maple. The turned knobs are of wood. This chest was made in the early nineteenth century in New England. In Colonial times no better gift could be brought back by the seafaring captains than a variety of spices. They were among the most precious possessions in the kitchen and had to have a place for safekeeping. The complete cabinet measures 20" wide by 25" high by 7" deep.

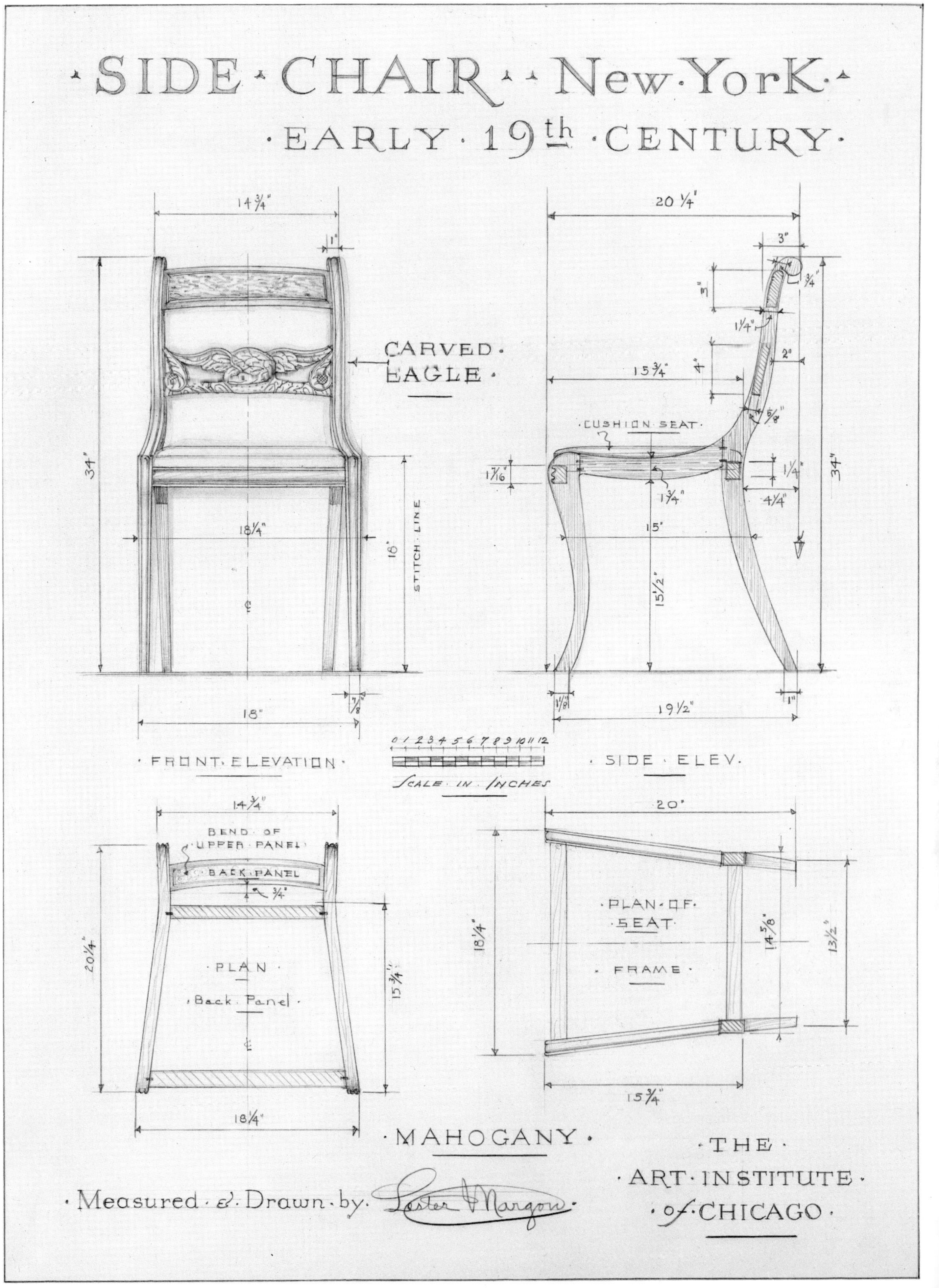

SIDE CHAIR · NEW YORK
EARLY 19th CENTURY

FRONT ELEVATION

SIDE ELEV.

CARVED EAGLE

SCALE IN INCHES

PLAN · BACK · PANEL

PLAN · OF · SEAT · FRAME

MAHOGANY

Measured & Drawn by

THE ART INSTITUTE OF CHICAGO

EAGLE CHAIR
Art Institute of Chicago
Gift of Mrs. Emily Crane Chadbourne

This mahogany Duncan Phyfe-type side chair is from New York, *circa* 1810-1820. It is an exceptionally fine model with a beautifully carved eagle as the center panel of the back. The top rail is slightly curved and paneled in a blistering crotch mahogany. This type chair was most popular at the turn of the century and may be called of late Sheraton inspiration. Of course the main interest in this side chair is the eagle as the center splat, which makes the chair positively unique. The line of the back post, which flows gracefully and becomes the actual front leg, suggests the Empire spell. The striped satin used as the upholstery of the seat is of the period. Many writers classify this chair as belonging to the American Directory style but we do not agree because it came into vogue in England while the Sheraton style was still at its height.

1812 CHAIR
Brooklyn Museum

This is one of those complex chairs that are difficult to classify. A mixture of many styles and influences, it looks like a strange combination of a wainscot chair and a Jacobean model with the twists. No doubt this chair was made for a certain purpose with the crown, the date and the many initials. You will remember that 1812 was a time of war and design was at a low ebb.

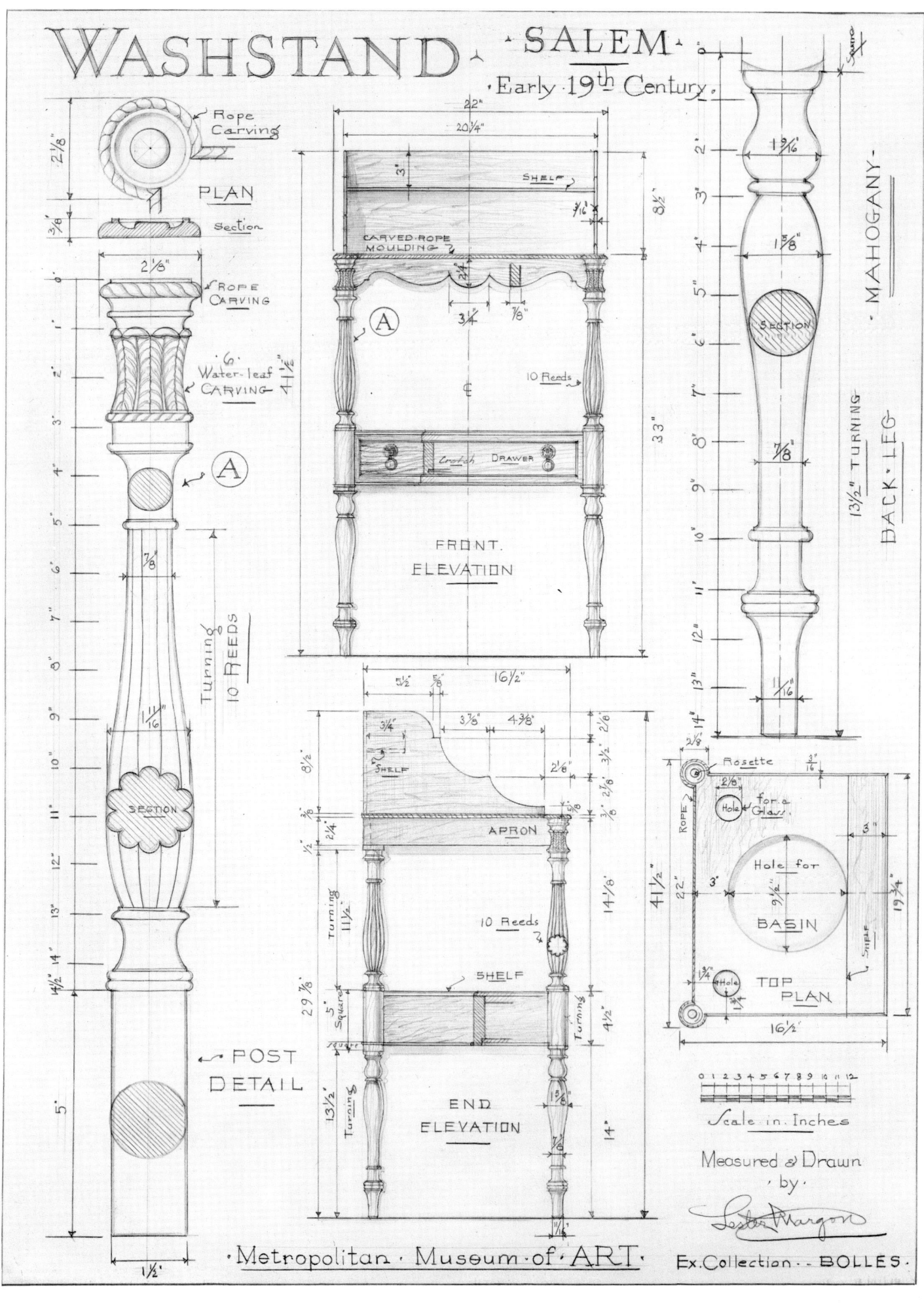

WASHSTAND
Metropolitan Museum of Art
Gift of Mrs. Russell Sage 1909

A washstand may seem a bit out of date in this day and age but in Colonial times it was a necessity in the bedroom. This model is from Salem, Massachusetts, and dates from the early nineteenth century. It is of mahogany in the Sheraton style. In this instance the designer has lifted a utilitarian piece of prosaic function to the exalted heights by reason of his imagination and skill. There are no finer turnings to be found anywhere and the carving is exquisite in its chastity. The inclusion of a drawer for toilet requisites and the adding of a shelf at the top are useful and surrounding it all with a backing which acts as splash is a masterly touch. The hole in the top proper is to receive the famous basin and pitcher and the two holes at the sides are for glasses. In these days of abundant plumbing we wonder how those Colonial Americans existed — yet look at this elegant washstand, created for an attendant purpose: it proves that the most ordinary piece of furniture may be treated reverently.

DECORATED WASHSTAND
Art Institute of Chicago

This Pennsylvania German washstand, *circa* 1795, is a good example of the crude but colorful decoration of these Amish farmers. The tulip again is featured. The wood used is cherry and all the decoration is confined to the inner side of the splash. The cut-out ends of the splash have a purpose and there is one drawer for the washing necessities. Much of this decoration was done by amateurs, hence the freedom with which the designs are handled. This washstand is the gift of Mrs. Emily Crane Chadbourne.

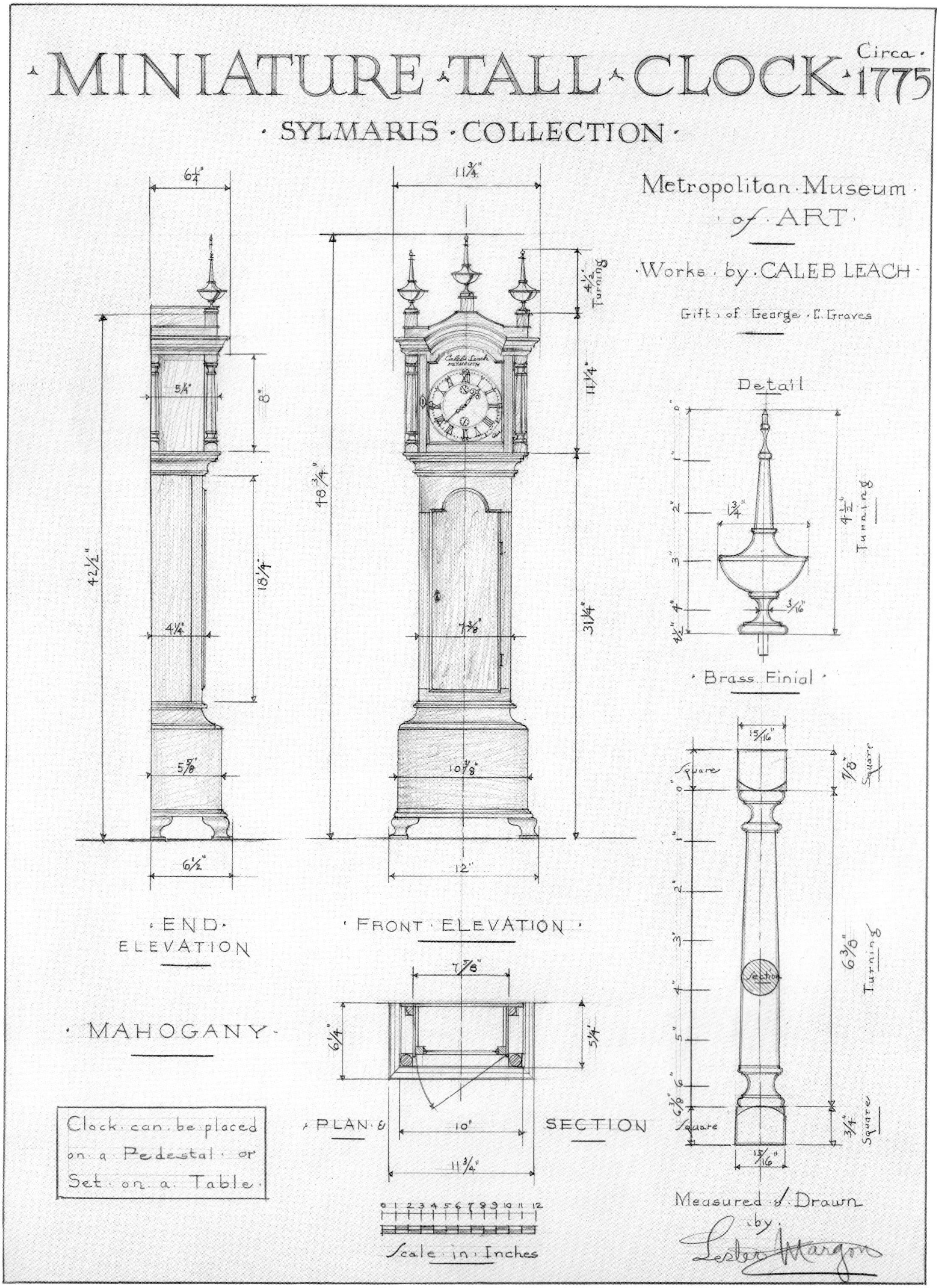

MINIATURE TALL CLOCK Circa 1775
· SYLMARIS · COLLECTION ·

Metropolitan Museum of ART

Works by CALEB LEACH

Gift of George C. Graves

· END ELEVATION ·

· FRONT ELEVATION ·

· MAHOGANY ·

Clock can be placed on a Pedestal or Set on a Table.

· PLAN & SECTION ·

Scale in Inches

Detail

· Brass Finial ·

Measured & Drawn by
Lester Margon

MINIATURE CLOCK
Metropolitan Museum of Art
The Sylmaris Collection
Gift of George Coe Graves 1930

This miniature tall clock in mahogany dates from 1775-1800. We are all familiar with the tall Grandfather clocks of this general design; these miniature ones were known as Grandmother clocks. The works are by Caleb Leach, who worked in Plymouth, Massachusetts, from 1776 to 1790. The design has all the features of the larger clocks along with a certain piquancy and charm due to the reduction in size. The rather large turned brass finials, resembling the towers of a cathedral, give the little clock an appearance of importance. The face is laid out well and the hands are jewel-like in delineation. The moldings are exemplary and the simple free-standing columns at the top are delicate and classical in design. These clocks were often set upon a shelf or placed on a platform prepared especially for them. In Revolutionary times they found great favor and graced many an important hall or drawing room.

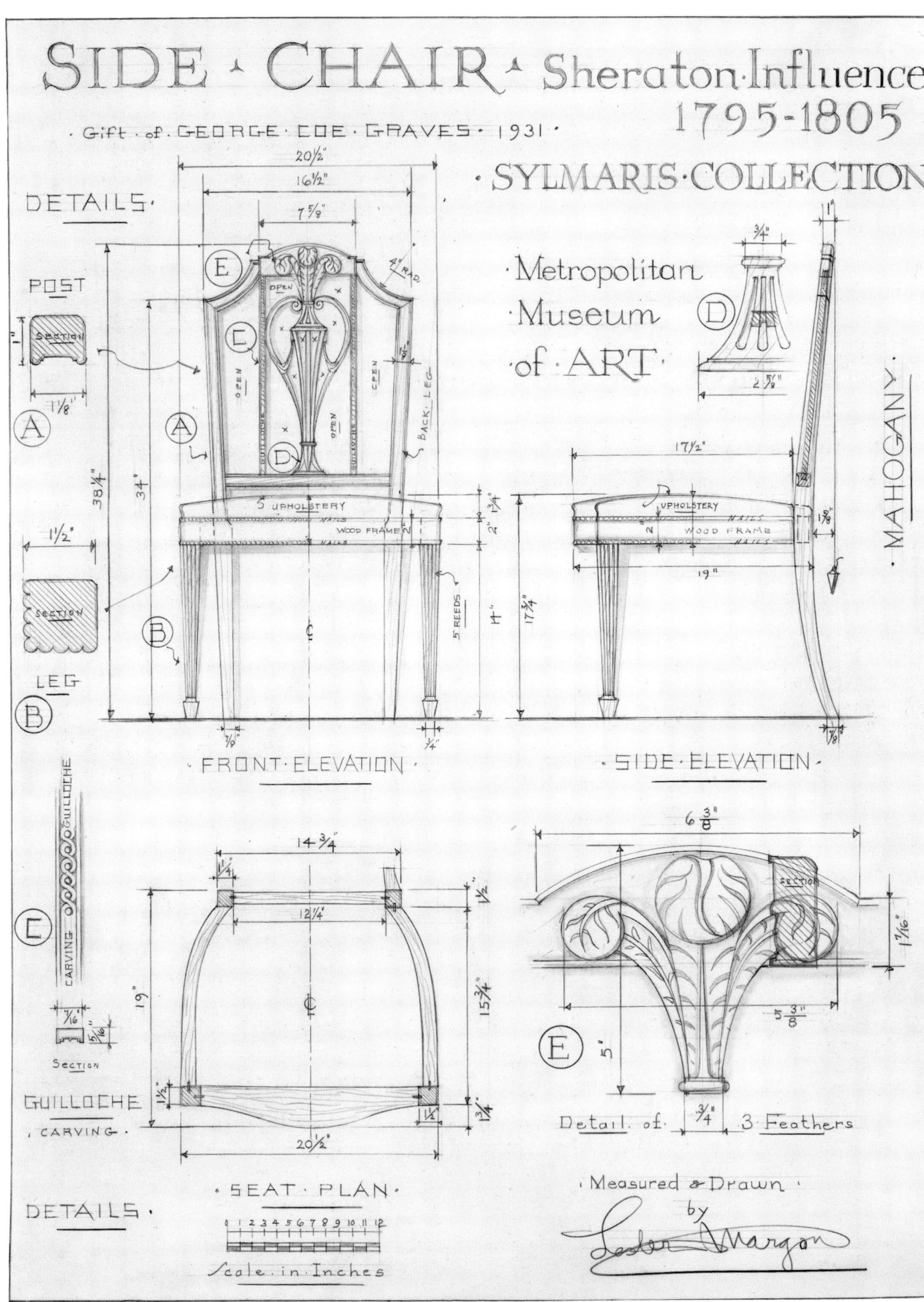

SIDE CHAIR

Metropolitan Museum of Art   Sylmaris Collection, Gift of George Coe Graves 1931

There are chairs and there are chairs but this model is superlative. Made of mahogany, 1795-1805, there is strong Sheraton influence evident, yet the chair appears distinctive and original in conception. This was one of the selected chairs that was in the exhibit, "The Anatomy of the Chair," in 1962 at the Museum. It no doubt was one of a set that graced the dining room of a splendid house; it is sufficiently pompous. This New York chair has a broad and ample seat typical of the chairs made in this locality. The urn-shaped splat is indicative of the Tory means of recognition. The squareness of the back is broken by the curves at the top and the center pierced and carved back, featuring the Crest of the Prince of Wales and the vase-shaped tracery, is so fine in detail that it could be said to resemble jewelry. There is nothing finer to be seen anywhere, as far as chair design is concerned, for delicacy and refinement. The square reeded leg with the spade foot fits perfectly into the scheme. Note the carved guilloche on the panel uprights and the elegant swags. All the carving is painstakingly beautiful. In sum, it is a breathtaking bravura performance.

A FANCY CHAIR
Los Angeles County Museum of Art

The term "fancy chair" is in no sense derogatory. It simply means that in this instance the designer has shown definite invention in the treatment of the design. The chair is cane-seated, painted an olive green with ivory striping, with decorations in gold and low-toned colors, the back having a landscape vignette. The date is *circa* 1800. The chair is from the Van Rensselaer family, one of a set of three formerly on loan to the Metropolitan Museum of Art. The maker, Thomas Renshaw (working 1814-15 at No. 37 South Gay Street, Baltimore); the decoration by John Barnhart, "ornamenteer."

HITCHCOCK ROCKER
Brooklyn Museum

This splendid example of a Hitchcock rocker is painted black, decorated with light-brown flower basket on the crest rail and a floral design on the front edge of the seat. This rocker, marked *Hitchcock – Alford & Co., Hitchcockville, Connecticut – Warranted 1832*, was exhibited in the Museum through the courtesy of Arthur W. Clement. There is no finer rocker made in America. For size, balance, comfort and rocking quality, it has no peer. Many of these were left in the wood finish.

HITCHCOCK CHAIR
Art Institute of Chicago

This model of a Hitchcock chair is very similar to the one from the Brooklyn Museum except that the back central panel is not decorated. Whether or not the decoration has been removed is a matter of conjecture. Nevertheless, this model has some excellent features. The splay of the back is superior and the front leg turnings are not so full. By leaving this chair in the wood finish the effect is quite different, a bit more provincial. This chair is the gift of that fine collector of Americana, Mrs. Emily Crane Chadbourne. The Art Institute of Chicago is especially favored with many of her pieces.

HITCHCOCK CHAIR
Brooklyn Museum

This is an original Hitchcock chair (marked), *circa* 1820, Hitchcockville. This is a typical model and clearly shows all of the characteristics. Here we see the fruit-and-leaf decoration on the central back panel, stenciled in metallics, the elaborate gold striping and the gilding of parts of the horizontal bead turnings. An interesting detail in the decoration is the arrow pointing downward on the back posts. Note the rush seat and the narrow wood enclosing it on the sides. The cushion back panel in the top rail is a feature of these chairs.

GONDOLA CHAIR
Metropolitan Museum of Art

This gondola chair in mahogany is of the Empire period in France, *circa* 1814. Note how it is fairly covered with ormolu mounts and shows to what extremes they went in the pursuit of pompously elaborate decoration. Perçier and Fontaine were the architects appointed by Napoleon to espouse his mania for regality. No wonder the American craftsmen could not reproduce this kind of furniture. It was in every respect foreign to their tendencies, liking and training.

LOUIS XV BERGÈRE
Metropolitan Museum of Art

Many chairs were brought into America after the French Revolution by the aristocrats who fled here to save their lives. Our cabinetmakers were unprepared to duplicate these French models: there were too many fanciful curves and too much unrealistic detail. They found the preponderance of exaggerated deviations beyond their desire and their comprehension. Happily they did not attempt this unholy task but proceeded on their way with logic and understanding. One clearly must be born French to understand their furniture making.

EMPIRE SETTING
Metropolitan Museum of Art

The French Empire style attained its highest distinction between 1804 and 1815. By the year 1825 it had deteriorated. Here may be seen a collection of Empire pieces showing the profuse use of ormolu mounts, leaving little of the wood showing. All this display and formality were totally foreign to the American way of thinking, which is why the French Empire style found few adherents in America. Even the great Duncan Phyfe did not succeed in working in this style, although some of his later pieces did show Empire tendencies.

SIDE VIEW OF EMPIRE CHAIR
Gothenburg Museum

The classical discoveries of the Pompeii and Herculaneum excavations had a worldwide influence on furniture design, as is evidenced by this interesting Empire chair from Sweden. The detail of the sphinx, incorporated as the arm support, is probably suggested by some mummy from an Egyptian tomb. It is fascinating to study the tremendous influence that past history can have upon design developments throughout the globe. Although all Europe seemed to adapt these tendencies, here in America we were loathe to do so and were the least successful.

ADAM PAINTED CHAIR
Metropolitan Museum of Art

The grace and charm of these Adam chairs are ever a source of wonder. They are almost feminine in their delicacy and their decorative treatment is altogether delightful. This model is definitely of Sheraton inspiration in design but it has been transformed into a piece of transcendent beauty by reason of the painted decoration. See how the garlands entwine the legs and the back posts, while the panels of baskets of flowers and the crossed torches on the seat frame complete the symphony.

EMPIRE ARMCHAIR
Gothenburg Museum

Here is still another version of the Empire influence that spread throughout Europe. Though more restrained, it still shows the Classic line and the fondness for gold and display. Note the design of the upholstery which incorporated much of the pomp and circumstance of the Empire period. How totally foreign from anything we can conceive as "Made in America"!

VICTORIAN

The Victorian Period in America presents an enigma because, in all its foreign aspects, it appeared to be so banal to our concepts of rational behavior. The reign of Queen Victoria lasted from 1838 to 1901 and it is quite understandable that her subjects would name their furniture and elegancies after their beloved Queen, but why on earth should we have become so servile as to designate that period in furniture after her? There seems to be a sly underground movement with wary commercial implications to foster this furniture in America by calling it the Second Baroque. We find this scheme totally unwarranted as a maudlin attempt to legitimize a bastard offspring. The Baroque style had a certain splendor and majesty, with richly carved ornamentation and voluptuous curves. The Victorian furniture is totally lacking in any such attributes. While much of the cabinetwork may be exemplary, the design element was totally lacking. The detail was heavy and crude and the composition elements were derogatory.

At this time in America there was no outstanding designer who could have stemmed the tide. It was left to the interior decorator to do the job. An effort was made to use Gothic forms but it did not succeed. All periods were drawn upon for inspiration which resulted in a hodgepodge of nothingness. When this furniture was set up in a room it appeared as a collection of unrelated objects. Confusion was the order of the day. Antique furniture was not wanted or appreciated and wood seems to have lost its favor. Much of this furniture was made of papier-maché, with insets of mother of pearl framed by naturalistic flower painting. Fantastic forms prevailed and the elegant cabriole legs assumed all sorts of preposterous curvatures.

Much of the upholstered furniture was made of rosewood or black walnut and the backs were deeply tufted, framed by galloons and enhanced by fringes. Every piece had to have its antimacassars over the arms and placed on the backs to protect them from the macassar oil from the hair. The square piano dominated the living room with its elephantine legs and pierced support for the sheet music. Wallpapers were used in furious stripes and colorings and bizarre patterns. Painted decorations appeared wherever possible. On ceilings and across beams painted cherubs pranced in glee. Above mantelpieces and surrounding arches decoration flourished. Crystal chandeliers held the center of the scene and supplied the needed sparkle. Parquet wood floors in Moorish design were popular. Windows, nooks and protuberances were swathed in multicolored draperies with the accompanying valances and cornucopias. Lavish lace curtains covered the windows, all as befitted the best brothels.

In furniture detailing it was bedlam. Turnings became frolicsome and oriental screens appeared everywhere. Whatnots, those utterly ridiculous contraptions, were made in every size and shape and became necessary adjuncts to accommodate the innumerable memorabilia collected by the Americans returning from the Grand Tour of Europe. But probably the most colorful anachronisms of the period were those heinous blackamoor statues in painted metallic getups and in coy postures. That demon atrocity, the family portrait album, was ever in evidence on the white marbletop table in the living room. There were many more homely idiosyncrasies, including spool-turned beds, fancy chairs, bureaux with teardrop pulls and table-desks. As for accessories, there were pressed glass, cast-iron trivets, hanging lamps with crystal dangles and a host of chromolithographs. This heterogeneous bewilderment need not be stressed or eulogized. The Victorian period in America spelled finis for furniture design for some time, and as such can be lamented.

Another reason for this floundering was the War Between the States. It is a well-known fact that all wars have a disconcerting effect upon the artistic and cultural advancement of nations. When opposing countries meet in battle, that is bad enough, but when brother fights brother, that is blasphemy. It was a time when this country was torn asunder by internal strife, and the end is not near in sight. The freedoms for which they fought and died are still hanging in the balance.

There are, however, some Victorian rooms that have merit. They were produced in the homes of the wealthy who still maintained a sense of the appropriate. Take for instance the Theodore Roosevelt House in New York City, dating from about 1860. Here the interior is homely and engaging, restrained and dignified, with few of the Victorian idiosyncrasies too evident. Another good example is the Old Merchant's House, also in New York City. It was built in 1830 as a residence for Mr. Seabury Tredwell and is now owned by the Historical Landmark Society; the location is 29 East 4th Street. Here one gets the impression of gracious living. The Museum of the City of New York, the Brooklyn Museum and the Metropolitan Museum of Art all have excellent examples of rooms and tableaux of the Victorian period.

EARLY VICTORIAN ROOM
Metropolitan Museum of Art

This Louis Philippe and Early Victorian-period living-room setting, 1830-1848, is a Museum recreation. The furniture shown here is eclectic. We see a square piano with elephantine multifarious carved legs and a square stool. The elaborately saw-cut panel to support the sheet music can be lowered. Note the large whatnot with mirror back and cut-out sides. The horsehair upholstered armchair and the overstuffed easy chair are grandiose. No doubt the engravings on the wall all tell a story.

VICTORIAN PARLOR
Brooklyn Museum

This parlor is from the house of Robert J. Milligan, built in Saratoga, New York, about 1853, at the time when this community was the center of racing and the gay life. It is one of the most exciting rooms of the Victorian period that has come to our attention, featuring many of the salient characteristics of that turbulent decade. Note the array of tufted upholstered chairs, the medallion portraits, the floral carpeting, the corner whatnot, the white marble-top center table and the globed crystal chandelier.

AFTER THE VICTORIAN

After the Victorian period came the deluge. Fortunately people were shocked out of their lethargy by the displays at the Philadelphia Exposition in 1876. It set them thinking. While no great revival of interest was evident at the moment, art and good design were presented in such a favorable manner that it prepared the way for greater understanding and appreciation of furniture. This was the time of industrial and business expansion. Railroads covered the continent, agriculture was becoming mechanized and national progress was unlimited. With wealth came the desire for display. Mansions sprang up like toadstools. The entire world was being scoured for its treasures and fine antiques. Indeed there was not enough to fulfill all the needs. Prosperity was going ahead in leaps and bounds.

There are two sides to every coin. With all this prosperity and material rapaciousness came the decline in apprenticeship in the arts and crafts. The supply of good craftsmen and cabinetworkers was becoming exhausted. This was the Mechanical Age. Men were being replaced by machines. The machine would take over, people thought, but soon it proved otherwise. The machine was found to have its limitations. Because of this fact detail in furniture had to be abandoned. There were few schools where the fundamentals of art education were taught, to say nothing of historic introspection and creative designing. Architecture had fallen into disrepute and the useful arts were subjected to disuse. The enlightened public was beginning to realize this, and leading publications began campaigns to urge persons of wealth to come to the rescue and subsidize schools for the furthering of the arts and the fulfillment of design.

The Metropolitan Museum of Art was dedicated and opened in 1880 and men of wealth set aside funds to further the development of art study. Even before that, Peter Cooper established the Cooper Union for the Advancement of Science and Art. This became a working model, with high standards for free education. In 1859, it established an art school with admission by competitive examinations. Mr. J. Pierpont Morgan was influential in the founding of the Society of Mechanics and

Tradesmen in New York City, with a night school offering free courses in art and technical subjects. The motto was "By Hammer and Hand All Arts Do Stand." It was not long before all schools of higher education included similar courses in their curriculum. The Beaux Arts, fashioned after the Paris Academy, held national competitions for university and art-school students in furniture, interior design and architectural design. Rapid and continued progress was made and the United States is now well on the way to becoming a world center of the arts and architecture.

7

FURNITURE DESIGN IN OUR TIME

Since furniture in the home continues to be one of the most intimate adjuncts of our daily lives, it is not only advisable but essential that its selection should be given careful attention and deliberation. Since this furniture surrounds us and plays a major rôle in our activities and well-being, it is only logical to surmise that it should reflect us, our natural inclinations and modes of expression. A room setting, with its furniture, accessories and color, is the stage setting against which our lives are enacted. If it enhances us, if it helps to bring to fruition our expectations and tends to diminish our vicissitudes, then it is a job well done with understanding and enlightenment. If the result is otherwise, the purpose is defeated.

WHAT is the status of furniture design in our time? That is a question that will concern everyone who is interested in furniture, the student, the designer, the architect, the furniture manufacturer, as well as the general public. It is a most controversial question that cannot be readily answered. Many have taken sides and will not budge an inch. The battle of Modernism versus Traditionalism has been going on for many years and the end is not nearly in sight.

Let us suppose that a piece of furniture could be made as finely today as it was in earlier times. This in itself is a spurious conjecture for, due to the fact that working conditions are so different, it would be practically an impossibility. Present-day demands that everything must be done in the shortest possible time preclude the respite necessary for trial and error. There is no time allotted for contemplation, study or repose. In many furniture factories there is so much pressure put on the workers that their one goal is to get the job done. Often employed on a piece-time basis, it is only natural that they should take every expedient and short cut to get the work done in the briefest possible time. They do not linger over a job one second longer than necessary. The machine is the master. The men are there only to see that the machine operates properly. Even that is only possible to a limited degree, for once the machine is set and goes into motion, it goes on its way unwittingly. The men's job is monotonous, wearisome and prostrating.

In this age of automation, man is fast becoming the robot, his initiative is no longer required, his free-thinking unnecessary and his integrity as a human being nullified. He becomes part of a mechanized procedure requiring little thought or initiative. This is the greatest affront to his creative potentialities, his freedom of thought and action, alienating his right to immortality. To the industrialist this is an inevitable situation that progress demands; to the humanitarian it is the most profound violation of human rights. Whether or not these two directly opposite philosophies can ever be reconciled is matter for consideration.

Under these circumstances the apprenticeship system in the field of cabinetmaking today is practically nonexistent, the young people having relegated it to the category of waste of time. In this electronic age, when boys just coming out of college are being offered a king's ransom, why should they bother about learning a trade? The high cost of living and the extravagant way in which they have been brought up make it necessary to sell themselves to the highest bidder.

At a furniture factory where I was to do some special designing recently, they did not have a wood carver or a decorator. It seems that a first-class finisher is a legendary figure. What the outcome will be no one can predict. We are reaching a point where craftsmanship is no longer to be followed. This would be altogether disconcerting were it not for the fact that all over the country there are many young industrial designers who possess that insatiable predilection to seek expression in the visual arts. As individual workers and as associates they are forging ahead and carrying the torch of study, progress, investigation and accomplishment. Their work is being shown at the Museum of Contemporary Arts in New York and in traveling exhibitions elsewhere. Much of their output is praiseworthy and some of this work is finding acceptance in commercial channels.

The last decade has seen furniture design and production that has been fallaciously called "Modern." The truth is that there is no such thing. What is "Modern" today may well become outmoded tomorrow.

Furniture Design in Our Time

When a man said, "I will have nothing of the old, I only want the new," he proved himself to be an uninformed duffer. Does he not know that all life is evolution and that all art is fruition from the past? Progress is based on our ability to add the knowledge and the accomplishments of the past to our present-day advantage. Tradition is our greatest heritage. It is the accumulation and the preservation of knowledge to be used for future growth and development. It is not possible to contemplate the future without investigating the past.

Today there are so many avenues of approach to furniture design that it will be well to investigate a few. Because of the inadequacy of the machine, detail, carving and intricacies have to be eliminated. What is left? Flat surfaces, straight lines, sharp corners and unfinished ends. This has led to the inevitable manufacture of furniture that is boxlike in perception, sharp in delineation and uninteresting in visualization. What then is a box? A box is a self-contained unit with four sides, a top and a bottom. The very structure of such a unit makes it limited for expansion or development. This may be the reason why so much of this "Modern" furniture is so deplorably blatant and deliberately hostile. It is altogether lacking in comprehension, variety and grandiloquence.

The public is up in arms. In the field of radio, television and hi-fi particularly, customers are no longer satisfied with those boxlike contraptions called cabinets. They are demanding finer cabinetwork of period inspiration, such as Early American, Georgian and Directoire, that will fit graciously into their present décor. Style again is becoming a sales factor, and rightfully so, because of its romantic appeal. Basically, we are all sentimentalists. Today traditional propensities are valid forces in our furniture selection.

Alas, another implication in contemporary furniture manufacture is the getting away from the use of woods and the substitution of all sorts of unrealistic materials. This includes such alternatives as formica, plexiglas, a host of laminated and phenol products, catalin and ever so many other plastics. It is a world of make-believe. These materials are sturdy, can be readily cast and molded and require little or no cleaning or assembling. Hence we see so many of these cast-in-one-piece chairs that are thoroughly ungainly and uncomfortable. Chrome, stainless steel and iron are more of the conspirators that are bent on replacing woods for furniture. While these metals might be all right for structural purposes, they are always cold and lacking in grace and comeliness.

However, woods can never be replaced for furniture — no, not as long as there is an adequate supply. Wood has a natural tenderness, a warmth that is akin to our body temperature. Wood has a humaneness that gives it an affinity for man. Wood is a faithful friend. It befits our sense of touch and ofttimes breathes forth the essence of rare perfumes. There are woods that are as light as a feather and there are woods that are as heavy as steel. No two pieces of wood are alike. The variety is infinite in color, pattern, texture and brilliancy. Woods are never monotonous or lacking in eloquence.

It is becoming more and more evident when walking through the better showrooms that the so-called "Modern" in furniture is on the way out. Very few samples are being shown and as things are shown so are they sold. The people are tired of it. The sense of novelty has worn off because its austerity is self-evident. Certainly the keyed-up factories would like to continue to turn it out indefinitely but there is little demand. It is cheap to manufacture and requires little or no handwork. Look at it! This furniture is dull, uninteresting, depressing. One cannot live with it for long. People desire furniture that has design, eloquence and perspicacity. Due to this unsettled condition, the furniture industry does not know which way to turn. There is no set plan. Every firm is taking chances, hoping that their choice will sell.

One season it is Danish, then Mediterranean, Swedish or Spanish. That is wonderful for the interior decorator with wealthy clients who can change their décor every season. Unfortunately for most people the purchase of furniture is a once-in-a-lifetime procedure. Why isn't there a stronger movement to use Colonial American furniture designs? It is our national expression, we understand it and can dwell with it comfortably. It is our natural heritage from the Founding of Jamestown and the Landing of the Pilgrims. Its development has been fine, progressive and exhaustive. When you enter a room furnished with Colonial appointments you immediately feel at home. Can this be said of any of the transient periods? Furniture of foreign inspiration may be all right but does it express us and our way of life? Take for instance the young, successful businesswoman who permits her interior decorator to do her living room in the Louis V style. It turns out to be most elegant but is it the proper background for her? Consider the young married couple who have just bought a tract house in the hills and are expecting. Their decorator insists that the entire house be done in Spanish. It is the vogue. Sure, it turns out to be most picturesque and would make a fine color page in the Sunday Home Section, but does it express the family who must dwell therein?

We hold that the time has come to sit back and try to evaluate calmly what actually constitutes good design in furniture. A well designed piece of furniture should fulfill the utilitarian demands, afford

Furniture Design in Our Time

esthetic pleasure to the beholder and express the taste, culture and milieu of the times. Design is a law unto itself. That is why furniture is such a boon. It is the reflection of our civilization and indicates the skill and imagination of the present. Furniture is so interesting because it is the most intimate of our personal possessions. A well furnished room is a delight. You sense it immediately upon entering, as though you are being taken in a fond embrace.

With the great advances in technology, the scope of the furniture designer has broadened. Everything is possible if he has knowledge and imagination and a sense of the appropriate. Furniture should be a handmaiden to make our lives fuller, richer and more colorful. Furniture should be practical, pleasing, light in weight, perceptive in structure, simple, sincere, gracious, economic in construction and above all utilitarian. Never before have designers been given such recognition. This is an indication that we are returning to the days of Duncan Phyfe, John Goddard and Samuel McIntire.

To conclude, only by a knowledge of the past, an appreciation of the present and a visionary outlook toward the future can we hope to arrive at a healthy premise for the furniture design of the future.

FINIS

INDEX

(Asterisks after page numbers refer to measured drawings.)

Accessories
  album, family, 240
  carpets, 99
  chandeliers, 40, 52, 102, 240, 242
  chromolithographs, 240
  Jasper vase, 206
  lamps, hanging, 240
  mantelpieces, 53, 102, 103, 221, 240
  photographs, 240
  pressed glass, 240
  statues, blackamoor, 240
  table tops, marble, 240
  trivets, cast-iron, 240
Architects
  Adam, Robert, 102
  Bulfinch, Charles, 221
  Fontaine, 207, 236
  Jefferson, Thomas, 97
  McIntire, Samuel, 185, 186
  Metcalf, Stephen O., 13
  Palladio, Andrea, 100
  Perçier, 207, 236
Associations
  Antique Dealers Association, 19
  Historical Landmark Society, 240
  New York State Historical Association, 10, 176

Beds
  cherry, 146
  four-poster, 58*, 59, 60
  spool-turned, 240
Benches
  storage, 170*, 171
  and table, 154
  window, 191
Bible boxes, 82*, 83, 84, 85, 99
Bookcases
  and secretary, 57
  tri-part, 54*, 55
Breadbox, Pennsylvania German, 164*, 165
Breakfront, secretary, 56

Cabinetmakers, *see* Designers and Cabinetmakers
Cabinets
  bric-a-brac, 128
  corner, 155, 212
  hanging, 53, 155, 255
  spice, 225
  tall, 213
  Welsh, 51, 52
  whatnot, 240, 241, 242
Cellarette, Southern, 122*, 123
Chairs, 99-100
  Adam, 238
  American Provincial, 208

armchairs, 21*, 23, 53, 92*, 93, 94, 100, 220, 238, 241
banister, 53, 92*, 93, 99
Brewster, 93, 99
Carver, 92*, 93, 99
Chippendale, 21*, 23, 100
Colonial, 21*, 23
double-decker, 100
Duncan Phyfe, 192
eagle, 226*, 227
1812, 227
Empire, 237, 238
fan-back, 100, 120
fancy, 234, 240
fiddle-back, 100
gondola, 236
Hepplewhite, 200
Hitchcock, 208, 234, 235
ladder-back, 94, 100
Louis XV, 236
McIntire, 199, 200
painted, 234, 238
Queen Anne, 100, 106*, 107
rocker, 100, 208-09, 234
roundabout, 126*, 127
Shaker, 119
Sheraton, 100, 218*, 219, 220
shield-back, 199, 200
side, 218*, 219, 226*, 227, 232*, 233
slat-back, 93
splat-back, 199, 200

251

swivel, 169
vase-shaped back, 94
Victorian, 241, 242
wainscot, 76*, 77, 99
Windsor, 100, 118*, 119, 120, 121
writing-arm, 121
Chests
  Bible, 82*, 83, 84, 85, 99
  block-front, 195
  carved, 84
  with cupboard, 172*, 173
  dower, 53, 160*, 161, 162, 163
  English, 87
  painted, 90, 91, 160*, 161, 162, 163
  Swiss, 84
  wedding, 53, 160*, 161, 162, 163
Chest of drawers
  chest on chest, 43
  dower, Pennsylvania German, 145
  high, 49, 111
  painted, 88*, 89
  shaped, 30*, 31, 196*, 197
  sunflower, 45
  tall, 87, 91
  Tudor, 86*, 87
  tulip, 44*, 45
Clockmakers
  Burnap, Daniel, 137
  Leach, Caleb (works), 231
  Massey, Edward (works), 137
  Terry, Eli, 223, 224
  Thomas, Seth, 223, 224
  Willard, Aaron, 137
Clocks
  bracket, 224
  grandfather, 136*, 137, 146, 231
  grandmother, 230*, 231
  mantel, 222*, 223
  miniature, 230*, 231
Collections
  Blair, Mrs. J. Imsley, 13
  Bolles, Eugene, 13, 219
  Geesey, Titus C., 14, 146, 213
  Hawley family, 191
  Karolik, M. & M., 14, 197, 199
  Morgan, J. Pierpont, 14, 29, 75
  Norton, Elizabeth B., 208
  Nutting, Wallace, 14, 29, 75, 88*, 89, 94, 116, 220

Pattison, Kenneth B., 94, 217
Pendleton, Charles Leonard, 13, 14, 35, 140, 196, 197
Sylmaris, 25, 140, 231, 233
"Trestle Board," 75
Verplanck, 135
Cradles
  Long Island Dutch, 117
  Pennsylvania German, 114*, 115
  Wetherfield, 116
Cupboards
  chest, 172*, 173
  corner, 146, 210*, 211
  court, 74*, 75
  press, 74*, 75

Designers and cabinetmakers
  Adam, Robert, 67, 68
  Adams, Lemuel, 217
  Affleck, Thomas, 43, 110
  Chapin, Eliphelet, 24
  Chippendale, Thomas, 67, 68, 69, 129, 181, 183
  Egerton, Mathew, 215
  Gillingham, James, 43
  Goddard, John, 183, 184, 195, 249
  Goddard, John Townsend, 183
  Gostelow, Jonathan, 43, 110
  Hepplewhite, George, 67, 68, 69, 181, 183
  Hitchcock, Lambert, 208
  Jones, Inigo, 67
  Langley, Batty, 67
  McIntire, Samuel, 185-86, 199, 200, 201, 221, 249
  Perkins, Thomas Handasyd, 42
  Phyfe, Duncan, 18, 67, 100, 180-82, 189, 190, 191, 192, 193, 206, 219, 237, 249
  Randolph, Benjamin, 43, 110
  Renshaw, Thomas, 234
  Savory, William, 110
  Seymour, John, 219
  Sheraton, Thomas, 67, 68, 69, 181, 183
  Swan, Abraham, 67
  Townsend, John, 195
  Tufft, Thomas, 43, 110

Wedgwood, Josiah, 206
See also Styles
Desks
  drop-front, 28
  on frame, 73
  Governor Winthrop, 28
  rolltop, 101
  slant-top, 72
  slope, 146
  on stand, 70*, 71
  storekeeper, 146
  table, 240
  tambour, 26*, 27
Donors
  Allerton, Robert, 30
  Antiquarian Society, 31, 215
  Avery Fund, Sewell L., 93, 163
  Balch Fund, 139, 199
  Carton Fund, Alfred T., 93
  Chadbourne, Mrs. Evelyn Crane, 32, 87, 109, 119, 120, 227, 229, 235
  Clement, Arthur W., 209, 234
  Davis, Charles K., 199
  de Forest, Mrs. Robert W., 211
  de Groot, Mrs. Adelaide, 191
  Denis Bequest, 24, 132, 220
  Du Pont, Mr. and Mrs. Lamont, 14, 51
  Du Pont, Mrs. Pierre S., 14, 51
  Egbert, George Drew, 127
  Fletcher Fund, 23
  Gardner Fund, John Lowell, 75
  Geesey, Titus C., 213
  Graves, George Coe, 140, 231, 233
  Kennedy Fund, 39
  Landon Fund, Jessie Spalding, 31
  Lorillard, Mrs. Screven, 121
  Phillip, Robert Simmons, estate of, 107
  Potter, Miss Mary Lemoine, 183, 195
  Rogers Fund, 71, 162, 195
  Runnells Fund, Mrs. Clive, 215
  Sage, Mrs. Russell, 14, 79, 90, 219, 229
  Smith, Alan Ross, 47
  Stokes, J. Stogdell, 87

Index

"Trestle Board," 75
Vaughan, Elizabeth R., 120, 212
Verplanck, James De Lancey, 135
Verplanck, John Bayard Rogers, 135
Walker Fund, Wirt D., 45, 73, 85
Dressers
  kitchen, Miller of Millbach, 50*, 51, 52
  kitchen, Pennsylvania German, 51, 152*, 153

Excavations
  Herculaneum, 186, 206, 237
  Pompeii, 89, 186, 206, 237
Expositions
  Art Décoratifs 1925, 8
  Hudson Fulton 1907, 13
  Philadelphia 1876, 243

Fireplace, Miller of Millbach, 167
Furniture centers
  Baltimore, Md., 101, 217, 234
  Boston, Mass., 101
  Charleston, N.C., 183
  Guilford, Conn., 90
  Newport, R.I., 35, 101, 183
  New York, N.Y., 13, 101, 119, 180
  Philadelphia, Pa., 101, 119
  Riverton, Conn., 208
  Salem, Mass., 101
  Wilmington, Del., 119

Highboys
  Chippendale, 38*, 39
  Colonial, 46*, 47
  maple, 46*, 47
  Philadelphia, 38*, 39, 110
  tiger-striped maple, 108*, 109
  walnut, 48
  William and Mary, 66
Houses
  Cook-Oliver, 221

Dodd, 42
Metcalf, Stephen O., 13
Miller of Millbach, 14, 51, 52, 87, 146, 155, 165, 166, 167
Milligan, Robert J., 242
Old Merchant's, 240
Peabody, 185
Pendleton, 60
Powel, 40, 41, 102
Roosevelt, Theodore, 240
Stuyvesant, 189
Van Cortlandt Mansion, 189
Van Rensselaer Mansion, 189

Interiors
  American Gallery (Boston), 42
  early Victorian room (Metropolitan), 241
  Eighteenth-Century Gallery (Boston), 197
  Empire setting (Metropolitan), 237
  Ipswich room (Boston), 75
  Lancaster County room (Metropolitan), 146-47
  Main Gallery (Metropolitan), 221
  Pennsylvania German (Metropolitan), 53
  Powel drawing room (Metropolitan), 40, 41
  Shaker Museum, Old Chatham, N.Y.
    Brother's room, 169
    Sister's room, 175
    sitting room, 173
    Trustees' Office, 171
  Verplanck room (Metropolitan), 135
  Victorian parlor (Brooklyn), 242
  Victorian room (Metropolitan), 241

Lighting
  fancy crystal chandeliers, 40, 240, 242
  wrought-iron chandelier, 52

Lowboys
  cherry, 138*, 139
  Chippendale, 140
  Colonial, 138*, 139
  Dutch, 80
  Philadelphia, 140
  Queen Anne, 138*, 139

Materials
  catalin, 247
  chrome, 247
  formica, 247
  glass, 211
  mother-of-pearl, 239
  papier-maché, 239
  phenol products, 247
  plastics, 247
  plexiglas, 247
  stainless steel, 247
  wood, 64, 65, 99, 143, 148, 181, 182, 183, 247-48
  wrought iron, 52, 72, 102, 147, 161, 166
Military insignia, U.S., 205
Mirrors
  "Constitution," 33
  cut-out, 33
  panel, 32
  phoenix, 30*, 31
Monarchs
  Charles I, 64
  George III, 103
  James I, 64
  Napoleon I, 207, 236
  Queen Victoria, 239
Motifs in furniture design
  American flag, 205, 208
  eagle, 57, 205, 206, 207, 208, 226*, 227
  Liberty Bell, 205
  lion's foot, 206
  "N" for Napoleon, 207
  peacock, 42
Museums
  Albany Institute of History and Art, 182
  Art Institute of Chicago, 10, 20, 31, 32, 45, 73, 85, 87, 93, 109, 119, 120, 163, 212, 215, 227, 229, 235
  Brooklyn Museum, 10, 20, 45, 49, 55, 80, 117, 123, 125, 127,

253

131, 209, 227, 234, 235, 240, 242
Cleveland Museum of Art, 182
Detroit Institute of Arts, 10, 28, 36, 57, 59, 113, 161, 182, 189, 191, 192, 217
De Young Memorial Museum, 208
Gothenburg Museum (Sweden), 237, 238
Los Angeles County Museum of Art, 10, 24, 47, 94, 132, 139, 199, 200, 217, 220, 234
Metropolitan Museum of Art, 8, 10, 13, 23, 25, 33, 39, 40, 41, 48, 53, 71, 79, 80, 81, 85, 90, 102, 110, 121, 135, 140, 145, 146, 153, 155, 162, 182, 185, 190, 195, 199, 211, 219, 221, 224, 229, 231, 233, 236, 237, 238, 240, 241, 243
Museum of the City of New York, 10, 189, 191, 193, 240
Museum of Contemporary Arts, New York, 246
Museum of Cooper Union, New York, 182
Museum of Fine Arts, Boston, 8, 10, 14, 42, 75, 197, 199
New York State Historical Association, 10, 28, 176
Nordiska Museum (Sweden), 91
Old Sturbridge Village, Mass., 10, 72, 81, 223, 225
Philadelphia Museum of Art, 8, 10, 14, 43, 51, 52, 56, 77, 84, 87, 115, 124, 146, 154, 155, 157, 158, 159, 165, 166, 167, 213
Rhode Island School of Design, 10, 13, 20, 35, 60, 107, 111, 133, 140, 183, 195, 197
Schlossmuseum, Berlin, 84
Shaker Museum, Old Chatham, N.Y., 10, 150, 169, 171, 173, 175
Taft Museum, Cincinnati, O., 182
Victoria and Albert Museum, London, 37, 77, 84, 128, 129
Wadsworth Atheneum, Hartford, Conn., 10, 14, 27, 29, 75, 83, 85, 89, 94, 116, 137
Williamsburg Restoration, 15
Winterthur Museum, Wilmington, Del., 14

Oddities
Pennsylvania German, 155
pipe rack, 53, 155
pressing board, 155

Painters
Barnhart, John, 234
Kauffmann, Angelica, 206
Selzer, Christian, 163
Utrillo, Maurice, 19
Personalities
Astor, John Jacob, 189
Cooper, Peter, 243
Hopkins, Stephen, 195
Humphrey, Doris, 149
Jefferson, Thomas, 97
King, Emma B., 149
Lee, Ann, 147
Morgan, J. Pierpont, 14, 29, 75, 243
Penn, William, 94, 143
Stephens, Sister H. Rosetta, 149
Tredwell, Seabury, 240
Washington, George, 28, 97, 102, 103
Wolcott, Oliver, 24
Young, Benjamin, 173
Piano, grand, Victorian, 239
Pole screens
Adam (Victoria and Albert), 37
Chippendale (Rhode Island), 34*, 35
Sheraton (Detroit), 36

Schools
Albany Institute of History and Art, 182
Beaux Arts, 8, 244
Brooklyn Museum, 20
Chicago Art Institute, 10, 20, 31, 32, 45, 73, 85, 87, 93, 109, 119, 120, 163, 212, 215, 227, 229, 235
Columbia College, 7
Cooper Union, 7, 243
Detroit Institute of Arts, 10, 28, 36, 57, 59, 113, 161, 182, 189, 191, 192, 217
New School of Social Research, 7-8
New York University, 7, 8
Pratt Institute, 8
Rhode Island School of Design, 10, 13, 20, 35, 60, 107, 111, 133, 140, 183, 195, 197
Society of Mechanics and Tradesmen, 243-44
Stevens Institute, 8
Sconce, Chippendale, 129
Secretaries
rolltop, 42
tall, 29
Settees
Shaker, 168*, 169
upholstered Chippendale, 25
Settlements
Easton, Pa., 143
Germantown, Pa., 143, 146
Hudson Valley, N.Y., 63
Jamestown, Va., 8, 63, 64, 69, 248
Lancaster, Pa., 143, 147
Plymouth, Mass., 8, 63, 97
Settlers
Balkan, 64
Dutch, 63, 69, 79, 98, 101
English, 63, 64, 69
French, 63
German, 63-64, 69, 143-47, 151
Irish, 64, 69
Italian, 64, 69
Russian, 64
Scottish, 69
Spanish, 64
Swedish, 64, 69
Swiss, 143
Sideboard, 214*, 215
Sofas
Duncan Phyfe, 188*, 189, 190, 193, 201
Empire, 190
Samuel McIntire, 185, 199, 201
Stairway, Miller of Millbach, 166
Styles, 179-80

Index

Adam, 37, 185, 186, 221, 238
American Colonial, *see* Colonial
Baroque, 239
Chinoiserie, 40, 41, 67
Chippendale, 21, 23, 24, 25, 30, 31, 33, 34, 35, 38, 39, 40, 41, 60, 100, 102, 129, 181, 183, 195
Colonial, 8, 13-18 *passim*, 23, 29, 38, 39, 41, 44-47 *passim*, 50, 51, 70-75 *passim*, 80-84 *passim*, 88, 89, 94, 179, 248
   and designers and cabinetmakers, 180-84
   origins of, 63-69
Contemporary, *see* Modern
Danish, 248
Directoire, 247
Duncan Phyfe, 180-82
Empire, 181, 207, 236, 237
Georgian, 179, 183, 247
Greek Revival, 186, 206
Hepplewhite, 27, 58, 59, 60, 137, 181, 183, 200, 215, 217
Louis XV, 67, 129, 236
Louis Philippe, 241
Mediterranean, 248
Modern, 9, 148, 245, 246, 247, 248
Pennsylvania German, 14, 85, 143-47, 151-67 *passim*, 213, 229
Queen Anne, 131, 139, 179, 183, 195
Regency, 181
Rococo, 67
Shaker, 147-50, 168, 169
Sheraton, 36, 42, 54-60 *passim*, 100, 181, 183, 197, 198, 199, 217, 219, 221, 223, 227, 228, 229, 238
Spanish, 248
Swedish, 248
Tudor, 87
Victorian, 179, 239-42
William and Mary, 46, 47, 66, 78, 79, 179
See also Designers and cabinetmakers

Tables
   "buro," 194*, 195
   card, 134*, 135
   console, 124
   dining, 80
   drop-leaf, 80, 81, 191, 216*, 217
   Duncan Phyfe, 191
   Dutch, 78*, 79
   gate-leg, 81
   marble-top, 240, 242
   occasional, 78*, 79
   peasant, 157, 159
   Pembroke, 101, 216*, 217
   Pennsylvania German, 154
   pine, 158
   refectory, 146, 154, 176
   sawbuck, 156*, 157
   serving, 101, 125
   Shaker, 176
   tailoress's, 176
   tea, 101
   tip-top, 130*, 131
   trestle, 53
   tripod, 130*, 131, 132, 133

Wallpapers
   American Gallery (Boston), 42
   Chinoiserie, 40, 41
   handpainted scenic, 102
   Powel House (Metropolitan), 40, 41
Wars
   American Revolution, 103, 105, 205, 206
   Civil War, 240
   French Revolution, 206, 236
   War of 1812, 207, 227
Washstands
   Colonial, 228*, 229
   Pennsylvania German, 229

Index of Museums and Displays

Art Institute of Chicago
   banister chair, 92*, 93
   Brewster chair, 93
   corner cabinet, 212
   decorated washstand, 229
   desk on frame, 73
   eagle chair, 226*, 227
   fan-back Windsor chair, 120
   Hitchcock chair, 235
   mirror and chest, 30*
   painted chest, 163
   panel mirror, 32
   sideboard, 214*, 215
   table box, 85
   tiger-striped highboy, 108*, 109
   Tudor chest, 44*, 45
   tulip chest, 44*, 45
   Windsor chair, 118*, 119, 120

Brooklyn Museum
   cellarette, 122*, 123
   cradle, 116
   dining table, 80
   1812 chair, 227
   high chest, 49
   Hitchcock chair, 235
   Hitchcock rocker, 234
   roundabout chair, 126*, 127
   serving table, 125
   sunflower chest, 45
   tip-top table, 130*, 131
   tri-part bookcase, 54*, 55
   Victorian parlor, 242

Detroit Institute of Arts
   drop-front desk, 28
   Duncan Phyfe chair, 192

Duncan Phyfe sofa, 188*, 189
Duncan Phyfe table, 191
four-poster bed, 58*, 59
Governor Winthrop desk, 28
painted chest, 160*, 161
Pembroke table, 216*, 217
pole screen, 36
secretary bookcase, 57
wing chair, 112*, 113

Gothenburg Museum
Empire armchair, 238
Empire chair, 237

Los Angeles County Museum of Art
Chippendale side chair, 24
fancy chair, 234
lowboy and mirror, 138*, 139
McIntire chair details, 199
maple highboy, 46*, 47
Pembroke table, 217
Sheraton armchair, 220
shield-back chair, 199, 200
tripod table, 132
vase-back chair, 94

Metropolitan Museum of Art
Adam chair, 238
Bible boxes, 85
block-front chest, 195
bracket clock, 224
card table, 134*, 135
Chippendale armchair, 21*, 23
"Constitution" mirror, 33
corner cupboard, 210*, 211
desk on stand, 70*, 71
details of carving, 201
drop-leaf table, 81
Dutch table, 78*, 79
early Victorian room, 241
Empire setting, 237
Empire sofa, 190
gondola chair, 236
kitchen dresser, 152*, 153
Louis XV bergère, 236
McIntire sofa, 198*, 199, 201
Main Gallery, 221
miniature clock, 230*, 231
occasional table, 79
painted chest, 90

Pennsylvania German interior, 53
Pennsylvania German oddities, 155
Philadelphia highboy, 38*, 39, 110
Philadelphia lowboy, 140
Powel drawing room, 40, 41
side chair (Seymour), 218*, 219
side chair (Sylmaris), 232*, 233
upholstered settee, 25
Verplanck room, 135
walnut highboy, 48
washstand, 228*, 229
wedding chest, 162
writing-arm Windsor chair, 121
Museum of the City of New York
Duncan Phyfe sofa, 193, 201
window bench, 191
Museum of Fine Arts, Boston
American Gallery, 42, 197
chest of drawers, 197
Ipswich room, 75

New York State Historical Association
Shaker table, 176
Nordiska Museum, Stockholm
painted tall chest, 91

Old Sturbridge Village
gate-leg table, 81
mantel clock, 222*, 223
slant-top desk, 72
spice cabinet, 225

Philadelphia Museum of Art
Bible box, 84
breadbox, 164*, 165
chest on chest, 43
console table, 124
cradle, 114*, 115
hanging cabinet, 155
kitchen corner, 52
kitchen dresser, 50*, 51
kitchen fireplace, 167
peasant table, 159

pine table, 158
sawbuck table, 156*, 157
secretary breakfront, 56
stairway and door, 166
table and benches, 154
tall cabinet, 213
tall chest of drawers, 87
wainscot chair, 76*, 77

Rhode Island School of Design
"buro" table, 194*, 195
four-poster bed, 60
high chest of drawers, 111
lowboy, 140
pole screen, 34*, 35
Queen Anne chair, 106*, 107
shaped chest of drawers, 196*, 197
tripod table, 133

Schlossmuseum, Berlin
Swiss chest, 84
Shaker Museum
chest cupboard, 172*, 173
dining table, 174*, 175
settee, 168*, 169
storage bench, 170*, 171
tailoress's table, 176

Victoria and Albert Museum, London
bric-a-brac cabinet, 128
Chippendale sconce, 129
oak chest, 84
pole screen, 37
wainscot chair, 77

Wadsworth Atheneum, Hartford
Bible boxes, 82*, 83, 85
Burnap tall clock, 137
cradle, 116
ladder-back chair, 94
painted chest of drawers, 88*, 89
press cupboard, 74*, 75
tall clock, 136*, 137
tall secretary, 29
tambour desk, 26*, 27